TRANSITIONAL JUSTICE AND THE PROSECUTION OF POLITICAL LEADERS IN THE ARAB REGION

The dramatic uprisings that ousted the long-standing leaders of several countries in the Arab region set in motion an unprecedented period of social, political and legal transformation. The prosecution of political leaders took centre stage in the pursuit of transitional justice following the 'Arab Spring'. Through a comparative case study of Egypt, Libya, Tunisia and Yemen, this book argues that transitional justice in the Arab region presents the strongest challenge yet to the transitional justice paradigm. This paradigm is built on the underlying assumption that transitions constitute a shift from non-liberal to liberal democratic regimes, where often legal measures are taken to address atrocities committed during the prior regime. The book is guided by two principal questions: first, what trigger and driving factors led to the decision of whether or not to prosecute former political leaders? And second, what shaping factors affected the content and extent of decisions regarding prosecution? In answering these questions, the book enhances our understanding of how transitional justice is pursued by different actors in varied contexts. In doing so, it challenges the predominant understanding that transitional justice uniformly occurs in liberalising contexts and calls for a re-thinking of transitional justice theory and practice.

Using original findings generated from almost 50 interviews across 4 countries, this research builds on the growing critical literature that claims that transitional justice is an under-theorised field and needs to be developed to take into account non-liberal and complex transitions. It will be stimulating and thought-provoking reading for all those interested in transitional justice and the 'Arab Spring'.

**Volume 15 in the series Studies in International
and Comparative Criminal Law**

Studies in International and Comparative Criminal Law
General Editor: Michael Bohlander

Criminal law had long been regarded as the preserve of national legal systems, and comparative research in criminal law for a long time had something of an academic ivory tower quality. However, in the past 15 years it has been transformed into an increasingly, and moreover practically, relevant subject of study for international and comparative lawyers. This can be attributed to numerous factors, such as the establishment of ad hoc international criminal tribunals and the International Criminal Court, as well as to developments within the EU, the UN and other international organisations. There is a myriad of initiatives related to tackling terrorism, money laundering, organised crime, people trafficking and the drugs trade, and the international 'war' on terror. Criminal law is being used to address global or regional problems, often across the borders of fundamentally different legal systems, only one of which is the traditional divide between common and civil law approaches. It is therefore no longer solely a matter for domestic lawyers. The need exists for a global approach which encompasses comparative and international law.

Responding to this development this new series will include books on a wide range of topics, including studies of international law, EU law, the work of specific international tribunals, and comparative studies of national systems of criminal law. Given that the different systems to a large extent operate based on the idiosyncracies of the peoples and states that have created them, the series will also welcome pertinent historical, criminological and socio-legal research into these issues.

Editorial Committee:
Mohammed Ayat (Rabat/Morocco)
Robert Cryer (Birmingham/UK)
Caroline Fournet (Groningen/NL)
Tomoya Obokata (Belfast/UK)
Alex Obote-Odora (Arusha/Tanzania)
Dawn Rothe (Norfolk (VA)/USA)
Silvia Tellenbach (Freiburg/Germany)
Helen Xanthaki (London/UK)
Liling Yue (Beijing/China)

Recent titles in this series:

The Defendant in International Criminal Proceedings: Between Law and Historiography
Björn Elberling

Counsel Misconduct before the International Criminal Court: Professional Responsibility
in International Criminal Defence
Till Gut

The Concept of Mens Rea in International Criminal Law: The Case for a Unified Approach
Mohamed Elewa Badar

Genocide and Crimes against Humanity: Misconceptions and Confusion
in French Law and Practice
Caroline Fournet

The Emergence of EU Criminal Law: Cyber Crime and the Regulation
of the Information Society
Sarah Summers, Christian Schwarzenegger, Gian Ege and Finlay Young

Transitional Justice and the Prosecution of Political Leaders in the Arab Region

A Comparative Study of Egypt, Libya, Tunisia and Yemen

Noha Aboueldahab

·HART·

OXFORD · LONDON · NEW YORK · NEW DELHI · SYDNEY

HART PUBLISHING

Bloomsbury Publishing Plc

Kemp House, Chawley Park, Cumnor Hill, Oxford, OX2 9PH, UK

HART PUBLISHING, the Hart/Stag logo, BLOOMSBURY and the Diana logo are
trademarks of Bloomsbury Publishing Plc

First published in Great Britain 2017

First published in hardback, 2017

Paperback edition, 2020

A catalogue record for this book is available from the British Library.

Library of Congress Cataloging-in-Publication Data

Names: Aboueldahab, Noha, author.

Title: Transitional justice and the prosecution of political leaders in the Arab region : a comparative study
of Egypt, Libya, Tunisia and Yemen / Noha Aboueldahab.

Description: Portland, Oregon : Hart Publishing, 2017. | Series: Studies in international and comparative
criminal law ; volume 15 | Includes bibliographical references and index.

Identifiers: LCCN 2017024449 (print) | LCCN 2017026545 (ebook) |
ISBN 9781509911349 (Epub) | ISBN 9781509911332 (hardback)

Subjects: LCSH: Transitional justice—Arab countries. | Human rights—Arab countries. |
Political crimes and offenses—Arab countries.

Classification: LCC KMC572 (ebook) | LCC KMC572 .A93 2017 (print) | DDC 340/.115—dc23

LC record available at https://lccn.loc.gov/2017024449

ISBN: HB: 978-1-78043-157-4
PB: 978-1-50993-640-3
ePDF: 978-1-78043-157-6
ePub: 978-1-78043-157-7

Typeset by Compuscript Ltd, Shannon

To find out more about our authors and books visit www.hartpublishing.co.uk. Here you will
find extracts, author information, details of forthcoming events and the option to sign up for
our newsletters.

For Andrew

ACKNOWLEDGEMENTS

The idea for this book emerged in 2011, a pivotal year for the Arab region. Ousted Arab leaders were either put on trial or negotiated their immunity from prosecution following mass anti-government uprisings. I began research for this book almost immediately, and am fortunate to have had the steadfast support of several colleagues, friends and family ever since then.

Professor Michael Bohlander provided direction and valuable support throughout the duration of my doctoral studies at Durham Law School and beyond. I am proud and honoured to have him as my foremost mentor.

Dr Catherine Turner and Dr Mohammad Hedayati-Kakhki provided invaluable guidance during the earlier stages of the research. Dr Thom Brooks offered helpful advice and support. Dr Mohamed Elewa Badar and Professor Jonathan Doak provided excellent feedback. I appreciate their encouragement and thoughtful critique.

The interviewees in Egypt, Libya, Tunisia and Yemen form the core of this book. I thank them for their generous time and for their in-depth reflections. Judges whose lives were at risk for the work that they do were very forthcoming with their thoughts while in exile. I am deeply appreciative of their insight.

I thank Bill Asquith at Hart Publishing for his editorial direction, cooperation and support. I am also grateful to the reviewers, whose suggestions strengthened the analytical scope of the book, and to Chris Myers for his excellent copyediting.

Advice from my more academically seasoned friends and colleagues provided reassurance. I thank, in particular, Edward Kolla, Beverley Milton-Edwards, Vasuki Nesiah, Chandra Sriram and Karine Walther for this.

Institutional and financial support greatly facilitated my ability to travel to Egypt, Libya, Tunisia and Yemen to conduct my interviews. I appreciate such support from the *Modern Law Review*, Durham Law School and Harvard Law School's Institute for Global Law and Policy/Santander Universities. Northwestern University in Qatar's library and the Brookings Doha Center served as welcoming places to write. I would like to thank the staff of both places for their cheerful disposition and encouragement.

I thank Fahad Al Dahimi for his research assistance in the final stage of the book edits.

While I am fortunate to have had the opportunity to pursue research on a matter that is deeply important to me, this book would not have been possible without the moral support of my friends and family. For this, I would like to thank my parents, Dr Hamed Aboueldahab and Dr Manal Said Eino, my sister Ghada and my brother Adel. I am also indebted to Hana Al Hirsi-Evans' friendship, which has been a great source of strength and comfort for many years.

Finally, the incredible support I had from my husband, Andrew Mills, was in many ways the engine that drove this book to completion. Our conversations about transitional justice were some of the most enjoyable moments in the years of research and writing for this book. I appreciate his patience, particularly during my travels while heavily pregnant in Egypt, Libya, Tunisia and Yemen. I benefited greatly from his close review of the manuscript, several times over.

Maya, Seif and Aziz were a source of joy and welcome relief from heavy bouts of work. I look forward to sharing stories with them of their very intimate participation both inside and outside the womb in the various stages of this book's development.

CONTENTS

1

Introduction

On the morning of 3 August 2011, shocking live images of former Egyptian President Hosni Mubarak in a courtroom cage lit up television screens in Egypt, the Arab region and beyond. When asked to confirm his presence in the courtroom, he responded: 'afandim, ana mawgood' ('your honour, I am present'). Mubarak's statement quickly became a popular ring tone for mobile phones in Egypt, as if to assert time and again that the impossible had now become reality. For many Egyptians, Mubarak's incarceration was a powerful symbol of the revolution's success in ousting him and in marking a new, post-Mubarak era. Alongside him in the dock were his two sons, former Minister of Interior Habib El Adly and several of his aides. The dock was thus teeming with some of Egypt's most notorious symbols of oppression.

Less than two months earlier, former Tunisian President Zine El Abidine Ben Ali was tried in absentia and the International Criminal Court (ICC) issued arrest warrants for Libyan leader Muammar Gaddafi, his son Saif al-Islam Gaddafi and the Chief of Intelligence Abdullah El Senussi. Meanwhile, Yemeni President Ali Abdallah Saleh agreed to step down in a deal that guaranteed his immunity from prosecution. Such was the rapid unfolding of decisions regarding the prosecution of political leaders in the Arab region, all within a matter of months following the massive anti-government uprisings of the Arab Spring. Prosecutions of former leaders and other high-level government officials emerged as the single most pursued route of transitional justice—something that was almost non-existent prior to the 2010/2011 uprisings in the Arab region.[1]

The jubilation that the images of Mubarak in the dock triggered, however, quickly subsided. Apart from the generic concerns surrounding politicised trials, deeper questions surrounding the premise of transition began to emerge. Is the toppling of a leader sufficient for a meaningful transitional justice process to unfold? What role do 'deep state', or entrenched, institutions play in shaping the direction of transitional justice? To what extent can the uprisings and their aftermath be described as *transitions*? With certain exceptions, the investigations and trials that took place in Egypt, Libya, Tunisia and Yemen were limited to crimes perpetrated during the uprisings, leaving decades of atrocities unaddressed. Moreover, while several high-level officials were prosecuted, many others did

---

[1] Exceptions include the trial of former Iraqi president Saddam Hussein.

not face trial. What explains this limited content and extent of the trials? To what extent can a 'global accountability norm' be invoked when international actors pursue it in one context (Libya) but completely ignore it in another (Yemen)? Whose interests does transitional justice serve and to what end?

This book argues that transitional justice in the Arab region presents the strongest challenge yet to the transitional justice paradigm, which presumes a shift from violent, non-liberal rule to peaceful, liberal-democratic rule. Through a comparative case study of Egypt, Libya, Tunisia and Yemen, this book presents a critique of mainstream transitional justice theory. This theory is built on the underlying assumption that transitions constitute a shift from non-liberal to liberal-democratic regimes, where measures—often legal—are taken to address atrocities committed during the prior regime.[2] Together with domestic prosecutions, this book also takes into account the role of international actors in shaping transitional justice decisions, especially within the context of the ICC's involvement in Libya and the role of international actors in negotiating an immunity law in Yemen. Using scholarly literature and the findings generated from interviews in each of the four case studies, the book challenges the predominant understanding that transitional justice uniformly occurs in liberalising contexts. The findings of this research therefore build on the growing critical literature that claims that transitional justice is an under-theorised field that must further develop to take into account non-liberal and complex transitions.

This book thus makes four principal arguments for how the Arab region cases challenge the transitional justice paradigm.

First, the nature of the transitions that took place in the Arab region was non-paradigmatic in that they did not constitute a shift from violent dictatorships to liberal democracies. This warrants a rethinking of transitional justice and its pursuit in varied contexts.

Secondly, the cases demonstrate that both domestic and international actors pursue competing accountability agendas, thereby weakening global accountability norm claims. The contradictory role of international actors in Libya and Yemen—pushing for criminal accountability in the former and immunity in the latter—exemplifies the need to deconstruct the varied objectives of transitional justice actors.

Thirdly, the limited content and extent of the investigations and prosecutions that have taken place in all four case studies further underline the need to develop transitional justice theory. The emphasis on corruption and economic crimes, particularly in Egypt and Tunisia, was used as a means to scapegoat certain high-level individuals to deflect attention from the lack of accountability for a more comprehensive set of human rights violations and their perpetrators.

Fourthly, the Arab region cases demonstrate the perils of pursuing prosecutions using weak and politicised judiciaries. Executive power meddling and inadequate

---

[2] See, eg, RG Teitel, *Transitional Justice* (Oxford, Oxford University Press, 2000); RG Teitel, *Globalizing Transitional Justice: Essays for the New Millennium* (Oxford, Oxford University Press, 2014).

legal frameworks are a principal challenge to the pursuit of fair prosecutions. The book therefore argues that a rethinking of transitional justice needs to take into account the absence of pre-existing democratic structures and what this absence means for criminal accountability prospects in diverse transitional contexts.

The term 'transitional justice' is used here to describe the processes that actors take to address past atrocities. Actors include the state, civil society, victims, the military, individual lawyers, politicians and the judiciary.[3] Transitional justice processes include a range of mechanisms, such as domestic and international prosecutions, institutional reform, vetting, reparations and truth commissions. This book, however, focuses on decisions regarding the prosecution of political leaders to ensure a rigorous comparison between the four country case studies. More importantly, the focus on prosecutions is driven by their centrality in the pursuit of transitional justice in the Arab region. The book therefore calls for a rethinking of transitional justice theory and practice. It does so by examining two principal questions.

First, what factors led to decisions regarding the prosecution of political leaders in Egypt, Libya, Tunisia and Yemen? The term 'political leaders' here includes heads of state, former ministers and other high-ranking government officials.[4]

Secondly, the book considers why there has been an emphasis on corruption and socio-economic crimes over civil and political rights crimes in the investigations and trials that have already taken place. The first question is addressed by examining the trigger and driving factors that led to the decision to prosecute or not. The second question is addressed by exploring the shaping factors that affect the content and extent of decisions regarding prosecution. 'Content' refers to the types of charges and accusations in the investigations and trials. 'Extent' refers to the selection of individuals who were prosecuted and/or investigated. This trigger–driving–shaping mechanism is used as a general prism through which the material gathered from the interviews is analysed.[5]

This book, then, does not aim to define what is meant by the term 'justice'. Nor does it seek to determine whether certain transitional justice mechanisms such as prosecutions or truth commissions should be implemented or not. Instead, the term 'transitional justice' is used primarily in reference to how the various actors in the four case studies pursue, shape and block criminal accountability for past atrocities. In doing so, the book provides a critical inquiry of the liberal assumptions of the transitional justice paradigm. Laurel E Fletcher and Harvey Weinstein note that the most influential transitional justice scholarship tests,

---

[3] Chapters 2–5 contain a more detailed explanation of the various actors involved in driving and shaping transitional justice processes.

[4] See the Methodology section for an explanation for why the term 'political leaders' encompasses these individuals.

[5] See the Methodology section for an explanation of the merits of the trigger–driving–shaping prism.

applies, evaluates or theorises the 'accepted transitional justice paradigm' and largely falls short in questioning the 'foundational assumptions of the field'.[6] This book aims to address this shortcoming of the field. It does so through scholarly research and a critique largely based on findings from almost 50 field interviews on the prosecution of political leaders in Egypt, Libya, Tunisia and Yemen between 2012 and 2017.

Significance of the Arab Region

The merits of examining how the Arab region is shaping transitional justice do not only have to do with challenging the predominant understanding that transitional justice occurs in liberalising contexts. Five additional points further illustrate the significance of this research.

First, most criminal prosecutions in the Arab Spring countries have dealt almost exclusively with crimes committed during the transition, as opposed to crimes during the decades of repressive rule prior to the political transitions. Moreover, most of the complaints and charges to date have had to do with corruption and financial crimes, as opposed to human rights violations. The reasons behind this duality of charges are unclear in the literature on the prosecution of political leaders. Scholars have flagged this as an area that requires closer attention.[7] Most transitional justice research focuses on the outcome of the decision to prosecute or not, without examining the shape that these decisions take as a result of the processes they emerge from and the contexts within which they unfold. The emphasis on corruption and socio-economic crimes in the investigations and trials that have taken place in the Arab region therefore warrants a closer examination. These practices have profound implications for the study of transitional justice because they weaken long-standing scholarly assumptions of the liberalising direction of transitions and of transitional justice.

Secondly, an inquiry into efforts to prosecute in the pre-transition period— before the 2010/2011 Arab Spring uprisings—is necessary in order to understand the development and execution of the prosecutorial strategy in the four countries after the uprisings.[8] Such an inquiry provides insight into the formative stages of these decision-making processes. Instead of judging the prosecutions and the decisions related to them solely on their outcome, the trigger–driving–shaping prism serves to ensure a focus on the very making of these decisions. For example, while many would label the Mubarak and Ben Ali trials in Egypt and Tunisia as

---

[6] LE Fletcher and HM Weinstein, 'Writing Transitional Justice: An Empirical Evaluation of Transitional Justice Scholarship in Academic Journals' (2015) 7 *Journal of Human Rights Practice* 177, 189.

[7] EL Lutz and C Reiger (eds), *Prosecuting Heads of State* (New York, Cambridge University Press, 2009) 280–82.

[8] This point is elaborated upon in the next section.

show trials or politicised trials that fell short in ensuring justice, this conclusion does not take into account the complex factors and the relationship between these factors that formed the processes leading up to the prosecutions. An inquiry into the formative stages of decisions regarding prosecutions, then, reveals that a variety of factors and actors shaped the decisions. As a result, attributing unfair trials to one factor, such as a politicised and weak judiciary, falls short of a more comprehensive explanation. Such simplistic inferences fail to take into account other significant factors, such as the nature of the transition, civil society, the role of international actors and legal challenges, that shaped transitional justice across the four countries. It is these factors that the research on which this book is based aims to identify and explain.

Thirdly, the four case studies are examples of the need to examine whose interests transitional justice serves and what those interests are.[9] Such an analysis is important for the deconstruction of the use and abuse of transitional justice in varied political contexts. The roles of the judiciary, the military, civil society and interim governments, for example, vary significantly and must be taken into account when addressing the use of transitional justice mechanisms. By examining the factors that triggered, drove and shaped decisions regarding the prosecution of political leaders in Egypt, Libya, Tunisia and Yemen, this research will enhance our understanding of how transitional justice is pursued in such non-paradigmatic contexts.

Fourthly, the timing of this research and of the questions asked in every interview conducted across the four countries is crucial. The book analyses the details of the early stages of decisions regarding prosecution from actors who were directly and indirectly involved in the prosecutions. As time passes, memory of such details will wane, as was the case in Latin America and other parts of the world. Kathryn Sikkink has described this dilemma and called it the 'frailties of human memory':[10]

> When I first started the research for this book, I wracked my brains for a memory of the first time one of the activists from Argentina or Uruguay mentioned the possibility of prosecuting state officials for human rights violations, and I could not pinpoint the moment. Surely Emilio Mignone or Juan Mendez, each immersed in the human rights legal culture of the time, was already talking about prosecutions in 1981? Emilio Mignone died in 1998, and I can no longer rely on his impeccable memory. Juan Mendez can't pinpoint the moment, either ... For almost two years I was part of a network that later became a main advocate for individual criminal prosecution, and yet I cannot identify the instant when the idea first appeared and started to flourish. So, my research began as a kind of detective work to locate the sources of the ideas and practices that I would later call the 'justice cascade'.[11]

---

[9] T Obel Hansen, 'Transitional Justice: Toward a Differentiated Theory' (2011) 13 *Oregon Review of International Law* 1, 2–3.

[10] K Sikkink, *The Justice Cascade: How Human Rights Prosecutions are Changing World* Politics (New York, WW Norton, 2011) 11.

[11] ibid, 10–11.

By conducting this research shortly after the investigations and trials began, I avoided having to pick at the vague memories of those I interviewed. Instead, I was able to draw a clearer and more accurate picture of what happened while the memories were still fresh. The novelty of the trials, then, serves as an advantage for valuable research into the emergence of individual criminal accountability in a region that is new to it.

Finally, the context of the Arab countries and their transitions are fundamentally different from previous studies on countries in other regions. Factors that have played an important role in countries in Latin America, such as international and regional human rights mechanisms and the use of universal jurisdiction laws, may not be as relevant to the Arab region.[12] This book thus presents an opportunity to think critically about how the Arab region is shaping transitional justice theory and practice.

This book does not attempt to propose a new theory of transitional justice. Rather, it seeks to challenge the predominant transitional justice paradigm, generally understood as a set of mechanisms to address past atrocities through the use of judicial and non-judicial measures, by arguing that it falls short in explaining non-paradigmatic transitions. The Arab region case studies herein present a strong challenge to the existing theory of transitional justice, which is rooted in liberal and hence non-universal values.

Significance of Pre-transition Decisions Regarding Prosecution

Certain iconic human rights cases in pre-transition Egypt, Libya and Tunisia served as major triggers, or turning points, that led to decisions to prosecute high-level officials in those three countries. These cases targeting pre-transition high-level officials have, with the exception of Yemen, trickled into post-2011 efforts to prosecute. Marked by the public outrage in response to the original crimes and the persistent efforts of civil society and individual lawyers to see the cases through, these triggers were milestones in the long and difficult road to accountability for political leaders in these countries. This is why it is crucial to identify pre-transition triggers and to analyse their impact, if any, in subsequent decisions to prosecute former political leaders.

One of the objectives of this book, then, is to explain the factors that led to decisions to prosecute political leaders or not. The research aims, in part, to explain what, if any, efforts were pursued to prosecute political leaders before, during and shortly after the 2010/2011 uprisings in Egypt, Libya, Tunisia and Yemen.

---

[12] Tunisia, however, benefited significantly from universal jurisdiction laws in pre-transition prosecution efforts, as explained in chapter 3.

The question regarding pre-transition decisions to prosecute is important for three reasons.

First, as explained above, the timing of this inquiry was crucial, as it allowed for interviews with individuals both directly and indirectly involved in the prosecutions shortly after they had taken place or, as in many cases, while they were still ongoing. This has helped to ensure an accurate explanation of the formative stages of the decisions regarding prosecution.

Secondly, an inquiry into efforts to prosecute in the pre-uprising period is necessary in order to understand the development and execution of the prosecutorial strategies in the four countries after the uprisings.[13] It provides insight into the formative stages of these decision-making processes. This is not to say that clear decisions to prosecute political leaders had begun before the ouster of the four leaders in 2011. On the contrary, the interview responses show that, for a variety of reasons, very little was done in terms of attempts to hold political leaders accountable in a court of law. However, certain iconic cases that implicated— whether implicitly or explicitly—high-level government officials reveal attempts to achieve some form of accountability within a difficult and opaque judicial environment pre-transition.

Finally, an inquiry into the formative stages of decisions regarding prosecutions reveals that a variety of factors and actors triggered, drove and shaped the decisions. As mentioned earlier, attributing unfair trials to one factor, such as a politicised and weak judiciary, falls short of a more comprehensive explanation. The scope of this part of the research is counter-intuitive in the transitional justice literature, which focuses primarily on post-transition efforts to prosecute. Before explaining the methodology used in more detail, the next section situates this book within the transitional justice literature.

The Arab Region: Rethinking Transitional Justice Scholarship

The Absence of a 'Return to a Liberal State'

The ambiguity of the transitions in the Arab region has led some to conclude that transitions simply did not take place.[14] However, transitional justice processes do take place in ambiguous political transitions. The fact that decisions regarding prosecution were taken—even in the case of Yemen, where an immunity law

---

[13] The implications of these prosecutorial strategies for transitional justice are discussed in chapter 6.

[14] RG Teitel, 'Transitional Justice and the Power of Persuasion: Philosophical, Historical and Political Perspectives', paper presented to the Panel, American Political Science Association annual conference, Chicago, September 2013.

was passed—is important in that it challenges the predominant understanding of transitional justice as a process that can only occur in a liberalising context. These arguments have profound implications for the study of transitional justice because they weaken long-standing scholarly assumptions of the liberalising directions of transitions and of transitional justice.

Trials are usually at the forefront of transitional justice mechanisms and serve as a strong symbol of a break with the former regime. Some argue that transitional justice is under-theorised, as it is increasingly unable to explain its divergent objectives in varied contexts.[15] Others, such as Paige Arthur, argue that there is no single theory or definition of transitional justice.[16] In their analysis of transitional justice scholarship between 2003 and 2008, Fletcher and Weinstein note that few scholars have questioned the foundational assumptions of the field.[17]

A rapidly expanding field, transitional justice is broad, inter-disciplinary and evolving in radical ways. Transitional justice and its various mechanisms, including truth commissions, reparations, vetting and prosecutions, are spread widely and draw scholarly attention from lawyers, political scientists, anthropologists, sociologists and historians. Prosecutions, however, are the most pursued mechanism of transitional justice, and the Arab region is not an exception to this trend.[18] It is, then, a field that possesses highly political attributes, but is heavily legalistic in its application. Sharp critiques the tendency of actors to pursue a top-down approach to transitional justice that is focused on 'technocratic legalism' that wrongly overlooks the 'underlying politics of transitional justice interventions'.[19] Nagy similarly critiques the heavy influence of the 'international legalist paradigm' and notes that 'The problem is not with law and human rights per se but with the depoliticised way in which "justice" can operate'.[20] Such calls to take the political and the contextual into account are certainly crucial to understanding both how transitional justice operates in various contexts and the limitations of the transitional justice paradigm as it currently stands.

Globally, the number of prosecutions of political leaders has increased significantly.[21] Since 1990, more than 85 heads of state have been prosecuted. Political and military leaders in Latin America, Europe, Africa and Asia have been put on trial for massive human rights violations and for corruption. In Latin America, leaders in Argentina, Chile and Peru have all faced prosecution. This

---

[15] See S Buckley-Zistel, TK Beck, C Braun and F Mieth (eds), *Transitional Justice Theories* (Abingdon, Routledge, 2014).

[16] P Arthur, 'How "Transitions" Reshaped Human Rights: A Conceptual History of Transitional Justice' (2009) 31 *Human Rights Quarterly* 321, 359.

[17] Fletcher and Weinstein, above n 6.

[18] Truth commissions have also increasingly become a popular mechanism of transitional justice.

[19] DN Sharp, 'Interrogating the Peripheries: The Preoccupations of Fourth Generation Transitional Justice' (2013) 26 *Harvard Human Rights Journal* 149, 150.

[20] R Nagy, 'Transitional Justice as Global Project: critical reflections' (2008) 29 *Third World Quarterly* 275, 278, 279.

[21] Lutz and Reiger, above n 7, 12.

phenomenon has been described as a 'justice cascade', which largely originated in Latin America and has reverberated throughout the world, leading to an increase in universal jurisdiction laws.[22] This wave of trials and legal transformations is also referred to as the 'Pinochet Effect', following one of the most notorious attempted prosecutions of former political leader, General Augusto Pinochet, who led Chile from 1973 to 1990.[23]

Neil Kritz's three volumes on transitional justice, published in 1995, in many ways set the stage for further scholarship on the dilemmas of what became known as transitional justice in various parts of the world.[24] Ruti Teitel's work on transitional justice in 2000 laid the foundations of transitional justice theory and highlighted it as a process of liberalisation.[25] Teitel's account of transitional justice is built on the underlying assumption that transitions constitute a shift from authoritarian, non-liberal regimes to liberal-democratic ones.[26] Recognising the extraordinary role of law in transitions and the thin line between fair prosecutions and politicised justice, Teitel describes transitional justice as:

> [C]ontextualized and partial: it is both constituted by, and constituted of, the transition. What is 'just' is contingent, and informed by prior injustice … While the rule of law ordinarily implies prospectivity, transitional law is both backward- and forward-looking, as it disclaims past illiberal values and reclaims liberal norms.[27]

Teitel attributes criminal justice to this 'liberalizing ritual' of states undergoing political transition and explains that criminal proceedings affirm 'the core liberal message of the primacy of individual rights and responsibilities'.[28] She emphatically denotes the significant role of criminal prosecutions as the 'leading transitional response' that is able to publicly and authoritatively convey 'the political differences that constitute the normative shift from an illiberal to a liberal regime'.[29]

The unfolding of decisions regarding prosecution in the Arab region, however, challenges Teitel's description of criminal prosecutions as a 'liberalizing ritual'. While Teitel begins with a caveat mentioning that her book rejects 'the notion that the move toward a more liberal democratic political system implies a universal or ideal norm', she provides no explanation for how transitional justice operates in non-paradigmatic, illiberal transitions. While she presents a powerful analysis of

---

[22] E Lutz and K Sikkink, 'Justice Cascade: The Evolution and Impact of Foreign Human Rights Trials in Latin America' (2001) 2 *Chicago Journal of International Law* 1, 5.

[23] N Roht-Arriaza, *The Pinochet Effect: Transitional Justice in the Age of Human Rights* (Philadelphia, University of Pennsylvania Press, 2005).

[24] NJ Kritz (ed), *Transitional Justice: How Emerging Democracies Reckon with Former Regimes*, vols 1–3 (Washington DC, United States Institute of Peace, 1995).

[25] Teitel, *Transitional Justice*, above n 2.

[26] ibid; Teitel, *Globalizing Transitional Justice*, above n 2.

[27] Teitel, *Transitional Justice*, above n 2, 96.

[28] ibid 30.

[29] ibid 104.

the role of law in transitions, or in times of political change, Teitel's point of departure is rooted in transitions constituting a shift from authoritarian rule to liberal democratic rule.[30] This is unhelpful in the case of the Arab Spring.

The Necessity of Pre-existing Democratic Institutions

Much of the scholarly work on transitional justice is based on the premise that democratically functioning institutions pre-existed the transition to a certain extent, allowing a legitimate transitional justice process to take place. Lutz and Reiger argue that 'accountability, by itself, is neither sufficient nor possible absent other functioning democratic institutions, including an independent judiciary'.[31] Luc Huyse argues that the democratic institutions that existed prior to the four years of repressive rule in Belgium, France and the Netherlands were able to survive and were not completely eliminated following World War II. This meant that 'four years of occupation and collaboration were insufficient time for the authoritarian regime's legal culture and codes to take root'.[32] This may, as Huyse suggests, explain the speed with which prosecutions were initiated.[33] In contrast, the communist regimes in Czechoslovakia, Hungary and Poland lasted for 40 years after World War II. This meant that decision making on crime and punishment was much slower and 'The legal culture created by communism was firmly established and [proved] hard to eradicate'.[34]

The early transitional justice literature contrasts ruptured and negotiated transitions. Despite, or perhaps in response to, this dichotomous approach, commentary on prosecution decisions in transitions that do not neatly fall within those two categories began to emerge almost simultaneously. Jose Zalaquett, for example, points to lingering political constraints, even in cases where a democratic election has taken place. In his discussion on Argentina, he contends that 'the government may have had the legitimacy of a democratic election, but the military remained a cohesive force with control over the weapons'.[35] Zalaquett attributes this to the initial failure of the Argentinian authorities to continue to carry out prosecutions of military chiefs. It points to an ethical dilemma undergirding decisions regarding prosecution. Zalaquett quotes Max Weber in his explanation of this dilemma:

> In ambiguous transitional situations, dealing with past human rights violations is indeed a wrenching ethical and political problem … The approach of democratic leaders in

---

[30] ibid 5.

[31] Lutz and Reiger, above n 7, 4.

[32] L Huyse, 'Justice after Transitions: On the Choices Successor Elites Make in Dealing with the Past' in NJ Kritz (ed), *Transitional Justice: How Emerging Democracies Reckon with Former Regimes*, vol 1 (Washington DC, United States Institute of Peace 1995) 111.

[33] ibid.

[34] ibid.

[35] J Zalaquett, 'Balancing Ethical Imperatives and Political Constraints: The Dilemma of New Democracies Confronting Past Human Rights Violations' in Kritz, above n 32, 205.

such difficult transitional situations should, then, be based on the ethical maxim that Max Weber lucidly characterized in his famous lecture, *Politics as a Vocation*: political leaders should be guided by the ethic of responsibility, as opposed to the ethics of conviction … He stressed the fundamental difference between acting according to an ethical precept regardless of the outcome, and acting while considering the predictable consequences of one's action. In Weber's view, politicians must always be guided by an ethic of responsibility.[36]

Ambiguous transitions, then, are not a new phenomenon that arose out of the Arab Spring experiences. The classic case of Argentina and several other Latin American countries point to the shortcomings of the ruptured versus negotiated transition argument. This is especially the case when analysing the course of decisions regarding prosecution over time. As Sikkink notes, the examples of Guatemala, Chile and Uruguay show that 'a ruptured transition was no longer a precondition for prosecutions'.[37] In fact, it may have never been a precursor to prosecutions, as the case of Argentina in the early post-transition period shows. Moreover, countries that underwent heavily pacted or negotiated transitions began to pursue prosecutions, especially since the 1990s. This, Sikkink argues, illustrates that 'the political world is not static'.[38] The dichotomy of ruptured versus negotiated transitions and their impact on the prosecution of political leaders is therefore no longer sufficient to explain decisions regarding criminal accountability for crimes of the former regimes. This point, however, has not been adequately developed in the literature, as the reflections on the Arab region in chapter 6 will discuss.

Critical Transitional Justice Literature

The proliferation of transitions that do not follow the path from dictatorship to liberal democracy have prompted some scholars to re-examine the principles and objectives of transitional justice. Cases such as Uganda, Colombia, Sudan and Morocco illustrate that transitional justice takes place in situations where there has been no fundamental transition, or where human rights abuses continue to be perpetrated.[39] Mainstream transitional justice theory, operating on the assumption that transitional justice occurs in liberalising contexts, has thus come under increasing scrutiny in recent scholarship. Obel Hansen, Hannah Franzki and Maria Carolina Olarte critique the limitations of this liberal conception of transitional justice by pointing to the simple fact that 'transitional justice occurs in radically different contexts'.[40] Cases displaying varied, non-liberal transitions

---

[36] ibid.

[37] Sikkink, above n 10, 83.

[38] ibid.

[39] T Obel Hansen, 'The Vertical and Horizontal Expansion of Transitional Justice: Explanations and Implications for a Contested Field' in Buckley-Zistel et al, above n 15, 109. See also N Roht-Arriaza, 'Editorial Note' (2013) 7 *International Journal of Transitional Justice* 383.

[40] Obel Hansen, ibid.

where transitional justice is actively pursued cannot, then, be explained by the mainstream theory of transitional justice.

Given that transitional justice can limit liberalisation and democratisation, it is important to examine whose interests transitional justice serves.[41] Rather than conform to a blueprint that was developed in Latin America or Eastern Europe, or by international NGOs, prosecutions and other transitional justice mechanisms are pursued for various reasons in varied contexts. On a theoretical level, critics of mainstream transitional justice theory point to its inherently political and liberal values, despite its proponents advocating it as a universal phenomenon that could and should apply across states.[42] Franzki and Olarte, for instance, reflect on transitional justice as part of a 'demo-liberal project'.[43] They go further and attribute transitional justice to the broader neo-liberal socio-economic order. They charge transitional justice with falling short in addressing structural inequalities, even enabling them.[44] Transitional justice, then, is a highly political project that aims to strengthen liberal democracy and market economy. As a result, it perpetuates social inequality in certain contexts, exacerbating injustices that the 'demo-liberal' project proclaims to address.

Paul Gready and Simon Robins similarly discuss the 'foundational limitations' of transitional justice.[45] They describe two principal limitations: the pursuit of liberal democracy as the endpoint of transitional justice and the overly state-centric approach to transitional justice processes. They argue for a transformative justice that places an emphasis on process rather than on predetermined outcomes.[46] This, they contend, should be done by involving victims and survivors as agents of change and through less top-down approaches whereby the state drives the transitional justice process.[47] They add that, 'In addition to the transitional justice agenda being externally driven in many contexts, the state-centric focus it brings to examining violent pasts discourages the engagement of affected populations'.[48] While Gready and Robins are critical of the overbearing role of external actors in local transitional justice processes, they note that certain types of external intervention can facilitate these processes. These external interventions, however, should take on a multi-dimensional approach that incorporates anthropology, social science, development and human rights. Finally, they argue that reparations are the best mechanism for addressing socio-economic grievances as they offer 'both corrective and distributive justice'.[49]

---

[41] Obel Hansen, above n 9, 18.

[42] See, eg, the International Center for Transitional Justice (www.ictj.org) and the Coalition for the International Criminal Court (www.coalitionfortheicc.org).

[43] H Franzki and MC Olarte, 'The Political Economy of Transitional Justice. A Critical Theory Perspective' in Buckley-Zistel et al, above n 15, 202.

[44] ibid 202, 206.

[45] P Gready and S Robins, 'From Transitional to Transformative Justice: A New Agenda for Practice (2014) 8 *International Journal of Transitional Justice* 339, 341.

[46] ibid 352, 358.

[47] ibid 360.

[48] ibid 343.

[49] ibid 347.

Socio-economic Accountability and Transitional Justice

Accountability for corruption and economic crimes and their role in prosecutions vis-à-vis human rights violations have important implications for transitional justice research. One debate centres on whether or not transitional justice mechanisms, including prosecutions, should expand to address corruption and socio-economic crimes. Sharp argues that economic violence has been the 'blind spot of transitional justice' as it is rarely scrutinised with regard to human rights violations.[50] Others question why trial charges are heavy on one set of crimes at the expense of the other. Lutz and Reiger emphasise that trends to prosecute perpetrators who engage in corruption have been 'largely unremarked by the international justice movement' and should be explored further.[51] They cite the Asian examples of South Korea, India, Pakistan, Nepal, the Philippines and Indonesia, where senior officials were tried for corruption and financial crimes, but not for human rights crimes. They posit that reasons for this include the lower costs of trying former leaders for financial crimes than for human rights crimes (as a smaller number of people are usually implicated in economic crimes) and political will. Significantly, they note that popular opinion may find a government official's involvement in corruption and financial crimes more disturbing than that official's perpetration of human rights crimes, such as murder and torture.[52] Still others critique the transitional justice project itself for enabling socio-economic inequalities, making it difficult to seek accountability for such crimes, as Franzki and Olarte explain.[53]

In her account of the status of transitional justice in Egypt, Reem Abou-El-Fadl argues that conventional transitional justice falls short in addressing key developments in Egypt. The former regime's violation of social and economic rights, she argues, is inadequately addressed in the transitional justice literature. She observes that stolen public funds and related crimes were a core focus of the 2011 uprising in Egypt and their articulation in the demands of the protesters played a key role in bringing former state officials to trial. She concludes that the Egyptian case points to the importance that transitional justice practitioners take historical context into account to ensure a more comprehensive implementation of justice measures that better suits the needs of Egypt.[54] The slogan of the Egyptian uprising, "ish, horreyah, 'adalah igtima'eyah' (bread, freedom, social justice), attests to the importance Egyptians attached to ensuring that both their socio-economic and human rights are respected.

---

[50] DN Sharp, 'Addressing Economic Violence in Times of Transition: Toward a Positive-Peace Paradigm for Transitional Justice' (2012) 35 *Fordham International Law Journal* 780, 782.

[51] Lutz and Reiger, above n 7, 10.

[52] ibid 281.

[53] Franzki and Olarte, above n 43.

[54] R Abou-El-Fadl, 'Beyond Conventional Transitional Justice: Egypt's 2011 Revolution and the Absence of Political Will' (2012) 6 *International Journal of Transitional Justice* 318.

Scholars and practitioners have thus been consumed with the tendency of transitional countries to include human rights crimes at the expense of socio-economic rights crimes in their transitional justice mechanisms.[55] As a result, two discernible attributes of the existing literature on this issue emerge. First, much of the literature on transitional justice is prescriptive and makes the case for how socio-economic rights should be included in transitional justice mechanisms.[56] A stronger account for the few yet significant cases in which corruption and socio-economic crimes were the focus of prosecutions, as in the Asian examples cited by Lutz and Reiger and others, should therefore take hold.[57] The Arab region's emphasis on accountability for corruption as opposed to civil and political rights violations presents an additional set of countries where this holds true. Secondly, several explanations have been proposed for why socio-economic rights have not been included. For example, transitional justice is largely drawn from international human rights law, which has traditionally viewed economic and social rights as entitlements rather than rights.[58] Other explanations include the difficulty in ascribing responsibility to individuals for socio-economic crimes and that social justice is a longer-term political process that short-term transitional justice mechanisms cannot fully take into account.[59] Moreover, scholarly discussions on the inclusion of economic and social rights in transitional justice mechanisms focus on their place in truth commissions and reconciliation deals, with limited discussion on their place in criminal prosecutions.

Transitional Justice and the Arab Spring: Emerging Scholarship

With the exception of a small body of emerging literature, the Arab region has been underexplored in the global transitional justice literature. This is in part because the Arab region is relatively new to transitional justice.[60] However, most of the transitional justice literature on the Arab region that has emerged since the Arab Spring uprisings does one or more of the following: it assesses how well

---

[55] See also Gready and Robins, above n 45, 339, although they argue that socio-economic crimes are best addressed through reparations, which can offer both 'corrective and distributive justice' (347, 356).

[56] See L Arbour, 'Economic and Social Justice for Societies in Transition', paper presented at the Second Annual Transitional Justice Lecture, New York University School of Law, 25 October 2006; L Waldorf, 'Anticipating the Past? Transitional Justice and Socio-Economic Wrongs' (2012) 21 *Social and Legal Studies* 171; L LaPlante, 'Transitional Justice and Peace Building: Diagnosing and Addressing the Socioeconomic Roots of Violence through a Human Rights Framework' (2008) 2 *International Journal of Transitional Justice* 331.

[57] Lutz and Reiger, above n 7. Also, General Augusto Pinochet was charged with corruption in Chile, including tax evasion and holding secret bank accounts abroad worth more than $25 million. See Transparency International, 'Chile Sets Precedent for Holding Dictators Accountable for Corruption', Press Release, 25 November 2005, available at www.transparency.org/news/pressrelease/chile_sets_precedent_for_holding_dictators_accountable_for_corruption.

[58] Arbour, above n 56.

[59] Waldorf, above n 56, 171.

[60] Exceptions include Morocco's transitional justice process and the Saddam Hussein trial in Iraq.

the Arab region cases 'fit' within the predominant transitional justice paradigm; it describes transitional justice processes as they have unfolded in some of the Arab region countries; or it calls for increased attention to socio-economic justice in transitional situations by drawing from examples from the Arab region, particularly Egypt and Tunisia.

With few exceptions, then, most of the literature on transitional justice and the Arab region is drawn from political science-based analyses with little rigorous comparative reflection.[61] Moreover, it is based on the assumption that the Arab region has experienced non-transitions or stalled transitions.[62] While there is welcome critique of the inability of mainstream transitional justice to explain the unfolding of transitional justice in certain cases in the Arab region, such critiques rarely question the foundational assumptions of the field.

Methodology

It is useful to briefly revisit the book's two principal research questions to explain the methodology pursued. First, what trigger and driving factors led to the decision to prosecute former political leaders or not? Secondly, what shaping factors affected the content and extent of decisions regarding prosecution? Although not explicitly framed as such, process tracing entails the identification of factors that play a triggering, driving or shaping role in processes. Alexander George and Timothy McKeown's definition of process tracing is particularly useful here:

> [Process tracing] attempts to uncover what stimuli the actors attend to; the decision process that makes use of these stimuli to arrive at decisions; the actual behavior that then occurs; the effect of various institutional arrangements on attention, processing, and behavior; and the effect of other variables of interest on attention, processing, and behavior.[63]

This definition sums up the function of and the relation between the trigger (stimuli), driving (decision process responding to stimuli) and shaping (institutional) factors.

The material collected for each case study is analysed by identifying what factors triggered, drove and shaped decisions regarding prosecution. The trigger–driving–shaping mechanism does not explain the process of prosecution from

---

[61] One exception to this is Ibrahim Fraihat's comparative study of Libya, Yemen and Tunisian, in which he argues for the importance of women, civil society and tribes in shaping national reconciliation in these countries: I Fraihat, *Unfinished Revolutions: Yemen, Libya and Tunisia after the Arab Spring* (New Haven, Yale University Press, 2016).

[62] CL Sriram (ed), *Transitional Justice in the Middle East and North Africa* (New York, Oxford University Press, 2016).

[63] AL George and TJ McKeown, 'Case Studies and Theories of Organizational Decision Making' in RF Coulam and RA Smith (eds), *Advances in Information Processing in Organizations*, vol 2 (JAI Press, 1985) 35.

start to finish. Rather, it is a prism through which the research collected is analysed and used to develop an explanation of how decisions regarding the prosecution of political leaders emerged and developed before and during the highly contentious period of transition. For instance, the identification of trigger factors provides insight into the formative stages of these decision-making processes. It contributes to an inquiry into efforts to prosecute in the past—before the 2010/2011 uprisings—which is necessary in order to understand the development and execution of the prosecutorial strategy in the four countries after the uprisings. Following a detailed presentation of findings from the interviews, each case study's conclusion summarises the key triggers, drivers and shapers based on these findings. Each case study begins with the trigger factors, which are the factors that led to decisions to prosecute or not. The various factors that drove these decisions and pushed and pulled them in different directions are subsequently addressed. Finally, the shaping factors that impacted the content and the extent of the prosecutions are discussed.

The significance of analysing the data through a trigger–driving–shaping prism lies in its facilitation of an in-depth understanding of the dynamics of the processes within which these factors operate. The primary function of this prism is to make sense of the processes that unfolded over time, while taking into account various contextual factors. This is particularly useful for a comparative case study and helps prevent false generalisations that do not take case-by-case specificities into account.

The arguments presented in this book are thus based on both primary and secondary sources. In addition to a critical analysis of the relevant scholarly literature, the research relied heavily on national, regional and international media reports to obtain details concerning the status of prosecutions in each country. An electronic database was compiled, consisting of news articles, reports and commentaries by both individual experts and NGOs for each country throughout the six years during which the research was conducted. Close monitoring of media reports and of new scholarly literature was important because of the developing nature of decisions regarding prosecution in the four case studies and the consequent emerging literature on the Arab region.

The core of the research is drawn from interviews conducted in the four case studies. Between 2012 and 2017, 48 interviews with 44 different interviewees were conducted in Egypt, Libya, Tunisia and Yemen. Twelve interviews were conducted in Egypt, nine in Libya, 15 in Tunisia and ten in Yemen. The interviews were conducted in Arabic, English and French. The interviews were with human rights lawyers and activists, independent experts, civil society leaders, national and international NGO officials, United Nations officials, government officials, including a former minister of justice, journalists and legal professionals, including lawyers, judges and a prosecutor. The interviews were semi-structured to ensure a focused comparison of data across the cases. This was done through the use of a set of questions asked of each individual, followed by additional questions generated by the responses received and by the particular context of the case study.

Challenges

Certain challenges resulted in a limited number of interviews conducted in Libya and Yemen, in comparison with the other case study countries. This was for four reasons.

First, the security situation in Libya was such that the mobility of some interviewees whose offices were difficult to visit was restricted. The first court hearing for Saif al-Islam Gaddafi and the 36 other defendants coincided with my visit to Tripoli, which created a precarious security environment. Precautions were therefore understandably taken by certain interviewees and by myself so as to avoid any danger during transport between interviews.

Secondly, given the high sensitivity of the Saif al-Islam Gaddafi and Abdullah El Senussi cases, and given that there had been several assassinations and death threats targeting lawyers and judges who were potentially involved in their defence, the Libyan human rights lawyers I interviewed refused to discuss the trial of those particular individuals.[64] However, I was able to access two Libyan judges, who have since moved to Tunis. One of them has made his views and analyses available through his writings in a number of online outlets. The other was interviewed via email. The insights from these two judges were particularly helpful in illuminating certain aspects of the Libyan case study. A third challenge to conducting research interviews in Libya was obtaining a visa to travel there. This challenge was eventually overcome with the help of friends, acquaintances and the Libyan ambassador to Qatar, and by the relentless efforts of the Office of the High Commissioner for Human Rights in Qatar, for which I was conducting a short consultancy at the time. Finally, the general opacity surrounding the legal cases in Libya made it difficult to obtain details on the status of the prosecutions.

There were similar challenges with regard to research interviews in Yemen. Thanks to the help of a friend and former colleague based in Yemen, I was able to obtain a visa and travelled to Sanaa in January 2014. There had been two security incidents involving a small bombing and an assassination on the same morning of my arrival in Sanaa. However, as is often the case in such contexts where there are regular fluctuations in the security situation, things returned to normal the next day and I was able to conduct more interviews than initially anticipated. I was also fortunate to have stayed at the hotel where the final stage of the National Dialogue Conference was taking place, which meant that I had relatively easy interview access to a number of key individuals who were attending the talks. The difficulty in accessing Yemeni judges for interviews was partially overcome through acquaintances, who put me in touch with a judge who had recently gone into exile. His views figure in the Yemeni case study in this book.

---

[64] Abdullah El Senussi was Muammar Gaddafi's intelligence chief and brother-in-law. His case is discussed in chapter 4.

No significant challenges were encountered during my research in Egypt and Tunisia. There were, however, certain risks in Egypt, such as surveillance by security officers due to the perceived controversial nature of the topic of the interviews. To reduce this risk, the interviews were conducted in safe, public spaces (eg an office or a café).

Access to prosecutors in Egypt, Libya, Tunisia and Yemen proved difficult. This is because they and other members of the judiciary in all four case studies faced security threats. A review of government and ministry websites in Egypt, Libya, Tunisia and Yemen reveals little more than general descriptions of the function of public prosecutors. As a result, one of the interviews was conducted with a former prosecutor. This stemmed from a number of challenges to do with the ongoing nature of the prosecutions and the general lack of security, which prevented prosecutors from providing commentary on such issues. Former Libyan prosecutor general Abdelaziz al-Hasadi was killed in February 2014, as was the former Egyptian prosecutor Hesham Barakat in June 2015. Both signify the highly controversial nature of their mandate and of the prosecutions in general. Once the trials come to a close, prosecutors may be more forthcoming with their insight into decisions regarding the prosecution of political leaders. Their reflections will be important in further research on criminal accountability within a non-paradigmatic transitional justice context.

An Expanded Definition of 'Political Leaders'

In this book, the term 'political leaders' is not restricted to heads of state, as in, for example, the work of Lutz and Reiger.[65] Rather, it includes other high-level regime officials, including former ministers, police chiefs and military chiefs. The reasons for this expanded focus are fourfold.

First, several high-level government officials other than heads of state have been investigated and/or tried, signalling a more extensive criminal accountability strategy than one that solely targets heads of state. Thus, a more limited focus on heads of state only would significantly limit the strength of the explanations surrounding the pursuit of transitional justice.

Secondly, scholarly literature on the prosecution of political leaders criticises the shortcomings of analyses focused on the prosecution of one individual, using the argument that the guilty individual (usually a head of state) does not necessarily reflect the wrongdoings of the entire regime.

Thirdly, some victims and other justice seekers prefer to see the prosecution of a particular leader, who is not necessarily the head of state. This is because certain individuals, such as the former ministers of interior in all four case studies, are

---

[65] Lutz and Reiger, above n 7.

in many ways regarded as having a more direct role in orchestrating the crimes committed, particularly torture.

Fourthly, the exclusion of certain former high-level officials from prosecution, such as Omar Suleiman and Moussa Kousa, former heads of intelligence in Egypt and Libya respectively, is in and of itself a question that requires examination. The selection of individuals who faced prosecution is a controversial issue in the case studies, revealing that various factors played a role in the inclusion and exclusion of certain individuals from the trials. The expansion of the term 'political leaders' in this way, then, is important for the purpose of addressing one of the book's central research questions: what factors shaped the extent of the investigations and trials?

Case Selection

The Arab region is important for the development of transitional justice research and practice, not least because of the varied types of transitions that have emerged since 2011 and the divergent transitional justice paths pursued. The cases around which the transitional justice field was formed are drawn largely from Eastern Europe and Latin America, which shaped the 'normative assumptions' of the field and represented transitions that resemble 'Western liberal market democracy'.[66] This contrasts with the varied transitions that have unfolded in the Arab region.

Egypt, Libya, Tunisia and Yemen share crucial attributes that make this comparative study possible. In all four countries, massive uprisings took place within the same time period, the leaders were toppled and a drastic political transition ensued. Almost simultaneously, a flurry of activity surrounding the prosecution of political leaders unfolded in all four cases. The absence of trials in Yemen did not mean that the question of prosecution was laid to rest definitively. On the contrary, several large protests in response to the immunity law took place, keeping the issue of accountability in the limelight.

The four case studies, however, are also sufficiently different to enable a meaningful comparative study. Egypt and Tunisia prosecuted their political leaders and issued verdicts. Libya's transition emerged from a violent civil war between Gaddafi loyalists and anti-Gaddafi militias, and with the North Atlantic Treaty Organization's military intervention to oust Muammar Gaddafi and his regime. Following arrest warrants issued by the ICC, Libya decided to prosecute its leaders domestically and refused to hand over suspects to the ICC in The Hague.[67]

---

[66] Sharp, above n 19, 149.

[67] ICC arrest warrants were issued for Muammar Gaddafi, Saif al-Islam Gaddafi and Abdullah El Senussi in June 2011. Following the death of Muammar Gaddafi on 20 October 2011, the ICC terminated its case against him. In April 2013, the ICC issued an arrest warrant under seal for Al-Tuhamy Mohamed Khaled, former head of the Libyan Internal Security Agency. The warrant was unsealed in April 2017.

It also won an admissibility appeal for El Senussi, resulting in the annulment of his ICC arrest warrant in July 2014. Former Yemeni President Saleh negotiated his ouster with heavy regional and international involvement. Geopolitics figured heavily in domestic decisions regarding prosecution in Yemen. The most influential regional and international players were Saudi Arabia and the Gulf Cooperation Council, the USA, the European Union and the United Nations. The Yemeni parliament passed an immunity law that protected Saleh and his aides from prosecution.[68] These varied transitions provide an abundance of material for the rethinking of predominant understandings of transitional justice.

Syria and Bahrain are countries whose mass anti-government uprisings in 2011 qualify them as Arab Spring countries. Iraq and Sudan are also countries that experienced either a trial of a former leader (Iraq) or efforts to prosecute leaders (Sudan) by the ICC. An in-depth study of decisions regarding prosecution in Syria, Bahrain, Iraq and Sudan, however, is beyond the scope of this book for several reasons. One question that arises when considering these cases is whether the ouster of political leaders in the Arab region is a necessary condition for any formal decision to be taken on whether to prosecute. Despite the fact that there have been recent efforts geared towards the establishment of human rights tribunals for Syria, access to the necessary data would have been and continues to be extremely difficult, given the ongoing nature and intensity of the conflict in Syria. Most importantly, the differences in the context within which decisions regarding prosecution have taken place in Bahrain, Syria, Iraq and Sudan are too great to warrant a comparative case study that extends to those countries. Iraq did not experience an Arab Spring uprising that toppled its leader, Sudan's leaders are still very much in power despite the ICC arrest warrants issued against them, and Bahrain and Syria's leaders have not been ousted by the uprisings that took place there.

As the first country in the Arab region to undergo a transitional justice process, Morocco is a well-known example in discussions on transitional justice in the Arab region. While it did not experience a mass anti-government uprising followed by a flurry of prosecutions, Morocco did undergo an elite-led transition that aimed to break with past human rights violations. This transition was very different from those of the Arab Spring in that it did not involve the overthrow of the leader. Rather, following pressure from civil society and victims, the leader agreed to establish an advisory council on human rights, which eventually led to a more comprehensive transitional justice process that has been in place for over a decade. This book, then, will discuss the implications of the Moroccan experience for the newer, core case studies.[69]

---

[68] Law No 1 of 2012 Concerning the Granting of Immunity from Legal and Judicial Prosecution, Amnesty International (22 January 2012) available at https://www.amnesty.org/download/Documents/24000/mde310072012ar.pdf (in Arabic).

[69] See chapter 6 for this discussion on Morocco.

Structure of the Book

In the chapters that follow, the findings for Egypt and Tunisia are presented first, followed by Libya and Yemen. This is because Egypt and Tunisia are the two case studies that are the most advanced with regard to the number of prosecutions and verdicts issued for former political leaders. The findings for Libya and Yemen will demonstrate similarities with Egypt and Tunisia, but will also highlight significant differences in the factors that triggered, drove and shaped decisions regarding prosecution there.

In Egypt (chapter 2), certain iconic legal cases concerning police brutality as well as high-level corruption cases related to the illegal sale of land figured in the pre-uprising period. Apart from the re-emergence of some of these iconic cases in accountability efforts in the post-2011 period, the human rights prosecutions were largely limited to the 18-day uprising. Corruption cases, on the other hand, spanned the pre-uprising period. The emphasis on such crimes was a way to shroud the neglect of accountability for widespread torture, killings, and other civil and political rights abuses committed for decades prior to the uprising. The military-controlled transition and the politicised judiciary in Egypt are two underlying and closely related factors that have shaped the content and the extent of prosecutions in this way. The military and other state agencies worked to ensure that investigations and trials did not extend 'too far' so as not to harm their political interests and subject themselves to human rights prosecutions. The victims, activists and lawyers who were active in pursuing prosecutions were preoccupied with the more recent crimes of 2011 because, practically, they are easier to prosecute. The emphasis on corruption and economic crimes in Egypt was a way to scapegoat certain high-level individuals to deflect attention from the lack of accountability for a more comprehensive set of human rights violations and their perpetrators.

The historic activism of the Tunisian Bar Association, workers' movements, human rights activism and significant pressure by a group of lawyers (the Groupe de 25) in the immediate aftermath of Ben Ali's ouster together formed a diverse protest movement in Tunisia (chapter 3) that contributed to efforts to prosecute Ben Ali and his aides. Moreover, a military that had been marginalised and victimised by both Ben Ali and his predecessor, Habib Bourguiba, served as a major driver of some of the decisions to prosecute former leaders of the Ben Ali regime. To a large extent, Tunisian workers' movements constituted one of the strongest opposition forces for the Tunisian government. Consequently, the role of these workers' movements and the history of deep inequalities and corruption in Tunisia significantly shaped the emphasis on corruption and socio-economic crimes in the prosecutions that have taken place. However, Tunisia's transitional justice process has seen a waning of the prosecutorial focus on corruption and economic crimes. This waning has been attributed to the establishment of the

Truth and Dignity Commission in 2014 and to a reliance on foreign models of transitional justice that foreground accountability for civil and political rights violations.

The anti-government uprising in Libya (chapter 4) was largely sparked by the harsh oppression and lack of accountability for the widespread and systematic crimes committed throughout Muammar Gaddafi's rule. With the exception of some politicised efforts by Gaddafi himself to hold certain high-level officials opposed to him accountable, there were no major efforts to prosecute political leaders in Gaddafi's Libya. There were, however, efforts aimed at accountability through financial compensation of the regime's victims. This was especially prominent in the case of the 1996 Abu Salim prison massacre, the impact of which continues to loom large over accountability efforts more than 20 years later. The Security Council's referral of the Libyan situation to the ICC has had significant implications for the domestic prosecution of former leaders. It has, perhaps more importantly, raised questions surrounding the motives of both international and domestic transitional justice actors, particularly in a transition characterised by ongoing violence. Moreover, rival governments in Libya have played a direct role in steering criminal accountability for certain former leaders, namely Saif al-Islam Gaddafi, in different directions.

Unlike Egypt, Libya and Tunisia, Yemen's ousted President Ali Abdallah Saleh stepped down after securing his immunity from prosecution. It is several years since the so-called transition, yet Saleh still retains significant control in Yemen (chapter 5). The country has been reeling from a devastating war, fought primarily between the 'Arab coalition', led by Saudi Arabia, and the Houthis and their allies. Prior to the outbreak of this war, Yemeni civil society activists worked hard to find ways to circumvent the immunity law, especially when it became clear that protests calling for its reversal would be completely ignored. Both the Libyan and Yemeni case studies raise questions about the merits of examining the unfolding of transitional justice there through the battered peace versus justice debate, not least because of the absence of any monolithic understanding of 'peace' or 'justice'.

Chapter 6 critically reflects on the findings from the four case studies by assessing their implications for transitional justice scholarship and practice. Several questions about the foundational assumptions of transitional justice emerge. To what extent can we speak of a 'transition' in the Arab Spring countries, particularly one that does not have attributes typical of the paradigmatic transitions that have largely shaped the transitional justice field? How can effective prosecutions run their course without pre-existing institutional structures that are equipped to implement and oversee them and other transitional justice processes? To what extent can we refer to a 'global accountability norm' when international actors pursue it in one context (Libya) but completely ignore it in another (Yemen)? The book ends with a brief conclusion (chapter 7) summarising the importance of the findings and with questions for further research.

Conclusion

This book constitutes the first empirical contribution of its kind with original material from 48 in-depth interviews across four countries. It expands the analysis of individual criminal accountability to high-level political, military and police chiefs in addition to heads of state. It investigates both pre- and post-transition efforts regarding the prosecution of such political leaders. This scope of the inquiry is, as explained, counter-intuitive in the transitional justice literature, which focuses primarily on post-transition efforts to prosecute. As such, it analyses the non-paradigmatic nature of the Arab Spring transitions by investigating the pre-transition period and by reflecting on its impact on post-transitional prosecutorial decisions.

Transitional justice scholarship is under-theorised.[70] There is a need for more nuanced, context-driven theories of transitional justice that take into account its use in non-liberal transitions. With few exceptions, Latin American countries underwent transitions that pushed the military back to the barracks and brought in civilian, democratic rule. Prosecutions of those responsible for the heinous crimes committed there are still ongoing, more than three decades later. But not all transitions occur in liberalising contexts. The Arab Spring thus presents an important opportunity to diversify the theory and practice of transitional justice.

---

[70] For discussions on the under-theorisation of transitional justice, see N Palmer, P Clark and D Grenville (eds), *Critical Perspectives in Transitional Justice* (Cambridge, Intersentia, 2012).

2

Egypt

Prosecutions were central to the transitional justice process in post-2011 Egypt. However, certain iconic legal cases concerning police brutality as well as high-level corruption cases related to the illegal sale of land also figured in the pre-uprising period. Apart from the re-emergence of some of these iconic cases in the efforts made to address accountability in the post-2011 period, human rights prosecutions were largely limited to the 18-day uprising. Corruption cases, on the other hand, spanned the pre-uprising period. This is a result of the ways in which certain actors, such as the public prosecution and the interim military authorities, drove and shaped decisions regarding prosecution. It is also reflective of a conscious effort by interim elites to separate the two sets of violations—the civil and political versus the socio-economic—in an attempt to highlight the 'exceptionality' of the human rights abuses. In other words, it was a way to portray the 18-day uprising as a temporary period of human rights abuses, rather than the culmination of decades of human rights violations leading up to it. This chapter discusses these and other factors that triggered, drove and shaped decisions regarding prosecution in pre- and post-uprising Egypt.

The anti-government uprising in Egypt began on the 25 January 2011. Mass demonstrations engulfed the country when hundreds of thousands of people took to the streets and chanted for the removal of former President Mubarak's regime. Mubarak had been in power for 30 years. Corruption, widespread torture and other human rights abuses were endemic. Criticism of the Mubarak government—whether in the press or through street protests and workers' strikes—was often met with swift repressive measures, such as arbitrary detention and torture. Presidential elections held every six years repeatedly resulted in dubious results, with 88–94 per cent of the vote claimed to be for Mubarak.[1] In the 2000s, public outrage directed at the Mubarak regime for various political and socio-economic grievances began to manifest itself in intensified protests, strikes and civil society pressure, despite the oppressive repercussions. Egyptians took to the streets to protest during the Palestinian Intifada in 2000 and again during the USA's invasion of Iraq in 2003, directing their anger at the Mubarak regime's close ties with the USA and

---

[1] 'Mubarak Wins Another Term', *BBC News*, 17 September 1999, available at http://news.bbc.co.uk/2/hi/middle_east/458754.stm; 'How Mubarak Won the Election', *The Guardian*, 13 September 2005, available at www.theguardian.com/world/2005/sep/13/worlddispatch.egypt.

Israel. Moreover, heightened tensions surrounding Mubarak's suspected grooming of his son, Gamal Mubarak, to become the country's next president led to the formation of the Kifaya protest movement. In 2005, judges in Egypt took a decisive and very public stand against electoral fraud and executive meddling in judicial affairs. This marked a major turning point in the decades-long struggle for judicial independence in Egypt.

Thus, the Egyptian anti-government uprising sprung from decades of political stagnation, social unrest and systematic human rights violations, mostly at the hands of the infamous Ministry of Interior and its agencies. On 11 February 2011, the eighteenth day of the uprising, Mubarak stepped down and the military took over as the governing interim authority until a new president—Mohammed Morsi—was elected in June 2012. Morsi was a member of the Muslim Brotherhood and led the Freedom and Justice Party, which was formed in June 2011. In July 2013, he was removed from office following a military coup backed by large protests, which saw the return of military rule in Egypt, this time headed by Abdel Fattah El Sisi, who then became president in June 2014.

Summary of Post-2011 Prosecutions

The most high-level prosecution that has taken place in Egypt is that of former President Mubarak, his two sons and the former Minister of Interior, Habib El Adly. All faced multiple charges of corruption, economic crimes and human rights violations. The human rights prosecutions were limited to violations that occurred during the 18-day uprising—specifically, the killing of protesters—whereas the corruption and economic crimes charges included the pre-uprising period.

Mubarak and El Adly were sentenced to life imprisonment in June 2012 for their roles in the killing of protesters during the uprising. They were charged with 'complicity in the killing of protesters', while four other high-level interior ministry officials were acquitted.[2] The verdict was appealed and, following a retrial, the charges against Mubarak and El Adly over the killing of protesters were dropped in a controversial verdict in November 2014. The court did not declare Mubarak guilty or innocent; instead, it referred to a technical error made by the court in 2011, when Mubarak's name was not included in the initial indictment listing El Adly and his aides in March 2011. Mubarak's name was added to the indictment in April 2011, following pressure on the interim military government by massive street protests.[3]

---

[2] 'Mubarak Sentenced to Jail for Life over Protest Deaths', BBC News (2 June 2012) available at www.bbc.com/news/world-middle-east-18306126.

[3] The nuances of this reasoning are discussed in H Bahgat, 'Q&A: The Mubarak Trial Verdict—What Just Happened?', *Mada Masr*, 29 November 2014, available at www.madamasr.com/opinion/politics/qa-mubarak-trial-verdict---what-just-happened.

However, the November 2014 verdict was also appealed, and a third and final retrial ended with a verdict declaring Mubarak innocent in March 2017.

Mubarak and his two sons, Gamal Mubarak and Alaa Mubarak, were also tried in several corruption cases.[4] In the *Presidential Palaces* case, Mubarak, his sons and four other defendants were accused of embezzling LE 125 million in state funds to adorn their private properties. The funds were falsely claimed to have been spent on maintenance for telecommunications towers. In reality, they were used to purchase furniture and for interior design purposes for the Mubarak family's homes. In May 2014, Mubarak was found guilty, sentenced to three years in prison and fined LE 120 million. The verdict was appealed and the appeal was upheld by the Court of Cassation in January 2015. Mubarak and his sons were released from the case. The charge against Mubarak and his sons of illegal possession of five villas worth LE 39 million in Sharm El Sheikh was dropped in November 2014 because of a ten-year statute of limitations. This was known as the *Sharm El Sheikh villas* case. In the *Al Ahram gifts* case, Mubarak was accused of illegally receiving gifts worth LE 18 million from the state-owned media institution Al Ahram. However, the case was dropped in August 2013 following Mubarak's repayment of the value of the gifts.

The *Israeli gas deal* case saw the prosecution of Mubarak along with former Petroleum Minister Sameh Fahmy and business tycoon Hussein Salem. They were accused of squandering public funds on a massive scale and of granting the Eastern Mediterranean Gas Company the right to sell Egyptian gas without a bidding process. They were also charged with failing to include provisions in the deal allowing Egypt to change gas prices in accordance with changes in international market prices. Nadia Ahmed summarises the magnitude of this case: 'The 15 year contract with Israel reportedly cost the Egyptian economy LE 4.2 billion. Hussein Salem allegedly made LE 2 billion in profit from the deal.'[5] The November 2014 verdict acquitted Mubarak and the other defendants on all charges related to this gas deal. While Hussein Salem was acquitted in the *Israeli gas deal* case, he was sentenced in absentia, along with his son and daughter, to ten years in a maximum security prison for his role in the *Selling Electricity* case. They were also fined LE 11.125 million. Through the Middle East Oil Refining Company, which Hussein Salem chaired and on which his son and daughter served as board members, they illegally sold electricity to organisations other than the Egyptian Electricity Authority. Hussein Salem fled to Spain during the 25 January 2011 uprising.

In August 2016, the Minister of Justice announced that a reconciliation deal had been finalised, in which Salem returned 75 per cent (LE 5 billion) of his financial assets to the state in exchange for the dropping of all charges against him and

---

[4] Gamal Mubarak, who was Deputy Secretary General of Mubarak's National Democratic Party, was active in Egyptian politics and was thought by many to be pushing his way to the presidency, following in the path of his father.

[5] N Ahmed, 'Show Me the Money: The Many Trials of Mubarak's Men', *Mada Masr*, 25 January 2015, available at www.madamasr.com/sections/politics/show-me-money-many-trials-mubaraks-men.

the unfreezing of his assets. However, the credibility of this deal has been challenged in an investigation that claims only 20 per cent of Salem's fortunes have been returned.[6] In what is known as the *Steel Licenses* case, former Trade Minister Rachid Mohammed Rachid was accused of issuing an illegitimate licence to steel tycoon Ahmed Ezz. Tried in absentia, Rachid was sentenced to 15 years in prison and fined LE 1.4 billion for squandering LE 600 million in public funds. In a similar reconciliation deal to Salem's, corruption charges against Rachid were dropped in February 2017 following his return of LE 500 million to the government.

Ahmed Ezz, steel tycoon and former chairman of Mubarak's National Democratic Party, was also tried in a number of corruption cases. In the *Money Laundering* case, he was released on an LE 100 million bail, 'reportedly the highest bail ever set in Egyptian history', for laundering LE 6.4 billion between 2003 and 2011 through deals related to his acquisition of the Al-Ezz Dekhelia Steel Company.[7] As mentioned above, in the *Steel Licenses* case, Ezz was charged, along with the former Trade and Industry Minister Rachid Mohamed Rachid, with squandering LE 660 million of public funds by obtaining two free licences to produce steel instead of obtaining the licences through a public bidding process. In March 2015, Ezz returned the second licence to the state. He was released in August 2014 after completing a three-year prison sentence for a previous corruption conviction.[8]

Three fact-finding committees were formed in Egypt after the 2011 uprising. The first was formed in 2011 and was tasked with gathering evidence for crimes committed during the 25 January uprising. Headed by Judge Adel Qoura, the committee issued its report in April 2011, in which it confirmed that Egyptian police used live ammunition against protesters on 28 and 29 January 2011.[9] Former President Mohamed Morsi formed the second fact-finding committee in July 2012, one month after he took office. This committee consisted of judges, an assistant public prosecutor, an assistant interior minister, the head of national security, human rights lawyers and relatives of victims.[10] The 2012 fact-finding committee's report was never made public, but its confidential findings led Morsi to order the reopening of the Mubarak trial. Given that the June 2012 Mubarak

---

[6] M Mohie, 'Hussein Salem's Wealth: What's Hidden Is More Important', *Mada Masr*, 19 October 2016, available at www.madamasr.com/en/2016/10/19/feature/politics/hussein-salems-wealth-whats-hidden-is-more-important/.

[7] Ahmed, above n 5.

[8] Several other high-level figures from the former Egyptian regime were tried for corruption and abuse of power. They include former Prime Minister Ahmed Nazif, former Finance Minister Youssef Boutros-Ghali, former Housing Minister Ahmed Al-Maghrabi, former Tourism Minister Zoheir Garana, former Information Minister Anas Al-Fiqqi, former Speaker of Egypt's Upper House in parliament Safwat El Sherif, and former Speaker of the People's Assembly Ahmed Fathi Sorour.

[9] 'Fact-finding Committee Releases Report on the January 25 Revolution', *Ahram Online*, 19 April 2011, available at http://english.ahram.org.eg/NewsContent/1/64/10374/Egypt/Politics-/FactFinding-Committee-releases-report-on-the-Janua.aspx.

[10] 'Morsi Expresses Gratitude to the Army Amid Demands to Release Confidential Report', *Daily News Egypt*, 12 April 2013, available at www.dailynewsegypt.com/2013/04/12/morsi-expresses-gratitude-to-the-army-amid-demands-to-release-confidential-report/.

and El Adly verdicts were appealed in January 2013, a retrial was set to take place later that year. Following the retrial, the charges against Mubarak concerning the killing of protesters were dropped in November 2014, as explained above. A third and final retrial resulted in a verdict declaring Mubarak innocent in March 2017.

The third fact-finding committee was formed in December 2013 by a presidential decree issued by interim President Adly Mansour. Headed by former international judge Fouad Abdel Moneim Riyad, this committee was tasked with investigating crimes committed during and immediately after the 30 June 2013 events, when former President Morsi was overthrown in a military coup backed by a large number of protesters.[11] While only an executive summary of the committee's report was made public, Egyptian civil society provided thorough responses to the published findings. One Egyptian NGO criticised the committee's failure to establish 'enforcement and accountability mechanisms to make it binding for state institutions to cooperate with the Commission' as well as its failure to specify whether it has the powers of subpoena, search and seizure.[12] The committee also apparently did not specify which human rights violations fell under its mandate, nor did it identify the time-frame covered in its investigations.[13]

While the above summary is far from comprehensive, it illustrates the centrality of prosecutions following Mubarak's ouster in February 2011. Efforts to prosecute political leaders were not, however, confined to the post-2011 period. The next section outlines pre-transition efforts to prosecute and highlights iconic cases that impacted subsequent criminal accountability efforts in Egypt.

The Prosecution of Political Leaders in Pre-transition Egypt

While there were no successful attempts to prosecute political leaders before the 2011 uprising in Egypt, lawyers filed many torture cases with the public prosecution.[14] These cases, however, targeted mid-level police and interior ministry officials, and most of them resulted in verdicts based on weak or incomplete

---

[11] Estimates vary, but some accounts state that 14 million protesters called for Morsi's removal, while others state that 30 million protesters backed the military coup. See 'Counting Crowds: Was Egypt's Uprising the Biggest Ever?', *BBC News*, 16 July 2013, available at www.bbc.com/news/magazine-23312656.

[12] Egyptian Initiative for Personal Rights, 'The Executive Summary of the Fact-Finding Commission's Report: Falls Short of Expectations', Press Release, 4 December 2014, available at http://eipr.org/en/pressrelease/2014/12/04/2293.

[13] ibid.

[14] Interview with anonymous senior expert on transitional justice in Egypt, International Center for Transitional Justice (14 June 2013); interview with Mohamed Al Ansary, human rights lawyer and activist, Cairo Institute for Human Rights Studies (Cairo, Egypt, 10 December 2013).

evidence and questionable judicial procedures.[15] The public prosecution blocked many cases. Interviewees cited several reasons for the weak verdicts and for the large number of cases that were blocked before 2011. First, there was no political will to push the cases forward 'because it was the regime that was committing torture'.[16] A lack of judicial independence, particularly where the public prosecutor is allied with the ruling political party, was a major obstacle to criminal accountability for both political leaders and mid-level officials. Several interviewees also explained that no one was 'bold enough' to pursue cases against high-level government officials, largely due to the systematic nature of the torture and intimidation tactics employed by the *amn el dawlah* (state security).[17] The human rights lawyer and activist Mohamed Al Ansary recalled testimonies from torture victims who said that when they attempted to report torture crimes at police stations, state security officials then posed as prosecutors and inflicted torture on them again for reporting the original crime.[18] This, of course, created a climate of fear, leading an increasing number of victims to refrain from reporting torture crimes. Al Ansary added that the difference between calls for prosecution before 2011 and those post-2011 is that civil society demands were formerly framed as 'we need more accountability' rather than the more recent, bolder and specific 'Mubarak should be prosecuted'. Naming high-level officials was too risky for torture victims in particular because of the systematic and widespread nature of torture practices in Egypt before 2011.

Difficult access to concrete evidence is another major reason for the lack of criminal prosecutions of high-level government officials before 2011.[19] As Judge Adel Maged explained, the problem with the Egyptian criminal system is that it requires 'direct evidence', such as eyewitnesses, for cases to be successful.[20] Maged explained that 'According to the ordinary criminal provisions, many cases both before and after 2011 resulted in acquittals because there was insufficient evidence according to this evidentiary requirement—direct evidence—in the current criminal system'.[21] The absence of a provision for command responsibility in the criminal code also makes it difficult, if not impossible, to establish the responsibility of leaders.

Before 2011, there were a few notable prosecution attempts that targeted the president, prime minister, ministers and intelligence chiefs. For example, a number of prominent human rights lawyers, including Khaled Ali and Ahmed Seif

---

[15] Al Ansary, ibid; interview with Mohamed El Shewy, Transitional Justice Programme Officer, Egyptian Initiative for Personal Rights (telephone interview, 24 November 2013); Anonymous, above n 14; interview with Gamal Eid, human rights lawyer, activist and Director of the Arabic Network for Human Rights Information (Cairo, Egypt, 8 December 2013).

[16] Eid, ibid.

[17] Al Ansary, above n 14.

[18] ibid.

[19] El Shewy, above n 15; interview with Judge Adel Maged, Vice President, Court of Cassation, Egypt (Cairo, Egypt, 7 December 2013).

[20] Maged, ibid.

[21] ibid.

El Dawla, filed complaints against former intelligence chief Omar Suleiman for the 2008 violent crackdown on protesters in Mahalla.[22] The public prosecutor blocked this case from going forward. The high-level corruption cases of *Madinaty* and *Palm Hills* in 2010 were filed against the president, prime minister and minister of investment.[23] Three influential cases, however, stand out in the string of failed attempts at prosecution before 2011. Several interviewees cited the *Khaled Said* case of 2010–14, the *Emad El Kebir* case of 2007 and the 2005 sexual harassment case, *Egyptian Initiative for Personal Rights and Interights v Egypt* (323/2006). These were relatively successful efforts to prosecute officials within the police and ministry of interior.

Khaled Said was a 28-year-old man from Alexandria who was arrested, beaten and tortured for posting a video on the internet of police officers conducting an illegal drug transaction. Said died as a result of the torture inflicted on him. Images of his mangled body went viral on social media and produced widespread and international outrage. Wael Ghonim, a Google marketing executive and computer engineer, created a Facebook page called 'We Are All Khaled Said' days after Said's death in June 2010. We Are All Khaled Said became a powerful social movement in the lead up to and during the Egyptian uprising in 2011. The two police officers accused of torturing Said to death, Awad Ismail and Mahmoud Salah, were initially put on trial in July 2010. The trial was then delayed until October 2011, when the officers were sentenced to seven years in prison. In March 2014, following a retrial, the sentence was increased to ten years in prison.[24] One year later, the ten-year sentence was upheld by the Court of Cassation following a failed appeal.

Emad El Kebir is a bus driver who was kidnapped by police officers in Alexandria, Egypt in 2006 and was beaten, raped and tortured while in detention. Videos of police officers beating and torturing El Kebir, recorded by the officers themselves, circulated on the internet and triggered widespread public outrage. The officers were found guilty and jailed for three years, and El Kebir was also offered

---

[22] Interview with Khaled Ali, Executive Director, Hisham Mubarak Law Center, former presidential candidate (2012), Co-Founder of the Bread and Freedom Party, lawyer and activist (Cairo, Egypt, 9 December 2013). In April 2008, a strike and protest by factory workers in the town of Mahalla was violently repressed by security forces. See O El Sharnoubi, 'Revolutionary History Relived: The Mahalla Strike of 6 April 2008', *Ahram Online*, 6 April 2013, available at http://english.ahram.org.eg/NewsContent/1/64/68543/Egypt/Politics-/Revolutionary-history-relived-The-Mahalla-strike-o.aspx. See also H Onodera, 'The *Kifaya* Generation: Politics of Change within Youth in Egypt' (2009) 34 *Journal of the Finnish Anthropological Society* 44, 52–61.

[23] Ali, ibid. See pp 48–49 for more on the *Madinaty* and *Palm Hills* cases. See also M Kassem and Z Fattah, 'The Man Behind Egypt's Real Estate Rebellion', *Bloomberg News*, 26 May 2011, available at www.bloomberg.com/bw/magazine/content/11_23/b4231041996189.htm. The *Madinaty* judgments and case summary are on file with the author.

[24] H Kortam, 'Two Sentenced to 10 Years in Khaled Said Murder Retrial', *Daily News Egypt*, 3 March 2014, available at www.dailynewsegypt.com/2014/03/03/two-sentenced-10-years-khaled-said-murder-retrial/; 'Khaled Said: The Face that Launched a Revolution', *Ahram Online*, 6 June 2012, available at http://english.ahram.org.eg/NewsContent/1/64/43995/Egypt/Politics-/Khaled-Said-The-face-that-launched-a-revolution.aspx.

monetary compensation.[25] Although high-level officials were not implicated in this case, its widespread publicity both within and outside Egypt turned it into an influential case that showed that holding the police accountable for their crimes was possible.

In 2013, the African Commission on Human and Peoples' Rights (African Commission) decided that the Egyptian state was in violation of several articles of the African Charter for the infamous harassment case of four women eight years earlier. On 25 May 2005, Shaimaa Abou Al-Kheir, Nawal Ali Mohammed Ahmed, Abir al-Askari and Iman Taha Kamel were beaten and sexually assaulted at a demonstration outside the Journalists' Syndicate in Cairo. Opposition groups protesting constitutional amendments that were viewed as an attempt to consolidate Mubarak's authoritarian rule led the demonstration. After a series of failed attempts to domestically prosecute those responsible for the harassment, the NGO Egyptian Initiative for Personal Rights and the international human rights group Interights filed a complaint with the African Commission in 2006.[26] The African Commission's decision in early 2013 and its call for Egypt to investigate, punish the perpetrators and provide monetary compensation to the victims is largely viewed as a significant victory in the difficult pursuit of accountability targeting Ministry of Interior officials. It also signified the first time that the African Commission had issued a decision on the duty of states to protect women from violence.[27] Moreover, human rights lawyers again filed complaints with the African Commission in 2012, this time against the military's use of 'virginity tests' on female protesters in Cairo's Tahrir Square.[28] While the African Commission is not regarded as influential as, for example, the Inter-American Court of Human Rights is in Latin America, it is a legal avenue that is increasingly used by Egyptian human rights organisations that are unable to effectively pursue criminal justice domestically.[29] That said, the decisions of the African Commission have yet to be implemented in Egypt.

[25] 'Egypt Police Jailed for Torture', *BBC News*, 5 November 2007, available at http://news.bbc.co.uk/2/hi/middle_east/7078785.stm. See also 'El-Kebir Vindicated', Al Ahram Weekly Online, 8–14 November 2007, available at http://weekly.ahram.org.eg/2007/870/eg8.htm.

[26] For details of the case, see 'Communication 323/06: Egyptian Initiative for Personal Rights v INTERIGHTS v Egypt', African Commission for Human and Peoples' Rights, available at www.achpr.org/files/sessions/10th-eo/comunications/323.06/achpreos10_232_06_eng.pdf.

[27] Egyptian Initiative for Personal Rights, 'Egypt Held to Account for Failing to Protect Women Demonstrators from Sexual Assault', Press Release, 14 March 2013, available at http://eipr.org/en/pressrelease/2013/03/14/1657.

[28] Egyptian Initiative for Personal Rights, 'African Commission Declares "Virginity Tests" Case Admissible: Lack of Accountability for Violations in Military Prisons Addressed in Regional human Rights Mechanism', Press Release, 3 December 2013, available at http://eipr.org/en/pressrelease/2013/12/03/1892.

[29] El Shewy, above n 15; Eid, above n 15. For more on the role of the African Commission, particularly post-2011, see the Role of International Actors section below.

Content and Extent of Prosecutions
in Post-transition Egypt

Since the 2011 Egyptian uprising, charges related to the embezzlement of state funds, the illegal sale of land and other illicit gains have figured quite heavily in the prosecution files. Moreover, some of these charges have dated back to periods from before the 2011 uprising. On the other hand, charges related to torture, arbitrary detention and other human rights abuses have been, with very few exceptions, limited to the 18-day period of the 2011 uprising, leaving previous decades of perpetual civil and political rights violations unaccounted for. This is not to say that there were no efforts to prosecute those responsible for human rights crimes in the pre-transition period. But, with few exceptions, such as those mentioned above, most of these efforts have met with failure. Also, certain high-level government officials were prosecuted in the immediate aftermath of Mubarak's ouster, while others were not. This section addresses why the content of the prosecutions—the types of charges—is focused on corruption and economic crimes and on a very limited set of human rights crimes. Using material from interviews with lawyers, activists, a judge and civil society organisations, this section also explains the selective extent of the trials—why certain leaders from the Mubarak regime were put on trial, while others ran free and even became candidates in presidential elections.

Why did prosecutions place heavy emphasis on corruption crimes as opposed to human rights crimes? One explanation pertains to the controlled nature of the transition that unfolded in Egypt, whereby the military and other state agencies worked to ensure that investigations and trials did not extend 'too far', so as not to harm their political interests and subject themselves to human rights prosecutions. Secondly, and linked to this explanation, is the absence of an enabling legal framework and the role of a politicised judiciary in blocking certain controversial cases, both of which made human rights prosecutions particularly difficult. Thirdly, the victims, activists and lawyers who were active in pursuing prosecutions were preoccupied with the more recent crimes of 2011 because they were 'fresher' and therefore easier to prosecute.[30] Fourthly, the emphasis on corruption and economic crimes is a means to scapegoat certain high-level individuals to deflect attention from the lack of accountability for a more comprehensive set of human rights violations and their perpetrators.

A Military-Controlled Transition

Many lawyers, activists and NGOs consider the military-controlled transition and a politicised judiciary in Egypt as the two underlying, and closely related, factors

---

[30] Eid, above n 15.

that have shaped the content and the extent of prosecutions.[31] Mohamed El Shewy, programme officer at the Egyptian Initiative for Personal Rights, explains: 'The government—the *feloul*[32]—controls the prosecutions. The military has been trying to control how much is prosecuted, what is prosecuted, how far back and how deep the prosecutions are going'.[33]

El Shewy's comments were made in 2013, when the Egyptian military had de facto executive power. The focus on crimes committed during the transition is itself also limited in scope. The majority of the human rights trials strictly addressed the 18-day period of the uprising, while rarely addressing crimes that continued to be perpetrated following Mubarak's ouster on 11 February 2011. One exception to this is the flawed trials of the police officers who shot and killed protesters during the November 2011 Mohamed Mahmoud Street demonstrations against the military. This limited scope is again attributed to the influential role of the military in limiting the extent of the prosecutions, aided by a powerful part of the judiciary that has loyalties to both the Mubarak regime and the military.

Human rights violations have continued and in some ways even intensified since the overthrow of Mubarak in February 2011, prompting the head of the Egyptian Centre for Economic and Social Rights (ECESR), Nadeem Mansour, to sum up the situation as follows: 'We have the same courts and the same human rights violations'.[34] Mansour's statement points to the military-controlled transition in Egypt, where the former regime still wielded significant influence on the shape of the transition and its politics. The former regime is often associated with the military because all of its leaders, including Mubarak, hailed from the military. Habib Nassar, former director of the Middle East and North Africa Programme at the International Center for Transitional Justice (ICTJ) argued that 'the army and interim authorities are afraid to open the human rights file'. This is because of the military's close ties with the former regime in the decades before the 2011 uprising.[35] Mansour elaborated on the impact of the controlled transition in Egypt on the limited nature of the human rights charges:

> The human rights charges in the prosecutions that have taken place in Egypt only have to do with the uprising because we are operating on the same system as before the revolution. We are dealing with the same system—the military which was part of the same violations is the group that led the so-called transition. It is the same court system that was running under the Mubarak regime. So it is very hard to conduct prosecutions, unlike

---

[31] Ali, above n 22; El Shewy, above n 15; Eid, above n 15; interview with Tamer Wageeh, Director, Economic and Social Justice Unit, Egyptian Initiative for Personal Rights (Cairo, Egypt, 8 December 2013); interview with Nadeem Mansour, Director, Egyptian Center for Economic and Social Rights (telephone interview, 13 May 2013); interview with Habib Nassar, Middle East and North Africa Director, International Center for Transitional Justice (New York City, New York, 18 May 2012).

[32] The Arabic term used in Egypt to describe 'remnants' of the former regime.

[33] El Shewy, above n 15.

[34] Mansour, above n 31.

[35] Nassar, above n 31.

in Argentina … The human rights charges are also limited because the prosecutions are governed by the prosecutor, who is totally controlled by the regime—whether the former or the current one. The whole system is very controlled in terms of what is prosecuted and what is not. The court system in the last two years has been focusing on resisting this temptation on focusing on before the uprising. The prosecution of old [pre-uprising] human rights violations would have been more radical for them. It would lead to real change in the regime and in the police. The old political violations are still being committed. We did not have a change in the governing elite. The Muslim Brotherhood joined, but they did not shift. And this is because the same political violations still exist.[36]

In his remarks on the lack of a definitive political transition in Egypt, the activist and writer Wael Eskandar distinguishes between social change and political change. He explains:

How would I describe the transition in Egypt? It's a matter of scapegoating faces of the same regime. Let's compare Egypt to the transitions in Latin America. Well, if Egypt didn't border Israel, things would be different. It would be more like Tunisia. It's too much of an important international actor. The change instead happened inside people. There is too much at stake with Egypt for a real transition to happen. What needs to happen is for there to be a system that reflects the social change that took place on the streets. There has been dramatic social change and without bringing people to account for what they did and do, there is no transition. Real criminal accountability is what is needed in order to have an effective transition.[37]

Of note, here, is Eskandar's reference to Egypt's geopolitical significance as Israel's neighbour, and the negative impact this has had on the emergence of a meaningful political transition. In other words, so long as the Egyptian government is committed to preserving peace with Israel, a primary foreign policy concern of the USA and other Western countries, no foreign pressure for a genuine democratic transition in Egypt will be applied. Instead, and as the years since 2011 have very clearly demonstrated, the Egyptian government will continue to enjoy political and financial support from long-time allies such as the USA, without having to bow to pressure to improve its human rights record. One glaring example is when the USA stopped short of declaring the removal of President Morsi a 'military coup', so as not to suspend its annual financial aid to Egypt of over one billion dollars. The Foreign Assistance Act of 1961 requires the USA to suspend foreign aid to countries where democratically elected governments are overthrown by a military coup.[38] The decision to avoid calling the overthrow of Morsi a coup, then, is a typical instance of bypassing legal provisions to protect political and national security interests. The absence of a meaningful political transition as well as of any major foreign pressure to bring about such a transition in Egypt has facilitated

---

[36] Mansour, above n 31.

[37] Interview with Wael Eskandar, prominent blogger, independent journalist and media commentator, and member of the Kaziboon campaign, which called for accountability for crimes committed by the Egyptian military (Cairo, Egypt, 8 December 2013).

[38] See S Aziz, 'US Foreign Aid and Morsi's Ouster', *Middle East Institute*, 31 July 2013.

farcical trials as no genuine reform of the judiciary and the political leadership has taken place.

El Shewy described a very similar situation to Mansour in his statements on the nature of the transition in Egypt and the consequent ways in which civil society had to adjust their advocacy efforts:

> This has been a controlled transition in the sense that there was a willingness to go after Mubarak and the National Democratic Party—especially the higher echelons of it—but I think that's where it stops and I think there is a lot of unwillingness to go beyond that and into how the 1952 state operated. Now of course, there is a lot of interest in trying Morsi and his people—but the way the transition has gone, it hasn't really been a transition. We've had one leader go, but the whole system is still exactly the same, so it's difficult to talk about a transition. So our belief is that there hasn't really been a transition and so [civil society's] approach is to go from the bottom up so instead of relying on the judiciary, we are attempting to go and archive and document things ourselves and try to have a strong series of cases that we can then—when there is political will—use to really have a serious transitional justice programme. We are reverting to the strategy we used to operate on before 2011 since there isn't much political will because there hasn't been much of a change.[39]

Mansour, Eskandar and El Shewy's observations also point to the problem of a non-independent judiciary. The history of the judges' struggle for independence in Egypt provides an important understanding of the context within which the judiciary operates, its various fissures and how they have shaped decisions regarding prosecution in Egypt. In the next section, I explain how obstacles to the judges' struggle for independence, anchored in the efforts of the Judges Club, were and continue to be crucial limiting factors to the content and extent of prosecutions.

Egypt's Judicial Struggle for Independence

Historical and contemporary accounts of the judges' struggle for independence in Egypt are useful in highlighting the origins of tensions between the executive and the judiciary, and their evolution in pre- and post-transition Egypt.[40] This section first provides a brief overview of how key judicial positions are filled, followed by a discussion of the major challenges judges in Egypt faced to assert their independence. It then addresses questions pertaining to the role of the judiciary in both facilitating and blocking the prosecution of political leaders in post-transition Egypt, thereby impacting on their content and extent.

---

[39] El Shewy, above n 15.

[40] For a historical analysis of the Egyptian judiciary, see N Bernard-Maugiron (ed), *Judges and Political Reform in Egypt* (Cairo, American University in Cairo Press, 2008); T Moustafa, *The Struggle for Constitutional Power: Law, Politics and Economic Development in Egypt* (Cambridge, Cambridge University Press, 2009). For a contemporary account, see also S Aziz, 'Theater or Transitional Justice: Reforming the Judiciary in Egypt' in CL Sriram (ed), *Transitional Justice in the Middle East* (New York, Oxford University Press, 2016).

Article 119 of the Law on Judicial Authority (Law 46/1972) states that the General Prosecutor and the President of the Court of Cassation are to be appointed by the President of the Republic. The Minister of Justice appoints presidents of courts of first instance for one year, which is renewable. Moreover, the judicial inspection department is affiliated with the Ministry of Justice, the composition of the Supreme Judicial Council (SJC) is controlled by the executive authority, and the Ministry of Justice and the President of the Republic make decisions regarding rules of transfer, secondment, and secondment abroad of judges. Moreover, the consent and opinions of the SJC are not always taken into account by the executive authority. Abdallah Khalil traces the evolution of the role of the General Prosecutor in Egypt and his office's relation to executive power since its introduction in 1875 and notes continued executive control throughout Gamal Abdel Nasser's rule:

> The 1952 Revolution government ... established a State Security Investigation Department to tighten its grip over investigation of political crimes and to ban the Office of Public Prosecution from conducting investigations of crimes allegedly perpetrated by public officials and security forces.[41]

The Judges Club, an informal but powerful association of judges, was formed in 1939. It has 9000 members and over 20 regional judges clubs, the most influential of which is the Alexandria Judges Club, which formed in 1941. In an attempt to curb the influence of these independent judges' associations, the Minister of Justice created other clubs in 1980.[42] Mohammed Sayed Said points to the Judge Club's refusal to join the Arab Socialist Union (ASU) as a major turning point that strengthened the Judges Club's resistance to executive control. Abdel Nasser established the ASU in 1962. Holding a judicial post was to be contingent on becoming a member of the ASU, a strategy seen by many judges as an additional tactic to weaken their independence. Said notes that 'The judges' refusal to join the ASU resulted in dozens losing their jobs in what is known as the Massacre of the Judiciary of 1969'.[43]

Throughout the 1990s and 2000s, the Judges Club exerted a significant amount of pressure to amend the Law on Judicial Authority. In 1991, it drafted an amendment to the law to put an end to executive appointment of the General Prosecutor and other judges. A particular objection was directed at the appointment of presidents of courts of first instance, who wield significant powers, including referral of particular cases to particular judges.[44] Part of the 1991 amendment, then, stipulated that the general assemblies of the courts of first instance should appoint judges and assign administrative duties to the presidents of these courts. Continued pressure by reformist judges in Egypt to amend judicial laws to allow

---

[41] A Khalil, 'The General Prosecutor between the Judicial and Executive Authorities' in Bernard-Maugiron, ibid, 62.

[42] Bernard-Maugiron, ibid, 12.

[43] MS Said, 'A Political Analysis of the Egyptian Judges' Revolt' in Bernard-Maugiron, ibid, 21.

[44] Bernard-Maugiron, ibid, 10.

for more independence eventually led to a significant judicial revolt in 2005. This marked a major turning point in the judges' struggle for more authority over their affairs. In the lead up to the judicial revolt of 2005, judges intensified their call for electoral transparency by linking it to judicial independence, firmly asserting that no free and fair elections are possible without independent judges closely monitoring the polls. Following the Supreme Constitutional Court's ruling in 2000 that, in accordance with Article 88 of the Constitution, members of judicial bodies should supervise all polling stations, judges quickly began to note widespread electoral fraud. This culminated in a judges' revolt through boycott threats, sit-ins and the use of the media to publicly report on such fraud. Noha El Zeiny, a senior judge, published a scathing op-ed in the newspaper *Al Masry Al Youm* on 24 November 2005, describing the electoral rigging she witnessed at a polling station in the city of Damanhour.[45] Reformist judges such as Hesham El Bastawissy and Ahmed Mekki faced negative repercussions as a result of their resistance to executive meddling in judicial affairs. Some were referred to the General Prosecutor for investigation.[46]

Only a limited number of proposals were incorporated into the amended Law on Judicial Authority in June 2006, leaving much of the executive authority's control intact. The Supreme Judicial Council's opinion on the draft law was never made public and the law was finally amended by the Political Affairs Committee of the National Democratic Party, leaving little room for suspicion that the amendments were made on a political basis. A major objection to the amended law in 2006 was that the executive retained the means 'to exert pressure on [judges] not to issue decisions that would displease the government'.[47] This, of course, bore significant implications for the transitional justice decisions taken five years later.

The challenges to prosecuting political leaders and high-level ministry officials have their roots in the role of the General Prosecutor before, during and after the 2011 uprising. As a judicial figure that has both investigation and conviction powers, the General Prosecutor has repeatedly neglected to ensure fair and effective investigations into torture cases, particularly those concerning political opponents of the Mubarak regime. Central to this failure of prosecuting for torture is that the police are often implicated as the perpetrators of torture crimes. The Office of the Public Prosecutor (OPP) works together with the police to gather evidence, arrest suspects, search homes and bring witnesses. As a result, the OPP delays forensic medical inspection, often with the intention of waiting for the torture wounds to heal, thereby weakening evidence of the crime.[48] Even when torture signs are evident, the victim is often unable to identify those who tortured him because he was

---

[45] N El Zeiny, 'Rigging Elections under the Supervision of the Judiciary', *Al Masry Al Youm*, 24 November 2005. See also Human Rights Watch, 'Elections in Egypt: State of Emergency Incompatible with Free and Fair Vote' (2010), available at www.hrw.org/sites/default/files/reports/egypt-1110WebforPosting.pdf.

[46] Bernard-Maugiron, above n 40, 13.

[47] ibid.

[48] Khalil, above n 41, 67.

blindfolded throughout the torture—and even when victims are able to identify their torturers, they are usually not held accountable because of the OPP's strong political links to the police and the Ministry of Interior and Ministry of Justice.[49]

While prosecutions concerning torture were largely unsuccessful in pre-transition Egypt, constitutional litigation through the Supreme Constitutional Court (SCC) had better success. Lawyers such as those working at the Center for Human Rights Legal Aid challenged legislation in the SCC courtrooms and initiated thousands of cases between 1995 and 1997. Other legal aid organisations followed suit. As Tamir Moustafa notes, 'By 1997, legal mobilization had become the dominant strategy for defenders of human rights', especially given the difficulties in building social movements without facing serious and negative consequences.[50] While litigation activism was successful only insofar as it exposed the 'chasm between the regime's rule-of-law rhetoric and the realities on the ground', it constituted a visible form of civil society protest.[51] Access to the courts for such litigation activism became central to civil society's partial success in raising awareness about the challenges of pursuing criminal accountability in an opaque judicial environment.

The SCC, however, also authorised a parallel court system that consisted of state security courts and military courts, which enjoyed fewer procedural safeguards. As a result, many civilian trials took place in military courts throughout the 1990s and have continued to take place throughout the Egyptian transition and in the post-transition period. Torture and the denial of basic rights to the detainees such as legal representation and family visits were all rampant during these trials, which were facilitated by the perpetual existence of the state of emergency law since 1958.[52] This law allows the president to refer crimes that would normally be penalised under ordinary laws to one of the exceptional courts in the parallel court system. The extent of executive authority in the decision-making process of these courts is astounding:

> The decisions of the courts have to be approved by the president of the republic (Article 12), who can commute the sentence, change it to a lighter penalty, cancel some or all of the penalties, suspend its execution, or order a retrial before another district of the court ... The decisions of these courts are not subject to any appeal before any court (Article 12).[53]

More than 1,000 civilians were tried in military courts en masse between 1992 and 1998, mostly targeting alleged members of extremist Islamist groups. From the start of the Egyptian uprising in 2011 until 29 August 2011, 11,879 civilians were tried in military courts. Between October 2014 and April 2016, at least 7420 civilians were tried in military courts. In October 2014, President Sisi issued a

---

[49] ibid.

[50] T Moustafa, 'The Political Role of the Supreme Constitutional Court: Between Principles and Practice', in Bernard-Maugiron, above n 40, 94.

[51] T Moustafa, 'Law and Courts in Authoritarian Regimes' (2014) 10 *Annual Review of Law and Social Science* 281, 288.

[52] Law No 162 of 1958.

[53] H Abu Seada, 'Exceptional Courts and the Natural Judge' in Bernard-Maugiron, above n 40, 170.

new law by decree that significantly expanded the military's jurisdictional powers. Under Law 136/2014, all public property, such as electricity stations, gas pipelines, railroads and road networks, were placed under military jurisdiction for two years. Human Rights Watch explains: 'To charge civilians under the law, military prosecutors filed charges such as blocking road and rail networks, burning electricity infrastructure or attacking government property.'[54] These vague provisions are in tandem with the repressive protest law passed one year before.[55] This law, issued in 2013 under the interim President Adly Mansour, grants security forces sweeping powers to ban protests through the use of lethal force, effectively putting an end to any kind of dissent and freedom of assembly.[56] Ironically, Adly Mansour was appointed President of the SCC a few days before he became interim President of Egypt in July 2013. He retained his position as head of the SCC until his retirement in 2016. By simultaneously holding the highest judicial and political positions of the state, Mansour's dual appointments embodied the problem of the murky separation of powers in Egypt.

Egypt's split and politicised judiciary was one of the hallmarks of the transitional period and a major shaper of decisions regarding the prosecution of political leaders. One stark example of the alliance between parts of the judiciary and the military is the discussions between Tahani el-Gebali, the deputy president of the SCC, and the military leadership in 2012. El-Gebali advised the military to delay the transfer of authority to civilians until a constitution was written so that the generals 'knew who they were handing power to and on what basis'.[57] El-Gebali's advice led the military to dissolve Egypt's first fairly elected parliament.[58] This example is indicative of the controlled nature of the transition in Egypt, whereby the military-led government and a fragmented judiciary worked together to shape key aspects of the transition, including who gets prosecuted and for what. As Tamer Wageeh, the director of the economic and social justice programme at Egyptian Initiative for Personal Rights explained, 'The judiciary has loyalties to the old regime and this has adversely affected the comprehensiveness of cases and investigations ... Previous human rights violations are not accounted for because it is the same regime'.[59]

In addition to 'rampant nepotism', Sahar Aziz describes the Egyptian judiciary as a 'formidable deep state institution' in which politicised loyalties to Mubarak and

---

[54] Human Rights Watch, 'Egypt: 7,400 Civilians Tried in Military Courts' (13 April 2016) available at www.hrw.org/news/2016/04/13/egypt-7400-civilians-tried-military-courts.

[55] Law 107 (2013) on the Right to Public Meetings, Processions and Peaceful Demonstrations, in addition to Law 84 (2002) on Non-Governmental Organisations.

[56] Law 107 (2013). For more on the human rights implications of this law, see Amnesty International, 'Egypt: New Protest Law Gives Security Forces Free Rein' (25 November 2013) available at www. amnesty.org/en/news/egypt-new-protest-law-gives-security-forces-free-rein-2013-11-25.

[57] See DD Kirkpatrick, 'Judge Helped Egypt's Military to Cement Power', *New York Times*, 3 July 2012, available at www.nytimes.com/2012/07/04/world/middleeast/judge-helped-egypts-military-to-cement-power.html?pagewanted=all&_r=0.

[58] ibid.

[59] Wageeh, above n 31.

the military are deeply entrenched.[60] Using the example of the military's ouster of former President Mohamed Morsi—Egypt's first elected president following the 2011 uprising—Aziz explains how the split in the judiciary along political lines was reinforced by a controlling executive:

> At the moment, over sixty judges who condemned the deposal of Morsi as a military coup are being investigated and systematically purged from the judiciary ... This explains, in part, why Adly Mansour's military-backed government permitted the ordinary judiciary to prosecute Muslim Brotherhood members, Morsi supporters that were not members of the [Muslim Brotherhood], and youth revolutionaries. The senior judicial leadership's cooperation with the executive's crackdown, coupled with a critical mass of judges that distrusted the [Muslim Brotherhood], transformed the judiciary into a political ally ... That the judges would suddenly transform into vanguards of transitional justice was improbable. Likewise, the prosecutors responsible for investigating the facts of prosecutions of Mubarak and his cronies were the same ones who for decades had propped up the Mubarak regime. Indeed, most judges were members of the same political elites that had benefited both financially and politically from the authoritarian state ... More than three years after Egypt's uprising, the judiciary has proven to be a formidable deep state institution, guarding its material interests in the status quo even if it means betraying the rule of law.[61]

The judiciary thus played a significant role in both allowing and blocking prosecutions from taking place without, as Aziz's damning critique of the judiciary shows, much regard for the rule of law. Judicial decisions regarding prosecution were thus very much tied to Egypt's military-controlled transition, fraught with the *feloul*[62] of the Mubarak era.

Other Legal Challenges to Prosecutions of Political Leaders

Other legal challenges further contributed to the limited content and extent of the prosecutions. Individuals who were prosecuted were tried under the regular criminal code for crimes that require a 'different set of legislations that could account for this transition'.[63] Judge Maged argued that the crimes committed during the 18-day uprising in 2011 are not 'ordinary crimes', such as murder.[64] Rather, they are

> serious crimes that require special techniques in investigations and prosecutions. The current criminal justice system cannot address such types of crimes because they are characterised by their systematic and widespread nature—especially if these crimes

---

[60] Aziz, above n 40, 233.
[61] Aziz, above n 40, 224, 228–30, 233. Adly Mansour is an Egyptian judge, former head of the Supreme Constitutional Court, who served as interim President of Egypt from July 2013 to June 2014.
[62] The Arabic term used in Egypt to describe 'remnants' of the former regime.
[63] El Shewy, above n 15.
[64] Maged, above n 19.

occurred in accordance with state policy, in which case they can be classified as crimes against humanity.[65]

Judge Maged also highlighted that without the inclusion of command responsibility in Egypt's criminal code, it will remain impossible to establish the responsibility of leaders.[66]

As several interviewees explained, access to the evidence necessary to build a strong case in court has been extremely difficult. This is because 'Evidence is with the police, the intelligence agencies, and the old regime—and the judiciary has no power to force these actors to submit the evidence they withhold'.[67] Judge Maged attributed the series of acquittals pre- and post-2011 to the lack of sufficient evidence to meet the evidentiary requirement in Egypt's current criminal system and summarised the legal challenges to the prosecution of political leaders in Egypt as follows:

> The 25 January crimes are grave crimes against protesters—they are not 'regular' crimes—not traditional or classic crimes such as murder, and they therefore require special techniques in investigations and prosecutions. The current criminal justice system cannot address such types of crimes, which are characterised by their systemic and widespread nature—especially if it occurred in accordance with state policy. I argue that these crimes can be classified as crimes against humanity. And the problem with the Egyptian criminal system is that you have to have direct evidence—such as eyewitnesses—to establish that such crimes occurred. To establish the responsibility of high-level officials, you need to incorporate in the criminal justice system new principles of command responsibilities which enable the judiciary to establish the responsibility of leaders ... If we had this legal tool, we could prosecute/establish criminal responsibility.[68]

Ali highlighted another challenge regarding the question of direct evidence. He argued that the interior ministry and the public prosecution were unwilling to release evidence because 'to hold El Adly responsible would implicate many other people'.[69] A strong indication of this deep-seated fear to prosecute is the shredding of thousands of classified documents by intelligence agency officials in March 2011.[70] Ali further explained that, as a result, limited prosecutions had taken place and they instead focused on corruption because the military, keen to appease public anger, wanted to give the impression that justice was being sought and that there had been a definitive break with the former regime.

---

[65] ibid.

[66] ibid. Maged referred to Article 28 of the Rome Statute on command responsibility and argued that Egypt should implement it in order to prosecute serious crimes. Maged has been active in pushing for a transitional justice law in Egypt that would cover crimes committed from 1981.

[67] Wageeh, above n 31.

[68] Maged, above n 19.

[69] Ali, above n 22. Habib El Adly was Minister of Interior in Egypt from 1997 to 2011.

[70] W Wan and L Sly, 'State Security HQ Overrun in Cairo', *Washington Post*, 5 March 2011, available at www.washingtonpost.com/wp-dyn/content/article/2011/03/05/AR2011030504356.html.

Popular Demands for Accountability

Retributive justice in the courts held a central place in the transitional justice psyche of Egyptians, particularly for victims and human rights defenders. While there is recognition that the trials have fallen short in addressing the societal desire for justice, Egyptian justice expectations, particularly in the immediate aftermath of Mubarak's ouster, point to strong popular support for trials.[71] Moataz El Fegeiry and others have noted that, for the Arab Spring protesters, justice means retribution, while reparations and truth commissions do not hold as much significance. People are not so much concerned with the justice process itself as wanting to see the outcome, such as imprisonment.[72]

The focus on crimes committed during the transition and on corruption crimes dating to periods from before the transition is also a result of the content of the public demands during the uprising. In fact, without the large number of people who took to the streets to demand prosecutions, decisions to prosecute may not have taken place to begin with. Protesters demanded accountability for the killing of demonstrators during the uprising and for the 'visible' and rampant corruption that plagued the country for decades.[73] Gamal Eid, lawyer for several victims, and Wageeh both explained that protesters emphasised accountability for corruption and for the limited set of human rights violations during the uprising because they were the most recent crimes and are still ongoing. Victims, activists and lawyers are more preoccupied with the recent crimes because 'it is more practical to deal with crimes that were committed during and since the uprising'.[74] This, coupled with the difficulty in obtaining access to evidence for previous human rights crimes, the lack of an independent judiciary and political will, and the continued perpetration of human rights violations throughout the transition, significantly shaped and limited the content of the prosecutions. As the post-transition period continued to unfold, however, the public desire for retributive justice in the courts began to shift, particularly with regard to accountability for corrupt businessmen. The next section discusses the practice of scapegoating in decisions regarding prosecution and the public's struggle to come to terms with reconciliation versus retributive justice.

---

[71] J Barsalou and B Knight, 'Delayed or Denied: Egyptian Expectations about Justice in Post-Mubarak Egypt' (The International Human Rights Funders Group, 14 January 2013) available at www.ihrfg.org/sites/default/files/Barsalou%20and%20Knight%20-%20Justice%20in%20Post-Mubarak%20Egypt.pdf.

[72] This point is elaborated on in chapter 6. N Aboueldahab, 'Rapporteur's Report: Prosecutions, Politics and Transitions: How Criminal Justice in the Arab Spring is Shaping Transitional Justice', panel discussion, Durham Law School, 6 May 2014.

[73] Ali, above n 22, during which he attributed daily corruption such as bribes to the visibility of corruption in Egypt and subsequent demands to fight it.

[74] Wageeh, above n 31; Eid, above n 15.

Prosecutions: A Scapegoating Strategy

The emphasis on charges of corruption and socio-economic crimes in the trials is, according to several interviewees, a form of scapegoating.[75] Mubarak, his two sons, Gamal and Alaa, and former Minister of Interior El Adly were used as scapegoats to appease public demands for accountability. In other words, the emphasis on such crimes was a means to shroud the neglect of accountability for widespread torture, killings, and other civil and political rights abuses committed for decades. Such corruption cases, Ali observed, often result in acquittals, worsening the problem of impunity in Egypt.[76] Only a select group of individuals were targeted for prosecution and many of the corruption cases have stalled.[77] As El Shewy noted, 'The corruption cases are politicised in that they have excluded certain individuals from prosecution. The exclusion of the military in particular, among various other elites.'[78] El Shewy continued to explain that the emphasis on corruption is 'an attempt to individualise what happened rather than look at it as a system … There is an attempt to say Mubarak was corrupt, but not necessarily the system he ran.'[79]

Mansour, who filed many corruption cases through his organisation ECESR, also pointed to the selectivity of the corruption cases, arguing that individuals such as Mubarak and his two sons could not be spared from corruption prosecutions because 'they are highly symbolic individuals'.[80] They were convenient scapegoats to give the impression that there was a break with the former regime, when in reality the former regime was kept intact. Mansour cited an example of corruption cases he had been working on involving around 50 ministers, only a handful of whom were tried. He also explained that the ECESR has been relatively successful in filing corruption cases because they are filed with the Administrative Court, which issues rulings on corrupt decisions rather than against individuals. The cases are then transferred to the criminal courts to identify the individuals who are criminally responsible for the corrupt decisions. However, a politicised public prosecutor's office meant that many of these criminal cases were blocked.[81]

Moreover, reconciliation deals meant that a greater number of individuals implicated in massive corruption crimes escaped prosecution. Given the vast extent of corruption, which involved the embezzlement of tens of millions of

---

[75] It is important to note here that there are additional explanations for the emphasis on socio-economic crimes and corruption in the charges. For example, the prominent role of workers' movements and labour unions before, during and after the uprisings have arguably been successful in ensuring some form of accountability for these crimes. See the Socio-economic Roots section below for a discussion of these factors.

[76] Ali, above n 22.

[77] Mansour, above n 31; El Shewy, above n 15.

[78] El Shewy, above n 15.

[79] ibid.

[80] Mansour, above n 31.

[81] ibid.

Egyptian pounds,[82] the military and other interim authorities decided to settle for reconciliation deals. Business tycoons such as Hussein Salem would pay the state the money they gained illicitly and this money would allegedly be used to help rebuild Egypt's battered economy. Legal steps were taken to facilitate these reconciliation deals, particularly the Supreme Council of the Armed Forces (SCAF) Decree No 4 of 2012, which 'gives immunity from criminal prosecution to businessmen accused of corruption under Mubarak and offers them the chance to settle their cases with government commissions'.[83] Wageeh explained that the military justified these reconciliation deals as a means to protect capitalism and restore economic security. On the question of holding the same business tycoons criminally accountable, Wageeh responded that the prevailing view of many Egyptians shifted to 'Our economy is in tatters—what will you gain from imprisoning them?'[84]

The extent of the human rights trials has also been selective. For example, despite crimes committed during the interim rule of the SCAF in 2011–12, no military officials have been prosecuted.[85] Other high-level former regime members also escaped prosecution, which points to a strategy that aims to show only a symbolic break with the former regime, rather than a genuine effort to achieve criminal accountability for past atrocities. Aziz gives an example of the selective extent of the trials:

> only one police officer is serving a three year sentence for shooting protesters during the bloody Mohamed Mahmoud protests in November 2011 wherein over 51 protesters were killed in five days. And only two police officers are serving time for the killing of at least 846 protesters in the protests of January 2011.[86]

As one interviewee explained, the objective was to 'sacrifice a part of the regime to save the regime'.[87] Ali gave a similar account of the motives behind the selective prosecutions and their link with the controlled nature of the transition:

> We have not taken serious steps in prosecutions because the revolution is not yet over. What is happening now is that the regime is prosecuting symbolic people just to 'show' that they are doing justice. But they are not serious—the regime is not individuals, the regime is a network of economic and social opportunists—and it's the same regime that is ruling. We succeeded in a part and failed in another part. I am not pessimistic; I am being realistic.[88]

---

[82] Ahmed, above n 5.

[83] M Abdelrahman, *Egypt's Long Revolution: Protest Movements and Uprisings* (New York, Routledge, 2014) 130.

[84] Wageeh, above n 31.

[85] See N Aboueldahab, 'No Generals in the Dock: Impunity Soldiering On in Egypt', *Al Jazeera*, 19 November 2013, available at www.aljazeera.com/indepth/opinion/2013/11/no-generals-dock-impunity-soldiering-egypt-2013111944842917230.html.

[86] Aziz, above n 40, 221.

[87] Anonymous, above n 14.

[88] Ali, above n 22.

Teitel's explanation of the limited criminal sanction is useful here as a point of reflection on the politicised prosecutorial strategy employed in Egypt. The limited criminal sanction provides insight into the exceptional uses of transitional criminal law in classic liberal transitions. It is essentially limited yet practical accountability for the sake of political liberalisation, security and peace.[89] However, this limited content and extent of accountability that has emerged in Egypt has been pursued for safeguarding the political interests of a controlled transition, rather than for the preservation of a secure, peaceful, liberal, democratic transition.[90] Teitel's limited criminal sanction theory and its relevance to the Arab Spring prosecutions are discussed further in chapter 6. Given the importance of socio-economic accountability in the Egyptian uprising, the next section is devoted to an analysis of this dimension of criminal accountability in Egypt and to its roots in the role of workers' movements and labour unions in the decades leading up to the uprising and beyond.

The Socio-economic Roots of the Transition

A prominent contextual factor that several interviewees discussed is the significance of the socio-economic roots of the uprising and their fundamental impact on the shape of criminal accountability in the transition. Deep socio-economic grievances led to partial socio-economic accountability in Egypt. Judge Maged argued that years of rampant corruption and a poor socio-economic situation in Egypt is a significant factor that led to the emphasis on corruption crimes in the trials. Like Wageeh and Eid, he points to the strong demands to end corruption during the mass uprising in 2011 and explained that 'corruption means money, resources—people want to remove corruption because they want the money back'.[91] This, in part, is what prompted the interim military authority to negotiate reconciliation deals with Egyptian business tycoons implicated in massive corruption cases.[92]

The poor economic health of Egypt, particularly the soaring unemployment rates among youth and significant structural inequalities, has not merely served as context or a background to the political developments of the Egyptian transition, but have been foregrounded as some of the most central concerns of Egyptian society—and this has manifested itself in the trials. The uprising was driven by economic injustices during which years of economic oppression and miserable

---

[89] RG Teitel, *Globalizing Transitional Justice: Essays for the New Millennium* (Oxford, Oxford University Press, 2014) 99–102.

[90] See chapter 6 for further discussion on Teitel's limited criminal sanction.

[91] Maged, above n 19.

[92] 'Egypt's Cash-strapped Rulers Woo Former Regime Tycoons', *Daily News Egypt*, 24 May 2013, available at www.dailynewsegypt.com/2013/05/24/egypts-cash-strapped-rulers-woo-former-regime-tycoons/.

living standards had no prospect of improvement because of the severely corrupt government and the absence of access to the most basic civil and political
rights. Here lay the nexus between socio-economic and civil and political rights
violations.

Significant socio-economic woes included poverty, high unemployment,
poor working conditions, lack of job security and the repression of unions. This
dreary state of economic affairs compounded the widespread frustration among
Egyptians, which in part resulted in the outburst of mass revolts that ousted
Mubarak. However, this explanation is insufficient because it does not explain the
concurrent high demand for human rights accountability and the link between
civil and political rights and socio-economic rights that activists had been pushing
for.[93] The drivers of the uprisings were just as much about socio-economic problems as they were about human rights problems. This explanation is therefore in
need of a more comprehensive account that addresses pre-transition factors that
contributed to the shape of post-transition prosecutions in Egypt. One of those
factors is the crucial role of the decades-long struggle of workers' movements and
labour unions in Egypt.

The Role of Workers' Movements and Labour Unions

Workers' movements and labour unions played a significant role before, during
and after the uprising in Egypt. In 2006, a strike took place in which 27,000 tex-
tile workers at the Misr Spinning and Weaving Company in the town of Mahalla
participated to demand better workers' benefits and better pay. The peaceful strike
was partially successful, resulting in a two-month incentive payment by manage-
ment that the workers fought hard for. Strikes continued into 2007 and peaked on
6 April 2008, when a general strike again took place in the town of Mahalla and
turned into a mini-uprising in Egypt. The heavy presence of state security officials,
the destruction of posters of Mubarak and the ensuing clashes between the police
and protesters during which tear gas, rubber bullets and live fire were used distin-
guished this strike from others.[94]

This strike led to the formation of the 6 April Youth Movement, which became
an influential workers' rights and human rights mobilising force. This movement,
along with other similar workers' rights movements, led mass protests during and
after the Egyptian uprising. In the lead up to the 2008 general strike in Egypt, the
6 April Youth Movement and a number of opposition groups and parties signed
this statement:

> All national forces in Egypt have agreed upon the 6th of April to be a public strike. On the
> 6th of April, stay home, do not go out; Don't go to work, don't go to the university, don't

---

[93] See, eg, the Egyptian Initiative for Personal Rights (www.eipr.org).
[94] El Sharnoubi, above n 22.

go to school, don't open your shop, don't open your pharmacy, don't go to the police station, don't go to the camp; We need salaries allowing us to live, we need to work, we want
our children to get education, we need human transportation means, we want hospitals
to get treatment, we want medicines for our children, we need just judiciary, we want
security, we want freedom and dignity, we want apartments for youth; We don't want
prices increase, we don't want favoritism, we don't want police in plain clothes, we don't
want torture in police stations, we don't want corruption, we don't want bribes, we don't
want detentions. Tell your friends not to go to work and ask them to join the strike.[95]

This statement clearly lays out the socio-economic and other human rights
demands of the Egyptian opposition and workers' movements in 2008—a year
that served as a 'rehearsal' for the 2011 uprising.[96] The statement demands both
social justice and civil and political rights. There is no prioritisation of one set
of rights over the other—the 6 April Youth Movement and its supporters clearly
viewed socio-economic rights as inseparable from civil and political rights.[97]

Prior to the 6 April Youth Movement, workers' protests and strikes constituted one
of the strongest opposition forces in Egypt. The Egyptian Trade Union Federation
(ETUF), established in 1957, repeatedly disappointed workers because of its politicised leadership, which was always appointed by the government as opposed to
being elected by workers. Increasingly disaffected by the non-representation of
ETUF, workers escalated their protests in the 1990s and eventually became 'the
largest component of the burgeoning culture of protests in the 2000s', posing a
significant challenge to the Mubarak regime.[98] Such labour mobilisation eventually led to the formation of the Egyptian Federation of Independent Trade Unions
(EFITU) soon after the 2011 uprising began. EFITU was established in response to
the overtly state-controlled ETUF, marking a turning point in the emergence of the
Egyptian independent labour movement.

The labour rights movements in Egypt continued to actively challenge government policies in the transitional and post-transitional period. According to the
Egyptian International Development Centre, 1354 social and labour rights protests took place in March 2013 alone, compared to 864 protests during the previous
month. This meant an average of 44 protests per day, or 1.8 protests every hour.[99]

[95] C Radsch, 'April 6th General Strike in Egypt Draws Together Diverse Groups Using Newest Tech-
nologies' (2 April 2008) available at www.radsch.info/2008/04/using-facebook-blogs-sms-independ-
ent.html.

[96] El Sharnoubi, above n 22.

[97] N Aboueldahab, 'Navigating the Storm: Ambiguous Transitions in Egypt, Libya and Tunisia' in
J Brankovic and H van der Merwe (eds), *Advocating Transitional Justice in Africa: The Role of Civil
Society* (New York, Springer, forthcoming). The 6 April Youth Movement was one of several organisations that was banned from operation in 2014. Since then, several of its leaders and members have been
detained and imprisoned.

[98] J Beinin, 'The Rise of Egypt's Workers' (Carnegie Endowment for International Peace, 28 June
2012) available at http://carnegieendowment.org/2012/06/28/rise-of-egypt-s-workers-pub-48689.

[99] S Shukrallah and R Ali, 'Post-revolution Labour Strikes, Social Struggles on Rise in Egypt: Report',
Ahram Online, 29 April 2013, available at http://english.ahram.org.eg/News/70384.aspx.

Through street protests and strikes, workers continued to demand an increase in the minimum wage, the replacement of temporary contracts with permanent ones and the right to strike. Some prominent figures from the independent labour movement, such as Kamal Abu Eita—the founder of EFITU—accepted ministerial positions and parliamentary seats in the interim transitional governments. This raised hopes that a draft Trade Union Freedoms Law would be enacted, which would legalise the establishment of independent trade unions in Egypt. However, thousands of workers continued to be jailed for staging demonstrations, sit-ins and strikes. Moreover, tensions between ETUF and EFITU persisted, and have led to a court case in which ETUF is charging EFITU with violating Trade Union Law No 35 of 1976, which prohibits the establishment of independent labour unions[100]

Labour rights movements in Egypt did not operate alone. The Kifaya movement, for example, was a coalition consisting of various opposition activists and politicians. It was established in the run-up to the parliamentary and presidential elections in 2005. Its members called for free elections, civil and political rights, and an end to authoritarian rule, particularly as suspicions rose regarding Mubarak's grooming of his son, Gamal, to become the next president.[101]

Nevertheless, some of the strongest forces of opposition in Egypt were labour rights movements. NGOs, independent activists and lawyers who demanded civil and political rights, such as the right to freedom of expression, the right to assemble, and the right to freedom from torture and arbitrary detention, were severely repressed through massive crackdowns led by the police and other state security forces. This significantly weakened the human rights movement in Egypt. In contrast, the labour rights movements were slightly better tolerated. This may, as discussed earlier, be explained by the involvement of the police and state security officials in the perpetration of human rights violations, particularly torture, and their alliance with the public prosecution and other key judicial and ministry of justice officials.

The Egyptian labour rights movements' success in bringing to the fore demands for social justice and an end to corruption eventually impacted the content of the prosecutions. Over the years, the build-up of their resistance through strikes, sit-ins and protests played a significant role in the emphasis on charges for socio-economic crimes in the prosecutions since Mubarak's ouster. Pressure for social justice, however, was also partially successful prior to the uprising, especially with regard to the illegal sale of land. This is most evident in, for example, the *Madinaty* and *Palm Hills* cases mentioned earlier, in which land was sold below market value through corrupt contracts between housing ministers and real estate tycoons and developers. A vast area east of Cairo, Madinaty was sold to real estate tycoon Hisham Talaat Mustafa without a public auction and below market value,

---

[100] 'Trial to Outlaw Independent Labor Unions Referred to Egypt's Highest Court', *Mada Masr*, 27 June 2016, available at www.madamasr.com/news/trial-outlaw-independent-labor-unions-referred-egypts-highest-court.

[101] Onodera, above n 22. Kifaya is also known as the Egyptian movement for change.

in violation of Egyptian law. Mustafa was also exempted from paying construction taxes and fees. Built to accommodate tens of thousands of luxury villas and a $3 billion commercial complex, the Madinaty contract signified blatant government corruption and waste, affecting millions of Cairenes without access to proper housing and public services. It intensified the visibility of corruption and socioeconomic inequality in Egypt.

Workers' movements and labour unions thus served as key drivers in ensuring some form of criminal accountability for socio-economic rights violations. This largely occurred through complaints filed by lawyers working in organisations such as the ECESR and the Hisham Mubarak Law Center. On the other hand, the harsh crackdowns on civil and political rights activists left a seriously weakened human rights movement that was largely unsuccessful in ensuring criminal accountability for human rights abuses committed before, during and after the uprisings.[102]

The Role of International Actors

What, if any, was the role of international actors in decisions regarding prosecution in Egypt? During the interviews, the term 'international actors' comprised foreign governments and regional and international NGOs. The overwhelming response from the interviewees was that international actors did not have a significant impact in driving the prosecutions both before and after Mubarak's ouster. Instead, international actors were active in monitoring and raising awareness about human rights violations. Nassar noted that investigations such as those conducted by Human Rights Watch and Amnesty International aided in increasing pressure on governments to improve the human rights situation.[103] But, he continued, 'things happened so quickly [during the uprising] that we cannot give too much credit to the international human rights movement. Domestic action was swift regarding the prosecutions.'[104] Nassar, however, added that the proliferation of the international criminal justice movement meant that it was more difficult to pass amnesty laws.[105] Activists also pointed to the role of international actors in supporting domestic civil society campaigns in Egypt by making legal and advocacy tools available to support their cause.[106] Overall, international actors did not have much of a role in driving prosecutions, which were 'very much a domestically

---

[102] Aboueldahab, above n 97.

[103] Nassar, above n 31.

[104] ibid.

[105] For developments that contrast with this argument, see the Yemen discussions in chapter 5. See also F Lessa and LA Payne (eds), *Amnesty in the Age of Human Rights Accountability: Comparative and International Perspectives* (New York, Cambridge University Press, 2012).

[106] Eid, above n 15.

driven process'.[107] Regional actors, such as the African Commission, had limited influence, but they nonetheless served a facilitating role when domestic processes were stalled.[108]

For example, Eid explained his organisation's decision to work with the African Commission on a case regarding the cutting of communications in Egypt during the uprising. On 28 January 2011, the government cut access to most internet and mobile phone services, resulting in a '90 per cent drop in data traffic to and from Egypt'.[109] Eid described the gravity of this move and his consequent decision to file a case against the Minister of Communications, among others:

> We have a case that we are filing with the African Commission—the communications case. We want to pinpoint the *individual* who took the decision to cut the communications on the 27 January—551 people died on the 28 January as a result. Between 16–90 individuals died because of inability to contact ambulances. This is [the Arabic Network for Human Rights Information's] estimation. Three communications companies and one internet company were probably responsible—we are filing for murder because of their role in cutting the communications. They keep transferring the case from this unit of the judiciary to that unit of the judiciary to tire us out. But we don't get tired.[110]

Eid noted that the case was buried by the Morsi government and then stalled with the military prosecution for over two years. 'This is why,' he said, 'we want to take the communications case to the African Commission.'[111]

Throughout the transitional and post-transitional period, international actors were regarded with great suspicion by the government. As early as July 2011, a fact-finding committee set up by the Ministry of Justice investigated the foreign funding of civil society groups in Egypt. Following the committee's report, 17 rights defenders from 12 organisations were charged with illegally receiving foreign funding, harming national security and founding organisations without the necessary administrative permits.[112] In addition, several international NGOs based in Egypt were ordered to close and many of their employees received jail sentences ranging between one and five years. The International Republican Institute, the National Democratic Institute, Freedom House, the International Center for Journalists and the Konrad Adenauer Foundation were all ordered to be closed by a Cairo criminal court in a continuation of this case in June 2013. The case was reopened in 2016, when travel bans and asset freezes were ordered for prominent human rights defenders, including Gamal Eid and Hossam Bahgat. The decision

---

[107] El Shewy, above n 15.

[108] Ali, above n 22.

[109] M Richtel, 'Egypt Cuts Off Most Internet and Cell Service', *New York Times*, 28 January 2011, available at www.nytimes.com/2011/01/29/technology/internet/29cutoff.html?_r=0.

[110] Eid, above n 15.

[111] ibid.

[112] 'Egyptian Human Rights Defenders Vow to Continue Work after Asset Freeze', *Mada Masr*, 17 September 2016, available at www.madamasr.com/news/egyptian-human-rights-defenders-vow-continue-work-after-asset-freeze.

to freeze their assets stemmed from the original investigation into receipt of foreign funding and the consequent harm to national security.[113] Gamal Eid best sums up the irony of case 173 and the charges therein:

> The main charge against us is that we harm Egypt's reputation by publishing information about human rights violations and that we receive funding from abroad. The charge itself is ridiculous, for it comes from the same regime that receives billions annually in aid from the United States, the Kingdom of Saudi Arabia and the United Arab Emirates.[114]

It is not surprising that, within this environment marked by heavy paranoia of foreign interference, international actors have had a minimal role in driving prosecutions of political leaders in Egypt. However, this perhaps more importantly points to the fact that the prosecutions were very much domestically initiated and domestically driven in both pre- and post-transition Egypt.

One attempt at the use of universal jurisdiction led to the opening of the case *R (Freedom and Justice Party and Others) v Secretary of State for Foreign and Commonwealth Affairs and Others* in 2014. In this case, which concluded in 2016, members of Egypt's Freedom and Justice Party attempted to use universal jurisdiction laws in the UK to prosecute Lieutenant Mohamed Hegazy, who was head of the Egyptian Military Intelligence Service in July and August 2013, for crimes committed during the Raba'a massacre of August 2013, including murder and torture. The High Court of Justice issued a judgment on 5 August 2016 stating that Hegazy could not be prosecuted due to the immunity he enjoyed under 'Special Mission Immunity' during his visit to the UK in September 2015. Despite the unsuccessful attempt to use universal jurisdiction, this case marked the first time that Egyptian claimants used universal jurisdiction laws to hold a military leader criminally accountable.[115]

The Role of Domestic Human Rights Civil Society Organisations

The stranglehold on foreign funding and the crackdown on international NGOs in Egypt had a direct impact on the work of domestic civil society both pre- and post-transition. The more recent legal attacks on the independence of civil society organisations, such as case 173 regarding the foreign funding of NGOs, have drastically intensified the crackdown. Moustafa tracks the repression of domestic human rights organisations to the late 1990s, during which law 153/1999 further

---

[113] ibid.

[114] G Eid, 'Chronicle of a Civil Society, Chronicle of a Death Foretold', *Mada Masr*, 17 July 2016, available at www.madamasr.com/opinion/chronicle-civil-society-chronicle-death-foretold.

[115] This is in contrast with Tunisia, which used universal jurisdiction laws more than once in attempts to prosecute high-level government officials. See chapter 3.

restricted an existing law regulating NGO activity (law 32/1964) by forbidding engagement in any political activity, giving the Ministry of Social Affairs the right to dissolve any association that threatens national unity, and by severely restricting the ability of domestic NGOs to receive foreign funding without prior government approval.[116] This, Moustafa explains, struck at the 'Achilles' heel of the human rights movement', which had relied heavily on leveraging international pressure to change Egyptian domestic policies: 'The greatest asset of the Egyptian human rights movement had became [*sic*] its greatest vulnerability.'[117] Sixteen years later, prominent Egyptian human rights NGOs, such as the Cairo Institute for Human Rights Studies, moved their regional and international programmes outside of Egypt for fear that they would be forced to close following the enactment of additional restrictive laws.

Documentation of human rights violations repeatedly emerged in the interviews as a strategy that was central to the work of civil society, particularly human rights organisations. When asked for what purpose civil society organisations documented human rights violations in Egypt, the responses revealed an array of reasons. Many cited the classic reason of raising awareness and putting pressure on the government to change its human rights practices. Eid and El Shewy explained that, despite working with a politicised judiciary, the aim of civil society documentation was to have enough evidence so that 'one day', when an independent judiciary is in place, 'we will be able to prosecute'.[118] Eid cited the lack of an independent judiciary as one of the strongest motivators for documentation and explained: 'We have archives, we have documents, we have testimonies. We need political will and a new government and an independent judiciary willing to prosecute for these crimes for the thirty plus years of Mubarak's rule.'[119] El Shewy described documentation as one of the powerful tools of a civil society struggling with authoritarian rule. He explained:

> Since there has been no real transition, our approach is to go from the bottom up. Through victims' families, we are archiving and documenting things ourselves to try and have a strong series of cases so that we can then—when there is political will—really have a serious transitional justice programme.[120]

A human rights lawyer said that while civil society documentation does not automatically count as evidence in a court of law, it was a powerful means to mobilise and pressure the government to respond to grievances.[121] That

---

[116] Moustafa, above n 50, 101.
[117] ibid.
[118] Eid, above n 15; El Shewy, above n 15.
[119] Eid, above n 15.
[120] El Shewy, above n 15.
[121] Interview with Ahmed Abdallah, Human Rights Officer and lawyer, 6 April Youth Movement (Cairo, Egypt, 4 December 2013). Khaled Ali also mentioned that the courts and the prosecution do not accept civil society documentation as evidence: Ali, above n 22.

said, documentation of electoral fraud by human rights activists during the 1995 and 2003 elections facilitated the opening of court cases by opposition candidates.[122]

Most civil society documentation in Egypt had addressed torture, police abuses, and other civil and political rights violations. However, as El Shewy explained, this changed following the 2011 uprising:

> There was never really a focus on how to document abuses of economic and social justice violations. We at EIPR began that much more strongly after the revolution because we realized [that both sets of rights] were linked—they are not mutually exclusive. They sustained one another. There was a realisation that if you simply went around prosecuting civil and political rights abuses then you wouldn't be getting into the structural reasons for why the revolution happened—and how Mubarak and his aides were able to maintain their power through their system of abuse.[123]

This link between civil and political rights and socio-economic rights, as discussed further in chapter 6, characterises the transitional justice discourse in Egypt. Unlike its predecessors in other parts of the world, the transitional justice that lawyers and activists sought in Egypt does not make a distinction between the two sets of rights. This is despite the fact that the prosecutions, for the various factors explained above, were heavy on corruption charges.

Conclusion

To conclude, this section sums up the trigger factors that led to decisions to prosecute, the various factors that drove these decisions and pushed them forward, and the shaping factors that impacted the content and the extent of the prosecutions. As explained in chapter 1, the material collected for each case study is analysed by identifying what factors triggered, drove and shaped decisions regarding prosecution. The trigger–driver–shaper mechanism does not explain the process of prosecution from start to finish. Rather, it is a prism through which the research collected is analysed and used to develop an explanation of how decisions regarding the prosecution of political leaders emerged and developed before and during the highly contentious period of transition.

Triggers

Two cases of police torture, one of which resulted in the victim's death, served as turning points in calls for accountability in Egypt before the 2011 uprising.

---

[122] Moustafa, above n 50, 102.
[123] El Shewy, above n 15.

The 2006 case of bus driver Emad El Kebir resulted in widespread publicity both within and outside Egypt. Although no high-level government or police officials were implicated, it became an influential case showing that holding the police accountable for their crimes is possible. The torture and killing in June 2010 of Khaled Said, who quickly became an iconic figure in Egypt because of his widely publicised fate, was investigated and two police officers were sentenced to 10 years in a maximum-security prison.[124] The case of Khaled Said is widely regarded as a major trigger for the uprising that took place just over six months after his death. It became a symbol of police brutality and impunity in Egypt, fuelling public anger and leading to the influential We Are All Khaled Said protest movement.[125] The cases of Emad El Kebir and Khaled Said were thus triggers, or turning points, that opened up the possibility of holding a much-feared arm of the Ministry of Interior—the police—criminally accountable. It is far from a coincidence that the Egyptian uprising started on National Police Day—25 January.

Prior to the Khaled Said incident, three other significant movements that had been brewing for years also served as turning points in the rise of the anti-Mubarak opposition. These were the Kifaya movement and the judicial revolt in 2005, and the decades-long labour rights movement that led to the formation of the 6 April Youth Movement in 2008.[126] Unlike the Emad El Kebir and Khaled Said incidents, which were shocking incidents that triggered sudden and widespread public anger, the judicial revolt, the Kifaya movement and the 6 April Youth Movement grew over time and were marked by periodic protests—even mini-uprisings—that increasingly drew ordinary Egyptians' attention and attracted widespread support.

Emad El Kebir, Khaled Said, the 2005 judicial revolt, the Kifaya movement and the 6 April Youth Movement thus served as some of the most influential trigger factors that led to the 2011 uprising and stronger demands for criminal accountability. While other factors may also have triggered a process that eventually led to decisions regarding prosecution, the named triggers were repeatedly cited by interviewees and often emerge in scholarly literature on the origins of the Egyptian uprising.[127] These triggers strongly represent police brutality, impunity, corruption, lack of democratic governance and economic grievances—all of which arguably led to the 2011 uprising and subsequent demands to hold high-level officials accountable for crimes that fall under each of those categories.

---

[124] Kortam, above n 24.

[125] See K Dawoud, 'Divided as Ever', *Al Ahram Weekly*, 7–13 June 2012, available at http://weekly.ahram.org.eg/2012/1101/eg4.htm.

[126] Onodera, above n 22.

[127] See, eg, G Achcar, *The People Want: A Radical Exploration of the Arab Uprising* (London, Saqi Books 2013); S Amin, *The People's Spring: The Future of the Arab Revolution* (Nairobi, Pambazuka Press, 2012); Onodera, above n 22.

Drivers

Like the trigger factors discussed above, it is not feasible to account for every factor that drove decisions regarding the prosecution of political leaders in Egypt. The interviewees, however, identified two drivers that they argue had the largest impact on decisions regarding prosecution: (i) public pressure, particularly during and immediately after the 2011 uprising; and (ii) individual lawyers, particularly those working for established NGOs. Together, these drivers pushed the judiciary and interim military authorities to respond by allowing certain prosecutions of high-level government officials. Many cases, however, were blocked—the reasons for which are explained in the subsequent section on shaping factors.

Calls for the 'fall of the regime' during the mass protests of January and February 2011 were quickly followed by calls for Mubarak to face trial. These demands intensified in March and April 2011, when Mubarak's continued exile in the resort town of Sharm El Sheikh angered a public still reeling from the crimes committed during his rule. In response to this pressure, Mubarak and his sons were arrested in April 2011 and subsequently faced a string of trials that began on 3 August 2011. El Adly, the infamous former Minister of Interior, had already been arrested on charges for the killing of protesters. His trial was then merged with that of Mubarak and his two sons, and their corruption and human rights charges were also merged. This was an ambiguous legal development that was frowned upon by several lawyers, especially as it weakened the investigation into individual criminal accountability.[128] Aziz noted the role of public pressure in driving prosecutions and the role of the public prosecution in shaping them:

> Because the public's demand for the criminal prosecutions of Mubarak-era officials was too great to ignore, [public prosecutor] Mahmoud had no choice but to charge them. However, he sabotaged the trials by assigning junior prosecutors to complex corruption cases, conducting poor investigations that could not withstand judicial scrutiny, and declining to prosecute police and security personnel accused of killing protesters. As a result, Mubarak's conviction and life sentence for complicity in the killings of protesters during the January 25th uprisings were reversed on appeal and on November 29, 2014 the charges were dismissed in their entirety.[129]

As noted earlier, the third and final retrial of Mubarak concluded in March 2017 with a verdict declaring Mubarak innocent.

Certain individual lawyers who are also veteran human rights activists, including Gamal Eid, Khaled Ali and Ahmed Seif El Dawla, were influential in successfully filing cases against former ministers. Only ten days after the ouster of Mubarak in February 2011, Eid's organisation, the Arabic Network for Human Rights Information (ANHRI), filed complaints against Safwat El Sherif (former

---

[128] Eid, above n 15; El Shewy, above n 15; Ali, above n 22; Al Ansary, above n 14.
[129] Aziz, above n 40, 221.

Minister of Information, former Speaker of the Shura Council and former Secretary General of Mubarak's National Democratic Party), Anas El Fiqqi (former Minister of Information) and Hassan Abdelrahman (Minister of Interior).
ANHRI also worked with the American Civil Liberties Union (ACLU) to try and
hold Omar Suleiman, the former intelligence chief who Mubarak had appointed
as his first vice president during the uprising, accountable for the torture of Guantanamo Bay detainees.[130] Given the unlikelihood that a prosecution involving
Suleiman for crimes committed in Egypt would take place, ANHRI opted to work
with ACLU on the Guantanamo Bay case as a means to bring Suleiman to court.[131]
Together with Seif El Dawla, Ali also filed complaints against Suleiman for the
crackdown on the 2008 Mahalla uprising. The public prosecutor blocked this case
and Suleiman died in July 2012.[132]

Shapers

A number of factors shaped the content and the extent of decisions regarding
prosecution.

First, there were explicit demands for socio-economic accountability by the
protesters. Stripped of their resources by a heavily corrupt government, many
Egyptians in Tahrir Square foregrounded their socio-economic grievances.[133]

Secondly, a politicised public prosecutor meant that many cases, particularly
those targeting human rights violations by high-level government officials, were
blocked. The Egyptian judiciary has struggled for independence in the past, most
notably in 2005, when some of its senior judges, including Noha El Zeiny, exposed
electoral rigging and fraud and demanded independence from the executive.[134]
Years later, and after the 2011 uprising, the judiciary is still split along several
lines, some of which are staunchly loyal to the former regime and to the military.
A divided judiciary thus significantly limited the number of human rights cases
and the number of individuals who faced trial, and contributed to the high number of acquittals.

Thirdly, the weak legal framework within which lawyers must build their cases
contributed to the problem of questionable acquittals. Judge Maged and others
outlined these legal challenges, citing difficult evidentiary requirements and a lack

---

[130] Eid, above n 15.
[131] ibid.
[132] Ali, above n 22.
[133] Maged, above n 19; Wageeh, above n 31. See also R Abou-El-Fadl, 'Beyond Conventional Transitional Justice: Egypt's 2011 Revolution and the Absence of Political Will' (2012) 6 *International Journal
of Transitional Justice* 318. As mentioned earlier, these demands went hand in hand with demands for
the respect of civil and political rights.
[134] See Human Rights Watch, 'Elections in Egypt: State of Emergency Incompatible with Free and
Fair Vote' (2010) available at www.hrw.org/sites/default/files/reports/egypt1110WebforPosting.pdf.

of provisions for command responsibility as major obstacles to a more compre-hensive set of cases.

Finally, a military-controlled transition in Egypt meant that certain individu-als, particularly from the military, are shielded from prosecution while others are scapegoated for the sake of appeasing public anger. The shaping factors affect-ing decisions regarding the prosecution of political leaders in Egypt are therefore complex: they pertain to deep structural and socio-economic problems, as well as lingering problems of the 'deep state', whereby powerful actors in the military, the judiciary and state security agencies mould transitional justice to protect their interests.

3

Tunisia

Tunisia's transitional justice process has seen significant developments since former President Zine El Abidine Ben Ali's ouster in January 2011. Several former political leaders were prosecuted and a transitional justice law was passed in 2013. A Truth and Dignity Commission (TDC) was subsequently established and has since heard thousands of testimonies concerning crimes committed since Tunisian independence in 1955. To a large extent, Tunisian workers' movements have constituted one of the strongest opposition forces to the Tunisian government. Consequently, the role of these workers' movements and the history of deep inequalities and corruption in Tunisia significantly shaped the emphasis on corruption and socio-economic crimes in the prosecutions that have taken place. However, Tunisia's transitional justice process has seen a waning of the prosecutorial focus on corruption and economic crimes. This waning has been attributed to the establishment of the TDC in 2014 and to a reliance on foreign models of transitional justice that foreground accountability for civil and political rights violations.

The historic activism of the Tunisian Bar Association, workers' movements, human rights activism and significant pressure by a group of lawyers (Groupe de 25) in the immediate aftermath of Ben Ali's ouster together formed a diverse protest movement in Tunisia that contributed to efforts to prosecute Ben Ali and his aides. Moreover, a military that had been marginalised and victimised by both Ben Ali and his predecessor, Habib Bourguiba, served as a major driver of some of the decisions to prosecute certain leaders of the Ben Ali regime. This chapter examines the role that these various actors played in triggering, driving and shaping decisions regarding the prosecution of political leaders in Tunisia.

The Tunisian anti-government uprising started on 18 December 2010, a day after the self-immolation of 26-year-old Mohamed Bouazizi, a fruit and vegetable street vendor, in the town of Sidi Bouzid. He had been frustrated by police corruption, harassment and the poor working conditions that made him struggle to make ends meet. Ben Ali was President of Tunisia for 23 years, during which time he maintained a firm grip over civil society and political opponents. The uprising claimed the lives of over 300 people and over 2,000 people were injured. Following pressure from the massive uprisings that engulfed Tunisia, Ben Ali fled to Saudi Arabia on 14 January 2011, where he has lived in exile ever since.[1]

---

[1] These casualty figures were released by an investigative commission in Tunisia in 2011, led by Taoufiq Bouderbala. 'La Commission Bouderbala présente son rapport final: elle a recensé 338 morts et 2147 blessés', *Leaders*, 4 May 2012, available at www.leaders.com.tn/article/8359-la-commission-bouderbala-presente-son-rapport-final-elle-a-recense-338-morts-et-2147-blesses.

When Ben Ali came to power in 1987, he renamed the ruling party the Democratic Constitutional Rally (RCD).[2] Over the course of the next 23 years, the RCD was for many Tunisians, and in particular for political opponents, synonymous with repression, dictatorship and torture. Immediately following Ben Ali's ouster, the RCD remained intact until it was dissolved on 9 March 2011. Tunisians then voted on 23 October 2011 for members of a new Constituent Assembly that would be responsible for drafting a new constitution. The Islamist party, Ennahda, won 41 per cent of the vote. A troika government was subsequently formed, with Hamid Jebali of the Ennahda party serving as the Prime Minister, human rights activist Moncef Marzouki as President of Tunisia and Mustapha Ben Jaafar of the secular Ettakatol party as head of the assembly. Marzouki remained President of Tunisia until 2014, when he lost the presidential election to Beji Caid Essebsi. Since his election, Essebsi's Nidaa Tounes party and the Islamist Ennahda party have formed a national unity government in which Ennahda made strategic power-sharing compromises, avoiding the fate of its Egyptian neighbour, the Muslim Brotherhood.

The Tunisian government's calls for Ben Ali's extradition to Tunisia have been repeatedly ignored by Saudi Arabia. As a result, his trials were all conducted in absentia. The Le Kef trial began on 28 November 2011 before the Permanent Military Tribunal.[3] Ben Ali, along with 22 other defendants, including two former interior ministers (Rafik Hadj Kacem and Ahmed Friaa) and a number of high and mid-level state security officers, faced charges relating to corruption, financial and human rights crimes. The majority of the human rights charges pertained to those committed during the uprising. Murder charges included the killing of protesters and attempted murder that took place in the governorates of Le Kef, Jendouba, Beja, Siliana, Kasserine and Kairouan.

A second group trial, involving 43 defendants, took place at the Permanent Military Tribunal in Tunis. In this trial, the defendants again included Ben Ali, the former interior ministers Kacem and Friaa, four former directors general of security forces and several other internal security officers and interior ministry officials. The charges included the murder of protesters in the governorates of Tunis, Ariana, al-Manouba, Ben Arous, Bizerte, Nabeul, Zaghouan, Sousse and Monastir. A third trial, also before the Permanent Military Tribunal of Tunis, was held for four state security officers accused of killing six members of the neighbourhood defence committees on 15 January 2011 in the town of Ouardanine. A fourth trial, before the Permanent Military Tribunal of Sfax, charged and sentenced two policemen (Omran Abdelali and Mohamed Said Khlouda) to 20 years in prison for the killing of a protester, Slim Hadhri, in Sfax on the 14 January 2011. The policemen were also fined almost $50,000.[4]

---

[2] Under Bourguiba, this party was called the Destourian Socialist Party and the Neo Destour Party.
[3] The trial took place in the governorate of Le Kef in Tunisia.
[4] Human Rights Watch, 'Tunisia: Q&A on the Trial of Ben Ali, Others for Killing Protesters' (11 June 2012) available at www.hrw.org/news/2012/06/11/tunisia-qa-trial-ben-ali-others-killing-protesters#2.

Ben Ali was sentenced to a total of 66 years in prison for graft and corruption charges in three separate trials between June 2011 and July 2012. In an exceptionally quick six-hour trial, Ben Ali and his wife Leila Trabelsi were both sentenced to 35 years in prison for embezzling public funds, after they were found guilty of unlawful possession of cash and jewelry at their palace. Ben Ali was then charged for the illegal possession of weapons and drugs found at another presidential palace in Carthage. He was sentenced to an additional 15 years in prison. In July 2012, he was charged with the corrupt purchase of property for his family at prices below market value and was sentenced to another 16 years in prison. In June 2012, he was sentenced to life in prison for his role in the killing of protesters during the uprising. He was convicted of complicity in wilful murder and attempted murder in accordance with Article 32 of the Tunisian Penal Code. Moreover, he and Abdallah Qallel, a former Minister of Interior, were sentenced for the torture of those who participated in the 1991 attempted coup plot—in what is known as the *Baraket Essahel* case, named after the town in which the events took place.

Other high-level government officials who were tried and given prison sentences include former Director General of National Security Adel Tiouiri, former Director of the Anti-Riot Police Jalel Boudrigua, former Director General of Public Security Lotfi Ben Zouaoui and the powerful former Director of the Presidential Guard Ali Seriati. However, almost 20 senior government officials from the Ben Ali era were set free in 2014, following a significant reduction in the sentences to time served.[5]

In January 2015, Human Rights Watch estimated that a total of 53 former government officials, including police and security officers, had been tried in military tribunals in Tunisia since late 2011.[6] Some verdicts had been issued, most of which were light sentences and acquittals, while several corruption cases that were filed in 2011 were still being investigated. Also, in the year following Ben Ali's ouster, 420 businessmen were banned from travelling outside of Tunisia pending investigation into their alleged involvement in corruption crimes.[7]

These trials took place following decades of political and economic deterioration in Tunisia. The northern and coastal regions of Tunisia have historically enjoyed social, political and economic privileges at the expense of the poorer interior regions of the country. This divide has been entrenched in the political governance of Tunisia for decades and perpetuated by the Ben Ali regime, which appointed those from the northern and coastal regions to high governmental and military positions. As a result, serious income inequality and social inequality

[5] C Gall, 'Questions of Justice in Tunisia as Ousted Leaders are Freed', *New York Times*, 16 July 2014, available at www.nytimes.com/2014/07/17/world/africa/questions-of-justice-in-tunisia-as-ousted-leaders-are-freed.html.

[6] Human Rights Watch, 'Flawed Accountability: Shortcomings of Tunisia's Trials for Killings During the Uprising' (12 January 2015) 1, www.hrw.org/report/2015/01/12/flawed-accountability/shortcomings-tunisias-trials-killings-during-uprising.

[7] Interview with Abderrahman El Yessa, Democratic Governance Advisor, UNDP Tunisia (Tunis, Tunisia, 26 April 2012).

led to higher unemployment rates in the interior regions of Tunisia. General discrimination against Tunisians from those areas meant they suffered from unequal access to basic services. Lawyers and mid-ranking military officers also suffered socio-economic grievances, as most of them hailed from the inner regions of the country. The police, on the other hand, enjoyed higher salaries and were rewarded for their loyalty to what Ben Ali transformed into a full-fledged police state, largely run by an intimidating interior ministry notorious for its widespread use of torture and arbitrary detention practices of political opponents of all stripes. While Tunisia was lauded by Western countries and international financial institutions for its 'economic miracle' in the 1990s, which allegedly saw economic growth and low unemployment rates, any success of such a miracle began to rapidly disintegrate in the 2000s. This is because, as Francesco Cavatorta and RH Haugbølle argue, Ben Ali and his associates took advantage of the progress made by private businesses in the 1990s by embezzling the profits.[8] As a result, the so-called economic miracle of Tunisia 'had a very dark side where under-employment, unemployment, difficult access to the labour market, income inequalities and wide regional gaps were the main features'.[9]

Such grim social, political and economic grievances were the subject of many testimonies heard at Tunisia's TDC. Tunisia was the first Arab Spring country to pass a transitional justice law in December 2013. Through this law, the TDC was established to cover crimes committed between Tunisia's independence in 1955 and 2013. Reparations, vetting, institutional reform and national reconciliation are some of the mechanisms that the transitional justice law intends to enforce. Moreover, the law establishes 'specialized chambers within the court system to try grave abuses committed between July 1955 and December 2013'.[10] The first victim testimony was heard at the TDC in May 2015.[11] Public hearings, in which victims of torture and relatives of the disappeared or killed spoke, were aired on television and radio in November 2016. Since the establishment of the TDC in 2014, it has received 62,000 submissions and 11,000 testimonies.[12]

Two fact-finding commissions were established in Tunisia in 2011. The first was established by former President Ben Ali on 13 January 2011—one day before his ouster. Its purpose was to investigate human rights violations committed during the 2010–11 uprising. The second commission was established to investigate corruption crimes. According to some interviewees, the capacity of these commissions

---

[8] F Cavatorta and RH Haugbølle, 'The End of Authoritarian Rule and the Mythology of Tunisia under Ben Ali' (2012) 17 *Mediterranean Politics* 179, 185.

[9] ibid, 184.

[10] Human Rights Watch, above n 6.

[11] Agence France Press, 'Tunisia "Truth Commission" Hears Victim Testimony', *Mail Online*, 27 May 2015, available at www.dailymail.co.uk/wires/afp/article-3099409/Tunisia-truth-commission-hears-victim-testimony.html.

[12] International Center for Transitional Justice, 'Revolutionary Truth: Tunisian Victims Make History on First Night of Public Hearings for TDC' (17 November 2016) available at www.ictj.org/news/tunisia-truth-dignity-public-hearings-live.

to carry out investigations was weak and their reports had little influence on the process of prosecution in Tunisia.[13] However, the commission investigating corruption reported in November 2011 that between 6,000 and 7,000 administrative officials were involved in corrupt, illegal practices.[14] Despite this, only 250 cases out of 16,000 complaints before the TDC relate to financial corruption. Some argue that a very controversial financial reconciliation bill that was proposed by the Essebsi government in July 2015 served as a deterrent for businessmen to step forward and resolve their disputes through the TDC.[15]

The Prosecution of Political Leaders in Pre-transition Tunisia

Domestic efforts to prosecute political leaders in Tunisia from before the 2010–11 uprising were almost non-existent.[16] However, through universal jurisdiction laws, two cases targeted former interior ministers Abdallah Qallel and General Habib Ammar in Switzerland, in 2001 and 2003, respectively. A third case, in 2001, targeted Khaled Ben Said, a police superintendent in Jendouba who later became Vice Consul for Tunisia in the French city of Strasbourg.[17] Severe repression, widespread torture by security forces and a 'judiciary strangled by the regime'[18] meant that domestic efforts to prosecute political leaders were 'impossible'.[19] Similar to Egypt, there were calls by well-known individual human rights activists, such as Moncef Marzouki and Hamma Hammami, for 'accountability' rather than for holding specific individuals accountable.[20] These calls, however, did not

[13] Interview with Solène Rougeaux, Director, Avocats Sans Frontières, Tunis Office (Tunis, Tunisia, 25 April 2012); interview with Anis Mahfoudh, Human Rights Officer, Office of the High Commissioner for Human Rights (OHCHR), Tunisia (Tunis, Tunisia, 27 April 2012).

[14] R Bendermel, 'Analysis: Amnesty for Corrupt Businessmen of the Ben Ali Era?', *Middle East Eye*, 13 October 2015, available at www.middleeasteye.net/news/corruption-tunisia-towards-state-failure-613657165.

[15] ibid.

[16] Rougeaux, above n 13; interview with Messaoud Rhomdani, Vice President, Ligue Tunisienne des Droits de l'Homme (Tunis, Tunisia, 25 April 2012); interview with Amor Safraoui, Coordinator, National Coalition for Transitional Justice and Head, Groupe de 25 (Tunis, Tunisia, 25 April 2012); interview with anonymous senior employee, OHCHR (24 April 2012); interview with Habib Nassar, Middle East and North Africa Director, International Center for Transitional Justice (New York City, New York, 18 May 2012).

[17] Jendouba is a city in Northwestern Tunisia. Habib Nassar brought my attention to this case, the details of which can be found here: Fédération Internationale des Ligues des Droits de l'Homme, 'The Conviction of Khaled Ben Said: A Victory against Impunity in Tunisia' (November 2010) available at www.fidh.org/IMG/pdf/Bensaid550ang2010.pdf.

[18] Interview with Amna Guellali, Tunisia and Algeria Researcher, Human Rights Watch (telephone interview, 23 April 2012).

[19] Rougeaux, above n 13.

[20] Interview with Amor Boubakri, lawyer and professor, University of Sousse; UNDP consultant (Tunis, Tunisia, 26 April 2012).

materialise into legal cases, they were not organised and those who called for accountability were severely repressed by Ben Ali's regime.

The *Baraket Essahel* Case: The Prosecution of Abdallah Qallel

The case of Abdallah Qallel, former Minister of Interior from 1991 to 1995, is one of the most well-known cases targeting a Tunisian high-level government official before the 2010 uprising. While Abdallah Qallel was in a Geneva hospital for heart surgery in February 2001, Abdennacer Naït-Liman filed a complaint with the prosecutor of the Geneva canton. Naït-Liman was tortured in a Ministry of Interior detention cell in Tunisia in 1992, following a violent crackdown by security forces on an alleged coup plot in 1991.[21] Over 240 members of the Tunisian military suspected of ties with the Islamist opposition party Ennahda were detained and tortured by interior ministry officials, who claimed that the military was planning a coup to overthrow Ben Ali and his regime. This case became known as *Baraket Essahel*, named after the town in which the alleged coup plot took place in 1991. The Swiss prosecutor cited the Convention against Torture and Other Cruel, Inhuman or Degrading Treatment or Punishment, under which any person, including foreigners, suspected of the crime of torture must be investigated and prosecuted. Following Naït-Liman's legal complaint, Abdallah Qallel fled Switzerland before the police were able to arrest him.

The *Baraket Essahel* case remained dormant until 2011, when 17 victims of the crackdown—mainly mid-ranking military officers—filed a case against Abdallah Qallel, Ben Ali and 12 other government and security officials for their alleged role in the torture of those detained in *Baraket Essahel*. The Permanent Military Court of Tunis sentenced Abdallah Qallel, Ben Ali, Mohamed Ali Ganzoui (the interior ministry's Director of Special Services from 1990 to 1995) and security officials Abderrahmen Kassmi and Mohamed Ennacer Alibi to four years in prison in November 2011. In April 2012, the Court of Appeal of the Military Tribunal of Tunisia reduced these sentences by half.[22] Moreover, these officials were charged with 'violence against others either directly or through others' as opposed to torture.[23] This is in part because the crime of torture was not incorporated into Tunisian law (Law No 89/2 August 1992) until 1999, eight years after the Baraket Essahel incident took place. Abdallah Qallel was also charged with embezzlement in 2011. He was freed, along with Ali Seriati, former Director of Presidential

[21] REDRESS, 'Reparation for Torture: A Survey of Law and Practice in 30 Selected Countries (Switzerland Country Report)' (May 2003) 18–19, available at www.redress.org/downloads/country-reports/Switzerland.pdf.

[22] Human Rights Watch, 'Tunisia: Reform Legal Framework to try Crimes of the Past: First Torture Trial Shows Need to Remove Obstacles to Accountability' (3 May 2012) available at www.hrw.org/news/2012/05/03/tunisia-reform-legal-framework-try-crimes-past.

[23] ibid.

Security Service, and Rafiq Belhadj Kacem, former Minister of Interior in 2010, in 2014 when an appeals court reduced their sentences to time served.[24]

Marzouki, who was President of Tunisia as part of a troika government in 2012, delivered an official state apology to the victims of Baraket Essahel. In June 2014, Law 28 elevated the ranks of the Baraket Essahel officers to where they would have been had they not been stripped of their uniforms and positions 23 years earlier. The officers of Baraket Essahel also formed a number of civil society organisations, such as the Association of Justice for Military Veterans. Sharan Grewal concludes: 'For the officers of the Barraket Essahel affair, perhaps more so than for other Tunisians, the revolution has truly brought transitional justice.'[25]

The Case of General Habib Ammar

The case of General Habib Ammar, Commander of the Tunisian National Guard from 1984 to 1987 and Minister of Interior in 1987, did not proceed as far as that of *Baraket Essahel*. Ammar was infamous for turning the offices of the interior ministry into 'centres of detention and torture'.[26] As a result, in September 2003, the international legal assistance NGO called TRIAL and the Organisation Mondiale Contre la Torture (OMCT) filed a criminal complaint against Ammar with the Attorney General of Geneva, during Ammar's visit to Switzerland. As a member of the Tunisian delegation to the International Telecommunications Union, however, the Attorney General stated that Ammar benefited from immunity.[27]

The *Khaled Ben Saïd* Case

A third Tunisian case—that of Khaled Ben Saïd—took place years before the 2010 uprising, again through the mechanism of universal jurisdiction laws, this time in France. As a police superintendent in the Tunisian town of Jendouba, Ben Saïd allegedly beat and tortured Zoulaikha Gharbi, a Tunisian lady, in October 1996. Gharbi was detained for questioning with regard to her husband and several others, who were suspected of having Islamist affiliations. Gharbi's husband, Mouldi Gharbi, had suffered a similar fate at the same Tunisian police station in 1991, after which he became a political refugee in France in May 1996. The Fédération Internationale des Ligues des Droits de l'Homme (FIDH) provides a concise

---

[24] Gall, above n 5.

[25] S Grewal, 'A Quiet Revolution: The Tunisian Military After Ben Ali' (Carnegie Europe, 24 February 2016) available at http://carnegie-mec.org/2016/02/24/quiet-revolution-tunisian-military-after-ben-ali-pub-62780.

[26] TRIAL, 'Habib Ammar (Tunisia)' (8 April 2015) available at www.trial-chapter.org/en/activities/litigation/trials-cases-in-switzerland/habib-ammar-tunisia-2003.html.

[27] ibid.

summary of the ensuing legal saga that led Gharbi to make use of France's universal jurisdiction laws to attempt to prosecute Ben Saïd:

> In October 1997, Mrs. Gharbi decided to leave Tunisia and went to the police station in order to get her passport. On this occasion, she recognised Khaled Ben Saïd, who was delivering her passport.
>
> On October 22, 1997, Mrs. Gharbi left Tunisia with her children in order to join her husband and settle in France.
>
> On May 9, 2001, having learned that Khaled Ben Saïd was on French soil in the capacity of Vice-Consul at the Tunisian Consulate in Strasbourg, Mrs. Gharbi, with her lawyer, Eric Plouvier, decided to file a complaint against him.
>
> A preliminary enquiry was initiated following this complaint, after which the superintendent in charge of the investigation contacted Khaled Ben Saïd on November 2, 2001 in order to inform him that a complaint had been filed against him and to summon him to a hearing. Khaled Ben Saïd never complied.
>
> In February 2002, the FIDH and its member organisation in France, the Ligue des droits de l'Homme (LDH), represented by Patrick Baudouin, lawyer and Honorary President of the FIDH, became *parties civiles* in the proceedings.
>
> On February 14, 2002, the judge in charge of the preliminary investigation attempted to contact Khaled Ben Saïd and was told by the Tunisian Consulate in Strasbourg that the Vice-Consul had returned to Tunisia.
>
> That same day, the judge issued an international arrest warrant against Khaled Ben Saïd, which was never enforced, similarly to the letter … issued a few weeks later.
>
> In spite of these obstacles, and after seven years of investigation, the indictment before the Criminal Court was finally issued on February 16, 2007.[28]

In December 2008, the Strasbourg Criminal Court found Ben Saïd guilty of torture and sentenced him to eight years in prison. The decision was appealed shortly thereafter and in September 2010, the Criminal Court of Nancy confirmed Ben Saïd's conviction, increased his sentence to 12 years imprisonment and issued an international arrest warrant against him.[29] It was never executed.

Of the three cases outlined above, the *Baraket Essahel* case against Abdallah Qallel seems to have had the largest impact on the pursuit of high-level government officials in Tunisia following the 2010 uprising. The initiation of the case in Switzerland in 2001, followed by its revival ten years later in Tunisia, is a strong indication of the case's importance for the victims and its symbolic value for many Tunisians, particularly during the transition. This is likely because of the terrible reputation of the Ministry of Interior and the highly symbolic value in targeting its chief. Moreover, Tunisia's military officers, long

---

[28] Fédération Internationale des Ligues des Droits de l'Homme, above n 17.
[29] ibid.

marginalised by both Bourguiba and Ben Ali, took advantage of the transition to file their complaints and raise a case against those responsible for the brutal crackdown in 1991. Recent judicial decisions, however, have undermined the momentum to prosecute political leaders in Tunisia: 'Of the approximately 20 former senior officials detained in the aftermath of the uprising, almost all are now free.'[30]

Content and Extent of Prosecutions in Post-transition Tunisia

As in the case of Egypt, there was a significant emphasis on corruption and socio-economic crimes in Tunisia, and a much more limited focus on human rights crimes in the investigations and prosecutions that took place. Corruption charges spanned a period dating back to years before the uprising, while the human rights trials were mostly limited to crimes committed during the uprising in December 2010 and January 2011. This is, of course, with the important exception of the *Baraket Essahel* case explained above. However, some scholars note that Tunisia's transitional justice process increasingly failed to take into account the social justice demands of the protesters and victims, particularly those relating to socio-economic inequality. Lamont and Pannwitz, for instance, attribute this waning of a prosecutorial focus on corruption and economic crimes to the impact of the reliance on foreign models of transitional justice, such as those in South Africa, Eastern Europe and Latin America. Those models focused more on 'traditional legal frameworks that centred around violations of civil and political rights such as police abuses and violations of due process'.[31] As a result, transitional justice in Tunisia was shaped more by elite politics than by the grievances voiced by impoverished victims since the bread riots of 1984.[32]

Lamont and Pannwitz's observation, however, pertains to the latter period of the transitional justice process in Tunisia, during which the controversial Economic and Financial Reconciliation Bill was proposed in 2015, thereby stalling further criminal cases involving corruption and economic crimes. There is no question that corruption crimes, including embezzlement of public funds, illegal possession of drugs and weapons, and the purchase of property at prices below market value for the benefit of Ben Ali family members, figured heavily in the early stages of the prosecutions. In addition, the meddling of the Ben Ali and Trabelsi families in the private businesses that boomed throughout the 1990s made such

---

[30] Gall, above n 5.

[31] C Lamont and H Pannwitz, 'Transitional Justice as Elite Justice? Compromise Justice and Transition in Tunisia' (2016) 7 *Global Policy* 278, 280.

[32] ibid 278.

high-level corruption all the more visible among a population suffering from economic marginalisation and high unemployment.

What explains the limited content and extent of the trials in Tunisia? Why were most high-level officials released? A number of explanations emerge. First, the resurfacing of old regime figures, or *anciens nouveaux*, in the post-transitional governments meant that the extent of the prosecutions was under close observation by a regime wary of a comprehensive accountability agenda that might target them and their past involvement in crimes. Secondly, the relative success of decades-long workers' movements, a history of very visible structural inequalities and specific public demands for prosecution all foregrounded the significant demand the Tunisian public had for accountability for corruption and socio-economic crimes. Thirdly, a politicised public prosecution, a weak legal framework and the anticipation of a truth and reconciliation commission further limited the content and extent of the trials. A preoccupation with political stability immediately following the uprising also stalled decisions regarding the prosecution of political leaders for human rights violations.

A Transition Muddled by the *Anciens Nouveaux*

While Tunisia is often lauded for striking a reconciliation deal in the form of a 'national unity' government, the unity itself is limited to Ennahda and the secular Nidaa Tounes party, which counts in its membership numerous former Ben Ali regime and RCD members. While Tunisia's transition was not as tightly controlled by certain elites as in Egypt, many figures from the Ben Ali era—the 'anciens nouveaux'[33]—retained power. Beji Caïd Essebsi, for instance, was Minister of Foreign Affairs and Minister of Interior in both Bourguiba and Ben Ali's governments and is now Tunisia's President. Since winning the presidency in December 2014, Essebsi nominated three Ben Ali regime officials to senior political positions, including Habib Essid as Prime Minister.[34] Marzouki, the former post-transitional President, laments this arrangement and argues that the praise for Tunisia as the beacon of hope for the Arab Spring does not accurately represent the reality on the ground:

> The corrupt media, business elites, and the politicians of the old regime have joined forces, with the support of some regional powers, to hijack our post-revolutionary institutions. The much-touted 'national unity government' that currently rules the country has become a vehicle for the revival of the old regime and the careers of its

---

[33] H Yousfi, W Majeri, C Hmed, S Djelidi and S Ben Abderrazak, 'En Tunisie, le retour de l'ancien regime n'est pas une rumeur', *Libération*, 21 November 2014, available at www.liberation.fr/debats/2014/11/21/en-tunisie-le-retour-de-l-ancien-regime-n-est-pas-une-rumeur_1147107.

[34] C Petré, 'Tunisia, Let's not Forget about Revolution Already', *Middle East Monitor*, 13 January 2015, available at www.middleeastmonitor.com/articles/africa/16310-tunisia-lets-not-forget-about-the-revolution-already. See also Yousfi et al, above n 33. After only 18 months, Essid lost a vote of confidence in parliament for failing to adequately address economic and security problems.

stalwarts. When current Prime Minister Youssef Chahed was appointed as the head of the government on August 3, his first act was to appoint 12 new governors—nine of whom were officials of the old regime.[35]

Concerned about the consequences of opening up 'too many' human rights cases implicating senior figures from a deeply entrenched and repressive regime meant that these incoming elites, many of whom have ties to the former Ben Ali regime, 'might not be spared' from prosecution.[36]

Tunisia's transition, then, has been marked by the return of old regime members who have morphed into new political parties. As a result, Tunisia has seen an 'elite instrumentalisation of transitional justice', resulting in a narrow accountability agenda fraught with 'limited investigations and a handful of symbolic trials'.[37] This scapegoating of certain individuals was motivated by an attempt by 'former ruling elites within Ben Ali's governing RCD … to limit political change—and by extension the scope of transitional justice—to Ben Ali's inner circle'.[38] As Lamont and Pannwitz point out, Essebsi's government refused the TDC access to presidential archives that may contain evidence of their responsibility for past crimes. This refusal led the TDC to file a lawsuit against the presidency.[39] Since then, the presidential archives have been made accessible to the TDC, but not the interior ministry archives. This, as president of the TDC Sihem Bensedrine noted, is a major obstacle to the work of the TDC 'because the police were the spine which supported the dictatorial system'.[40]

Workers' Movements and Labour Unions: The Leading Role of the UGTT

The social and political processes that unfolded in Tunisia point to the significant role workers' movements and labour unions played before, during and after the uprising. Prior to the eruption of the Tunisian uprising in December 2010, the General Union for Tunisian Workers (UGTT) played a leading role in challenging government policies for years. It was the country's strongest opposition.[41] The mass revolt against unemployment and economic inequality in the Tunisian

---

[35] MM Marzouki, 'The Grim Reality Behind Tunisia's Fairy Tale', *Foreign Policy*, 22 September 2016, available at http://foreignpolicy.com/2016/09/22/the-grim-reality-behind-tunisias-fairy-tale-mohamed-moncef-marzouki/.

[36] Interview with anonymous senior employee of the Tunisian Ministry of Foreign Affairs (22 May 2012).

[37] Lamont and Pannwitz, above n 31, 278, 279.

[38] ibid 278, 281.

[39] ibid.

[40] Sihem Bensedrine, quoted in 'Tunisia Struggles to Hold Former Regime to Account', *Financial Times*, 25 February 2016, available at www.ft.com/content/501f8704-d34a-11e5-8887-98e7feb46f27.

[41] H Yousfi, 'Ce syndicat qui incarne l'opposition tunisienne', Le Monde Diplomatique, November 2012, available at www.monde-diplomatique.fr/2012/11/YOUSFI/48348.

town of Gafsa in 2008, which resulted in several deaths and many injuries, is widely seen as a turning point in the lead up to the uprising two and a half years later.[42] 'This six month revolt,' Messaoud Rhomdani explained, 'may have opened the door to what happened in Sidi Bouzid.'[43] Gafsa and its aftermath helped chip away at the fear barrier that prevented many Tunisians from challenging the regime's repressive policies. It also demonstrated the strength of mobilisation in the face of an often brutal police force. The UGTT led a general strike during the uprising and oversaw the sit-ins at the Casbah thereafter, all of which strengthened their influence and stature as the government's most serious opposition.

The fight against economic injustice in Tunisia was, however, well established long before the Gafsa revolt. In 1978, the UGTT led a nationwide strike that was brutally suppressed and signified the start of a decades-long workers' movement that demanded better contract terms, working conditions, a solution to rampant unemployment, particularly in the interior regions of the country, and higher salaries. In 1984, following a request by the International Monetary Fund to temporarily lift subsidies on primary foodstuffs in order to relieve the strain on hard currency reserves and to fulfil certain requirements for international loans, the cost of bread rose by 108 per cent. This led to massive bread riots (*intifadat al khubz*) in Tunisia and resulted in the deaths of almost 100 people, with almost 1,000 injured.[44] So, to a large extent, the anti-government protest movement has its roots in Tunisian workers' movements, starting with the strike in 1978 under Bourguiba. The UGTT and other workers' movements subsequently served as major actors in the mass uprising of 2010 and in its aftermath.

These labour rights movements in Tunisia did not operate alone—human rights activists, such as Moncef Marzouki (who served as President of Tunisia from 2011 to 2014), Sihem Bensedrine and Hama Hammami, were persistent in their calls for democracy and respect for human rights. But the strongest forces of opposition in Tunisia were labour rights movements, especially the UGTT. Those calling for civil and political rights, such as the right to freedom of expression, the right to assemble and the right to freedom from torture and arbitrary detention, were severely repressed through massive crackdowns led by the police and other state security forces, resulting in a significantly weakened human rights movement in Tunisia. In contrast, the labour rights movements were slightly better tolerated. The UGTT's complicated relationship with the Ben Ali regime, for instance, often meant that the union's executive office was staffed with individuals loyal to the regime.[45]

---

[42] Rhomdani, above n 16; Boubakri, above n 20; Anonymous, above n 16). See also G Achcar, *The People Want: A Radical Exploration of the Arab Uprising* (London, Saqi Books, 2013).

[43] Rhomdani, ibid. Sidi Bouzid is in reference to the town in which the self-immolation of Mohammed Bouazizi, the fruit-seller whose act ignited the Tunisian revolution of 2010/2011, took place.

[44] 'Tunisia Report Places Blame for Bread Riots', *New York Times*, 23 April 1984, available at www.nytimes.com/1984/04/23/world/tunisia-report-places-blame-for-bread-riots.html.

[45] Interview with Anis Morai, lawyer, professor, columnist and host of 'Dans le Vif du Sujet' (telephone interview, 2 May 2013).

The relative success of the Tunisian labour rights movements in bringing to the fore demands for social justice and an end to corruption impacted the content of the prosecutions. The build-up of their influence over decades played a major role in the consequent emphasis on financial corruption crimes in the prosecutions, such as the embezzlement of public funds and money-laundering charges faced by Ben Ali and others in the first few years after the uprising. Like in Egypt, the workers' movements and labour unions in Tunisia thus served as drivers that ensured a certain degree of criminal accountability for socio-economic rights violations. On the other hand, the harsh crackdowns on civil and political rights activists left a seriously weakened human rights lobby that has been largely unsuccessful in ensuring criminal accountability for human rights abuses committed both before and during the uprisings.

The visibility of corruption throughout Ben Ali's reign is, as several interviewees explained, a major factor that fuelled public demands for prosecution.[46] The lavish lifestyles of the Ben Ali and Trabelsi families funded by ill-gotten funds is just one example of the ways in which corruption upheld the authoritarian regime. The continued marginalisation of the interior regions compared to the more privileged northern and coastal regions compounded the grievances caused by such socio-economic inequality. The demands for human rights prosecutions were thus largely focused on the killing of protesters during the uprising, whereas demands for socio-economic justice spanned the 23 years of Ben Ali's rule.

Abderrahman El Yessa noted that the demography of the protesters during the uprising impacted directly on the content of the demands for prosecution:

> The human rights charges are limited to the period of the revolution because the demands of the protesters were limited in this way. This is because most of the protesters were young and leftist and they see themselves as the owners of the revolution. Their vision is therefore limited to the violations that they faced during 'their' uprising.[47]

El Yessa added that the poor economic situation in Tunisia prompted jurists to propose reconciliation deals with hundreds of business tycoons banned from travelling, as a way to help boost the country's battered economy. When it comes to corruption, El Yessa explained, 'everyone is a victim'.[48] Amor Boubakri, a Tunisian academic, lawyer and United Nations consultant, echoed this explanation: 'People want to hold [political leaders] accountable for poverty and widespread socio-economic malaise. To prosecute them would help resolve economic problems.'[49] Anis Morai, a Tunisian legal expert and political commentator, suggested that the

---

[46] Anonymous, above n 16; El Yessa, above n 7; Boubakri, above n 20; Mahfoudh, above n 13.

[47] El Yessa, however, added that the Youssefists—or the Islamists—played a significant role in pushing for an expansive time period for Tunisia's Truth and Dignity Commission. The 'young and leftist' protesters thus did not apply pressure alone: 'These [justice] demands were made by everyone—ordinary citizens, political activists, Islamists and non-Islamists.' El Yessa, above n 7.

[48] El Yessa, above n 7. The original quote was in French: 'tout le monde est victime'.

[49] Boubakri, above n 20.

scale of corruption and poverty meant that other rights were not a priority for the average Tunisian: 'Tunisians do not dwell on freedom of thought, on the freedom to form an association. And I can understand that, because it is *they* who are hungry.'[50]

The Islamists and Youssefists also voiced specific demands for accountability, much like the 'young' and 'leftist'[51] protesters had specific demands regarding who should be prosecuted and for what. Salah Ben Youssef was a nationalist who led an opposition against the diplomatic solution Bourguiba pursued to end the French occupation of Tunisia. Ben Youssef thus became Bourguiba's arch-enemy, and his supporters, the Youssefists, were regularly detained, beaten and tortured in Bourguiba's prisons. The Islamists, on the other hand, were Ben Ali's largest opposition and they also suffered repression, including torture, under his rule. Moreover, Ben Ali's mistrust of the military meant their continued marginalisation throughout his rule, mainly in the form of a low budget, especially in comparison to the budget granted to the police and interior ministry, but also through brutal practices such as torture and detention, as happened during the Baraket Essahel incident. As a result, the Youssefists, the military and the Islamists emerged as some of the most vocal actors with demands for the prosecution of leaders who had overseen widespread torture since Tunisia's independence.[52] This became particularly clear when 17 military officers filed a court case against Qallel and others for the brutal crackdown of Baraket Essahel.[53]

Legal Challenges

The absence of certain critical reforms to Tunisia's criminal code severely limited prosecutions in two ways. First, all trials took place in military courts because they involve actions by military personnel. Human Rights Watch explains the problem of military jurisdiction in Tunisia:

> the Tunisian president appoints civilian judges to serve in military courts by decree, pursuant to the recommendation of the ministers of justice and defense. The general military prosecutor is appointed by the minister of defense and works under his supervision. All prosecutors and investigative judges who serve in the military courts are members of the military. Thus, military courts cannot be considered as structurally independent from the executive branch. This lack of independence of military courts understandably heightened suspicions among victims and their families that the courts remained

---

[50] Morai, above n 45. The original quote was in French: 'Les tunisiens ne réfléchissent pas à la liberté de pensée, à la liberté de faire une association. Et je peux le comprendre, parce que c'est eux qui ont faim au ventre.'

[51] As described by Abderrahman El Yessa. El Yessa, above n 7.

[52] Boubakri, above n 20; El Yessa, above n 7.

[53] See the Baraket Essahel section above.

susceptible to political pressure, leading to lenient sentences for those convicted in relation to the uprising killings and the acquittal of other accused.[54]

Secondly, the lack of the principle of command responsibility in Tunisia's penal code significantly weakened the extent of the prosecutions and resulted in many acquittals. While Ben Ali was found guilty of failing to stop the killings of protesters in his capacity as commander of security forces, the military courts did not use the same legal reasoning in the trials of the former Minister of Interior and other high-level officials. In its 2015 report on accountability in Tunisia, Human Rights Watch observed:

> The military appeals court sentenced former president Ben Ali to life in prison when delivering its April 12, 2014 verdict. It found that as head of state he commanded the security forces, in accordance with article 2 of law 70 of 1982 specifying that the president has direct or indirect supervision of all of Tunisia's security forces ... The court did not follow this same reasoning with regard to the former minister of interior and the former directors general of the security forces. The court sentenced these defendants to three years in prison for 'dereliction of duty' or 'failure to act'. This discrepancy between the severity of the sentence imposed on Ben Ali and the leniency of the sentences imposed on other former senior officials underscores the court's failure to analyze the command and control structures of the Ministry of Interior in depth, in order to determine the responsibility of each defendant.[55]

The report also notes that the military appeals court did not take into account elements that it had itself listed as evidence for the trials of other senior officials. It adds that: 'Article 32 of Tunisia's penal code encompasses the notion of aiding and abetting, stating that an accomplice is someone who assisted the offender in the commission of a crime.'[56]

Finally, a lack of political will, together with a politicised public prosecution and a weak legal framework, contributed to the limited scope of the content and extent of prosecutions in Tunisia. The majority of the complaints filed against former leaders were instigated by individual plaintiffs and by a group of lawyers called the Groupe de 25. The Groupe de 25 was formed on the 14 January 2011—the day that Ben Ali was ousted from power. Amor Safraoui, the head of the Groupe de 25, explained the initial efforts aimed at prosecution:

> Between the 14 January 2011 and the 8 February 2011, we were waiting for the Public Prosecutor to begin the process of prosecution. We were also waiting for the Minister of Justice to take action. As a group of concerned lawyers and citizens, we met often during this time period. We realised that there was no political will to prosecute, and so we decided to act on the 8 February 2011. Although [this was not our role as lawyers], we ... decided to take the place of what should have been the Public Prosecutor and we went ahead and filed a complaint against two former ministers of interior and the

---

[54] Human Rights Watch, above n 6.
[55] ibid.
[56] ibid.

former president for corruption crimes and human rights violations committed during the uprising.[57]

A lack of action on the part of the Public Prosecutor thus led the Groupe de 25 to initiate prosecutions. When I asked the Groupe de 25 why they were more active in filing for corruption rather than human rights crimes, Charfeddine Kallel, a human rights lawyer for several victims of the uprising and a prominent member of the Groupe de 25, cited capacity and expertise challenges:

> We, the Groupe de 25, have limited capacity. We are unable to pursue human rights violations on the same scale as financial corruption cases because first of all, we do not have the resources and second, we need the training on how to prosecute crimes such as torture.[58]

Furthermore, a public prosecution allied with the ruling political party has thus meant that many human rights cases continue to be blocked.[59]

While the lack of an enabling legal framework to prosecute for serious human rights crimes was a major challenge that limited the content of prosecutions, the transitional justice law adopted in December 2013 aimed to redress this. It has also tamed demands to prosecute decades of torture crimes. This is because specialised chambers will be established to try serious crimes committed between July 1955 and December 2013.[60] The law also set up the TDC that will cover crimes committed during the same time period. Amna Guellali observed that:

> in the beginning, popular demand for prosecutions was focused on social justice, but then it also encompassed demands for justice for human rights abuses. The reason for this limited content is that everyone is waiting for the Truth and Dignity Commission.[61]

Boubakri and El Yessa made similar arguments, stating that the Islamists and the Youssefists took the lead in pressuring the interim governments to expand the scope of the TDC to ensure that it addresses the crimes committed against them between the 1950s and the 1990s.[62]

The Role of International Actors

The role of international actors in steering Tunisia's decisions regarding prosecution was, as in Egypt, minimal. Several lawyers and civil society activists noted

---

[57] Safraoui, above n 16.

[58] Interview with Charfeddine Kallel, lawyer and member, Groupe de 25 (Tunis, Tunisia, 25 April 2012).

[59] Rhomdani, above n 16; Safraoui, above n 16.

[60] Human Rights Watch, 'Tunisia: Hope for Justice on Past Abuses: Specialized Chambers Should be Independent, Fair' (22 May 2014) available at www.hrw.org/news/2014/05/22/tunisia-hope-justice-past-abuses.

[61] Guellali, above n 18.

[62] Boubakri, above n 20; El Yessa, above n 7.

that the prosecutions of political leaders were domestically driven, with little involvement from external actors. Rhomdani was emphatic in his response to the question of international actors' involvement: 'The decision to prosecute was directly in response to the demands of civil society and the protesters. It was entirely domestically driven—there has been no role played by the international human rights movement in the decision to prosecute.'[63] Despite this, Rhomdani continued to argue for the importance of working with international actors to advance transitional justice in Tunisia, as well as reforming the judiciary:

> Tunisians do want transitional justice for torture and corruption crimes, but they don't quite understand how important it is to do it right. Transitional justice is not necessarily understood well—some consider it 'turning the page' and not dealing with the crimes of the past. We must learn from the experiences of Latin America, South Africa, Portugal and Spain. Morocco's experience with its truth and reconciliation commission has not been thorough. We need to work both internationally and nationally. But justice has been slow. The snipers, for instance, have not been held to account. We have a very corrupt judicial system. The Groupe de 25 has done a good job of fighting this, but a lot still needs to be done.[64]

While the role of international actors was minimal in the immediate aftermath of Ben Ali's ouster in January 2011, however, it was much more prominent in the decade leading up to the uprising. Prior to the uprising, international NGOs such as Human Rights Watch, FIDH and Amnesty International were influential in raising awareness about human rights violations in Tunisia and in documenting abuses. As head of the Groupe de 25 Safraoui explained, 'We reached out to the international community in the past: FIDH, the Paris Bar, etc, in an effort to put pressure on the European Community to put pressure on the Ben Ali government to respect human rights'.[65] Moreover, the use of universal jurisdiction laws in Switzerland and France were critical in triggering prosecutions pre-uprising and also in raising awareness among Tunisians regarding criminal accountability for its leaders.[66] Post-uprising, international actors have largely taken on a training role, rather than one that triggers or drives decisions to prosecute.[67]

The systematic documentation and monitoring of human rights abuses, particularly with the help of international actors, has, however, had a significant impact in the post-uprising transition period. For instance, Amnesty International worked relentlessly with the United Nations Committee Against Torture, Tunisian victims and civil society organisations on a gruelling 22-year-long campaign to establish the truth surrounding the torture case of Faysal Baraket.[68] The exhumation of

[63] Rhomdani, above n 16.
[64] ibid.
[65] Safraoui, above n 16.
[66] See The Prosecution of Political Leaders in Pre-transition Tunisia section below.
[67] Guellali, above n 18; Rougeaux, above n 13; Safraoui, above n 16; Boubakri, above n 20; El Yessa, above n 7.
[68] Amnesty International, 'Tunisia: When Bones Speak: The Struggle to Bring Faysal Baraket's Torturers to Justice' (October 2013) available at www.amnesty.org/en/library/asset/MDE30/016/2013/en/cf6715f8-e1a7-426b-9635-8dd5289bc1e0/mde300162013en.html.

Baraket's body took place in March 2013, 22 years after his death from torture by police officers. While at the time of writing nobody has been prosecuted, the collaboration between international actors and Tunisian actors has been crucial in moving Faysal's case forward.[69] Nevertheless, the pervasive repression throughout Ben Ali's police state in Tunisia meant that international and domestic civil society actors faced massive challenges in ultimately ensuring prosecutions, particularly of high-level officials.

Strikingly, none of the interviewees mentioned any role or impact of Tunisia's accession to the Rome Statute on 24 June 2011. A senior employee in the Middle East and North Africa section of the Office of the High Commissioner for Human Rights (OHCHR) stated that his office banked on both the optimism and uncertainty of the transition period immediately following Ben Ali's ouster and, together with international human rights groups, launched a campaign calling on the interim authorities to join the International Criminal Court.[70] He added that the timing of the campaign—when government policies were in flux—was key to its success. On the other hand, when I specifically asked whether Tunisia's accession to the Rome Statute had had any impact on domestic decisions to prosecute, Safraoui replied:

> People are not so much interested in the goings-on of the international criminal justice movement, even after Tunisia ratified the Rome Statute. At the moment, Tunisians are caught up with internal politics—particularly the 'Islamist versus the secularist' discourse that has become so dominant now.[71]

It should be noted, however, that Safraoui's observation came just over one year after the ouster of Ben Ali and a few months short of Tunisia's one-year anniversary of its accession to the Rome Statute.

When Samir Dilou became Minister of Human Rights and Transitional Justice, he advocated for an internationalised model of transitional justice. By reaching out to international actors such as the International Center for Transitional Justice and the United Nations Development Programme (UNDP), 'the national dialogue on transitional justice served to filter local voices into internationally established and pre-fixed normative frameworks'.[72] As mentioned earlier, some scholars claim that such an alignment of a local transitional justice process with international models reduced the emphasis on social justice. Instead, it focused more on civil and political rights violations in the more recent transitional justice processes in Tunisia.[73] The televised hearings organised by the TDC in November 2016 are an example of the very public way in which civil and political rights violations have been exposed.

---

[69] ibid.
[70] Anonymous, above n 16.
[71] Safraoui, above n 16.
[72] Lamont and Pannwitz, above n 31, 278, 280.
[73] ibid 278.

The Role of Domestic Civil Society

The preservation of historical memory and the documentation of human rights abuses guided the work of Tunisia's civil society in the decades before the uprising. Working within a repressive environment, civil society organisations such as the Tunisian Human Rights League (LTDH) began to document and disseminate information, particularly following the 1978 general strike by the UGTT.[74] As a result of this strike, labour union members were tortured and faced other repressive measures. This, Rhomdani argued, is what motivated the LTDH to make as its goal the documentation and dissemination of information on human rights violations. It also marked the start of a Tunisian civil society that was predominantly made up of labour union activists. Rhomdani explained:

> Trade and labour unions in Tunisia have historically played an important role in politics. Because of the severe repression practiced by the RCD, Tunisia's ruling political party, it was extremely difficult to form political parties. Political dissidents thus either joined the LTDH or the trade unions. A number of 'governmental NGOs' were formed, but they were just that—GONGO's.[75]

While there were very few explicit attempts by civil society to trigger prosecutions of political leaders before the 2010–11 uprising,[76] documentation of abuses signified anticipation of a time when prosecutions would be possible. As an anonymous Tunisian interviewee explained:

> [Civil society documented abuses] because they knew one day that the dictatorship would fall. Also, they did it for the sake of historical memory. The CNLT developed a list of who they thought was responsible for abuses from the 1990s. OCTT has also documented testimonies. We all knew one day that the regime would disappear. That is why documentation took place.[77]

Nevertheless, despite severe restrictions on the work of civil society under Ben Ali, a creative use of universal jurisdiction laws with the help of international organisations such as the OMCT helped bring about the cases of Abdallah Qallel, Habib Ammar and Khaled Ben Said.

Tunisian lawyers are key actors who sustained demands for accountability before, during and after the uprising. Eric Gobé and Lena Salaymeh outline the 'profound transformation' of the Tunisian legal profession, which saw a shift from

---

[74] Rhomdani, above n 16.

[75] Referring to the term 'governmental NGOs'. ibid.

[76] See the *Baraket Essahel*, *General Habib Ammar* and *Khaled Ben Said* cases in The Prosecution of Political Leaders in Pre-transition Tunisia section below. Note that these three cases were initiated by individual plaintiffs and the *Khaled Ben Said* case was later taken up by international lawyers and NGOs, such as the OMCT in Switzerland.

[77] Anonymous, above n 36. CNLT is the Conseil National pour la Liberté des Tunisiens. OCTT is the Organisation Contre la Torture Tunisienne.

strictly professional activities to 'activist lawyering'.[78] At the centre of this activist lawyering is the Tunisian Bar Association (TBA), which posed a significant challenge to the Bourguiba and Ben Ali regimes. Gobé and Salaymeh explain the progression of the TBA's evolution since Tunisian independence through 2014 as a shift from 'professional objectives, to socioeconomic concerns, to political engagement that divided the membership and leadership, to relatively unified political mobilization of the legal profession'.[79]

The Tunisian legal profession essentially saw a shift from activity in the courtrooms to activity in public spaces, with the 2010–11 uprising as a major turning point that redefined activist lawyering in Tunisia. Its democratic structure and elected leaders meant that the TBA was one of only a few platforms where lawyers were able to discuss sensitive political issues.[80] This was important as judges and prosecutors were largely aligned with the regime while lawyers were more independent. Throughout the 1990s, Ben Ali repeatedly attempted to limit the TBA's autonomy. For example, Ben Ali pressured parliament to pass a bill in 1989 that allowed judges and prosecutors to infiltrate the TBA after serving as magistrates for ten years. It also allowed judges to unilaterally declare that an attorney's arguments or statements in court were made in bad faith and to refer the attorney to appear before other judges to defend him or herself.[81] Also, Islamist lawyers who were members of the TBA were often harassed and tortured during Ben Ali's rule.

The activist lawyering practised by the TBA, particularly during the uprising, was key in supporting the protests against socio-economic grievances in a very public manner—mainly through political mobilisation and street protests. This is unsurprising, given that a majority of TBA lawyers came from working-class neighbourhoods and served clients struggling with family law, petty crimes and neighbourhood disputes. A small number of lawyers who were members of the RCD, however, were rewarded with responsibility for much larger projects involving public funding, thereby reaping larger benefits from the cases they took in comparison to their working-class colleagues. As Gobé notes, 'In exchange for these economic benefits, these pro-regime attorneys monitored and challenged the collective actions of their colleagues in the legal profession'.[82] Such lawyers went so far as to litigate against 'activist lawyers' who posed a challenge to the Ben Ali regime.[83] However, such manoeuvres by the Ben Ali regime and those loyal to it were unsuccessful, particularly as grievances emerging from poor socio-economic

[78] E Gobé and L Salaymeh, 'Tunisia's "Revolutionary" Lawyers: From Professional Autonomy to Political Mobilization' (2016) 41 *Law and Social Inquiry* 311, 312.

[79] ibid 313.

[80] ibid 315.

[81] ibid 320. Art 46 of the bill.

[82] E Gobé, 'Of Lawyers and Samsars: The Legal Services Market and the Authoritarian State in Ben 'Ali's Tunisia (1987–2011)' (2013) 67 *Middle East Journal* 44, 49–53.

[83] Gobé and Salaymeh, above n 78, 324.

conditions strengthened over time and 'led a majority of lawyers to be receptive to activist lawyering (opposed to the regime) well before the Tunisian uprising'.[84]

Immediately following Mohamed Bouazizi's self-immolation in December 2010, lawyers began to participate in street protests and sit-ins outside courts throughout Tunisia while wearing their black robes. As the uprising progressed, lawyers were not spared in the government's violent crackdown on peaceful protesters. As a result, the TBA escalated its anti-government protest by publicly condemning police aggression and organising a general strike on 6 January 2011 and again on 14 January 2011.[85] At the same time, the UGTT also organised general strikes throughout Tunisia from 12 January 2011. Strikingly, the TBA made specific demands following Ben Ali's ouster for criminal accountability for those who benefited under the regime. It set up its own Working Group on Transitional Justice in February 2012, which drafted transitional justice legislation and made recommendations regarding arbitration and reconciliation. The technical committee that developed the legislation for transitional justice, which resulted in the enactment of the Transitional Justice Law in December 2013, apparently took into consideration the TBA's recommendations.[86]

The historic activism of the TBA and the UGTT, and the intensive pressure and activity led by the Groupe de 25 in the immediate aftermath of Ben Ali's ouster, all formed a diverse protest movement in Tunisia that contributed to the downfall of Ben Ali. As explained earlier, a military that had been marginalised and victimised by both Bourguiba and Ben Ali was an additional domestic actor that, together with activist lawyering by the TBA and the Groupe de 25 and the pressure from the UGTT, served as major drivers of some of the decisions to prosecute former leaders of the Ben Ali regime. Strong public support for criminal accountability has recently emerged again in the very vocal protests against the proposed economic reconciliation bill that the Essebsi government floated in June 2015. Campaigns such as 'Manich Msamah' ('I do not forgive') voiced strong concerns over reconciliation with former cronies of the regime and instead called for their prosecution in the courts. Centres such as I WATCH give access to citizens to report corruption practices and provide investigation services with a view to offering legal advice on judicial proceedings. A group of legal experts offer these services free of charge and are licensed to process personal data from the National Authority for the Protection of Personal Data.[87]

---

[84] ibid.

[85] ibid 327.

[86] S El Gantri, 'The Role of Lawyers as Transitional Actors in Tunisia' *Lawyers, Conflict and Transition Project* (August 2015) 11.

[87] A Nadhif, 'Who Protects Tunisian Corruption Whistleblowers?', *Al Monitor*, 29 July 2016, available at www.al-monitor.com/pulse/originals/2016/07/tunisia-watchdog-fight-corruption-high-index.html#ixzz4NbeGo1yS.

Conclusion

Triggers

At least three events in Tunisia's recent past served as turning points in the momentum behind decisions to prosecute the country's leaders. The 1978 general strike, the Baraket Essahel torture practices in 1991 and the Gafsa revolt of 2008 each fuelled resistance to repression and civil society advocacy for accountability for human rights violations. The *Baraket Essahel* case specifically led to the initiation of a case against former Minister of Interior Abdallah Qallel in Switzerland in 2001, and was reignited domestically in Tunisia in 2011. As Rhomdani argued, the general strike in Tunisia in 1978 was critical in that the torture that took place at the time triggered a civil society movement for accountability.[88] The six-month revolt in Gafsa, violently repressed by state security forces in 2008, had a similar, if not even more significant, impact on later decisions to prosecute leaders. While there may not have been calls aimed specifically at the prosecution of leaders for the repression that marked both the general strike and Gafsa, they were still cited regularly as early turning points that triggered a movement that ultimately turned into a call for criminal accountability.[89] Speaking about Gafsa, an anonymous interviewee stated, 'It was the spark'.[90]

Immediately following the ouster of Ben Ali in January 2011, individual plaintiffs, members of the TBA and groups of lawyers such as the Groupe de 25 filed complaints on behalf of victims and against former leaders for both human rights violations and corruption. These actors were key in initiating the process of prosecution. However, pressure from 'the street' (protesters) during the uprising and also immediately following Ben Ali's ouster was, as several interviewees noted, the strongest trigger that led to decisions to prosecute.[91] This demonstrates the significant role of mass mobilisation and repeated calls by civil society for accountability, particularly following a long period of repression. As Nassar declared, 'Impunity is one reason the uprisings started'.[92] He added that the timing of popular calls for prosecution was key, despite the fact that they were not organised and there was no clear prosecutorial strategy.[93] Amor Safraoui, head of the Groupe de 25, echoed this observation.[94]

[88] Rhomdani, above n 16.
[89] Anonymous, above n 36; Rhomdani, above n 16; Boubakri, above n 20.
[90] Anonymous, above n 36.
[91] Mahfoudh, above n 13; Guellali, above n 18; El Yessa, above n 7; Nassar, above n 16; Anonymous, above n 36; Rougeaux, above n 13.
[92] Nassar, above n 16.
[93] ibid.
[94] Safraoui, above n 16.

Drivers

Some of the trigger factors described above also served as drivers of decisions regarding prosecution. In particular, the Groupe de 25's early efforts, immediately following Ben Ali's ouster, were successful in pushing for prosecutions. Continued protests and pressure from victims' families made it difficult for interim authorities to ignore the question of prosecutions for former leaders. The appeasement of public anger was therefore a key driver of decisions regarding prosecution.[95] A military that had long been marginalised and victimized, by both Bourguiba and Ben Ali, was an additional domestic actor that, together with activist lawyering by the TBA and the Groupe de 25 and pressure from the UGTT, served as major drivers of some of the decisions to prosecute former leaders of the Ben Ali regime.

Shapers

The demands for human rights prosecutions were largely focused on the killings of protesters during the uprising, whereas demands for socio-economic justice spanned the 23 years of Ben Ali's rule. Moreover, most of the 20 senior officials from Ben Ali's regime who were prosecuted have since been set free. Several factors shaped this limited content and extent of the prosecutions. Poverty, inequality and widespread corruption contributed to the emphasis on accountability for socio-economic crimes in the mass protests of 2010–11. The highly symbolic tragedy of Mohamed Bouazizi's self-immolation illustrates this state of affairs well. The government's plans to establish a commission (the TDC) to cover crimes committed since Tunisia's independence in 1955 further contributed to the very limited scope of the human rights charges in the prosecutions. Moreover, a corrupt judiciary and a politicised public prosecutor, along with the use of military jurisdiction to try former leaders, put into question the legitimacy of the legal steps taken to ensure criminal accountability. A lack of command responsibility provisions led to many acquittals and light sentences. The financial reconciliation bill introduced by President Essebsi slowed down corruption and financial crimes prosecutions. Finally, a transition that increasingly saw the return of the *anciens nouveaux* meant that human rights prosecutions in particular, but also corruption prosecutions, would be limited to protect those with former regime ties. In much the same way that prosecutions were used to sacrifice a part of the regime to save the regime in Egypt, former Minister of Interior Abdallah Qallel, prosecuted in the *Baraket Essahel* case, was, as his daughter proclaimed, 'designated as a scapegoat for torture' while other former ministers were exempted from prosecution.[96]

---

[95] Nassar, above n 16.

[96] J Thorne, 'Tunisian Ex-minister Fights Torture Verdict: What Did He Know, When Did He Know It?', *The National*, 29 February 2012, available at www.thenational.ae/news/world/middle-east/tunisian-ex-minister-fights-torture-verdict-what-did-he-know-when-did-he-know-it#full.

4

Libya

The anti-government uprising in Libya was largely sparked by the harsh oppression and lack of accountability for the widespread and systematic crimes committed throughout Muammar Gaddafi's rule. With the exception of some politicised efforts by Gaddafi himself to hold certain high-level officials opposed to him accountable, there were no major efforts to prosecute political leaders in Gaddafi's Libya. There were, however, efforts aimed at accountability through financial compensation of the regime's victims. This was especially prominent in the case of the 1996 Abu Salim prison massacre, the impact of which continues to loom large over accountability efforts more than 20 years later. Political developments in Libya, particularly since the intensification of conflict in 2014, have resulted in the emergence of rival governments and militias violently fighting each other for the control of territory and resources. These rival governments have played a direct role in steering criminal accountability for certain former leaders, namely Saif al-Islam Gaddafi, in different directions. While there was initial support for his prosecution domestically, an elusive general amnesty law issued by one of Libya's governments in 2015 led to his alleged release in the town where he has been incarcerated since 2011. This chapter discusses such developments and the role of Libya's judiciary, civil society and international actors in decisions regarding the prosecution of political leaders in Libya.

On 15 February 2011, the arrest of Fathi Terbil sparked protests in Libya's eastern town of Benghazi. Terbil was a prominent lawyer who represented the families of the victims of the Abu Salim prison massacre.[1] The protests then grew into

---

[1] Thousands of political opposition activists were imprisoned in Abu Salim, following orders by Gaddafi and his regime. The following is a description of the Abu Salim massacre obtained by Human Rights Watch: 'on the evening of June 28 the prisoners protested over harsh prison conditions and captured two guards, one of whom died. Guards opened fire, killing six prisoners and wounding about 20. The government sent senior officials to negotiate, including Muammar Gaddafi's brother-in-law and intelligence chief, Abdullah Sanussi. Five prisoners met Sanussi to present their demands, including a stop to torture, trials for prisoners, and improved food, health care, and family visits. Sanussi said he would meet the prisoners' demands, except for trials, if the prisoners released the other captured guard, one of the prisoner negotiators told Human Rights Watch. The prisoners agreed and about 120 sick prisoners were taken away, allegedly for medical care. Instead, many of them were shot and killed. The next morning, hundreds of prisoners from different cell blocks were brought into a courtyard in the civilian side of the prison. Between 10 am and 11 am, gunmen on the roofs opened fire with automatic weapons for at least one hour. In total over the two days, more than 1,200 prisoners lost their lives'. Human Rights Watch, 'Libya: Abu Salim Prison Massacre Remembered' (27 June 2012) available at www.hrw.org/news/2012/06/27/libya-abu-salim-prison-massacre-remembered.

82

Libya

a full-fledged massive uprising on 17 February 2011, with mass demonstrations in other parts of the country calling for the ouster of former leader Muammar Gaddafi and his regime. Terbil's arrest and the protests that ensued show the key role the government's campaign against criminal accountability played in triggering the Libyan uprising. The desire of victims' families to bring the Abu Salim perpetrators to justice also played a significant role in mobilising the protesters. As Amel Jerary, the Communications Director for former Prime Minister Ali Zeidan, declared, 'The aim of the revolution was to establish a state of law and to achieve justice for the Abu Salim victims'.[2]

A NATO-led military campaign against the Gaddafi regime began on 19 March 2011. Backed by the United Nations Security Council, this intervention ended on 31 October 2011, 11 days after Muammar Gaddafi was captured and killed by Libyan rebels. Gaddafi's son, Saif al-Islam Gaddafi, was captured near Sabha on 19 November 2011 and has since been held by armed Libyan rebels in Zintan. Former military intelligence chief Abdullah El Senussi was extradited from Mauritania to Libya on 5 September 2012. Former Prime Minister al-Baghdadi al-Mahmoudi was extradited from Tunisia to Libya on 24 June 2012. Both El Senussi and al-Mahmoudi have since been detained in Al Hadba prison, along with over 30 former high-level Gaddafi regime officials.

On 26 February 2011, the Security Council passed Resolution 1970, in which it referred the situation in Libya to the International Criminal Court (ICC). The same resolution imposed an arms embargo on Libya as well as a travel ban and asset freeze targeting high-profile members of the Gaddafi regime.[3] On 27 June 2011, the ICC issued three arrest warrants, for Muammar Gaddafi, Saif-al Islam Gaddafi and El Senussi, for crimes against humanity, including persecution and murder.[4] Following the capture and killing of Muammar Gaddafi in October 2011, the ICC dropped its case against him.

Muammar Gaddafi ruled Libya for 42 years. He overthrew King Idris, a pro-Western Libyan monarch, in a bloodless military coup in 1969. In the four decades that ensued, the Gaddafi regime violently clamped down on dissent, going so far as to hold public and televised executions of university students opposed to Gaddafi in the 1970s. Many of Gaddafi's critics and political opponents suffered arbitrary detention, torture and death in custody. The practice of enforced disappearance at the hands of the brutal Internal Security Agency claimed thousands of victims over a period of decades. The Gaddafi regime also targeted its opponents in exile, killing them through the use of a Libyan intelligence network operating at a global level. Under Gaddafi, Libya was regarded as an international pariah state, particularly following its involvement in the bombing of the Pan American flight

---

[2] Interview with Amel Jerary, Director of Communications, Prime Minister's Office (for former Libyan Prime Minister Ali Zeidan) (Doha, Qatar, 8 November 2012).

[3] S/RES/1970 (2011).

[4] United Nations Support Mission in Libya (UNSMIL) and Office of the United Nations High Commissioner for Human Rights (OHCHR), 'Report on the Trial of 37 Former Members of the Qadhafi Regime (Case 630/2012)' (21 February 2017).

over Lockerbie, Scotland in 1988. Subsequent UN sanctions against Libya further marginalised the country. The USA bombed Libya in 1986 in retaliation for Libya's involvement in the bombing of a Berlin nightclub in which two American soldiers were among the dead. However, following Gaddafi's renunciation of Libya's weapons of mass destruction programme in 2003, Libya's status as a pariah state quickly changed. It began to forge political and economic ties with an increasing number of states, particularly in Europe.

Libya's improved relations with European states and the USA did not, however, mean things improved at home. Civil society organisations under Muammar Gaddafi were strangled by heavy legal restrictions on their formation and independence. The government secured its control over NGOs through the Associations Act of 1970 and again in 2001. Moreover, government officials were placed in leadership positions within civil society organisations and foreign funding was severely restricted and controlled by the General People's Committee. According to Mercy Corps, an estimated 22 NGOs operated in Libya before Muammar Gaddafi's fall in 2011.[5] Pre-transition Libya was thus marked by a crippled civil society that was unable to effectively push for a better human rights situation without being brutally repressed by Gaddafi's authoritarian regime.

Since the fall of Muammar Gaddafi in October 2011, Libya has had several governments amidst ongoing violence and military campaigns by various armed groups and militias, all vying for control of Libya's territory and resources. In 2011 and 2012, the National Transitional Council (NTC) served as the first internationally recognised government in Libya, despite its relatively small constituency of rebel leaders. In August 2012, the NTC transferred power to the General National Congress (GNC), an elected parliament with Mohammed Al Magarief as President and Ali Zeidan as Prime Minister. After the expiration of the GNC's 18-month mandate to move Libya towards a democratic constitution, a new House of Representatives (HoR) replaced the GNC in August 2014. This government is widely referred to as the 'internationally recognised' Tobruk government, in the East of Libya. That same year, General Khalifa Haftar launched Operation Dignity, a military campaign against the GNC and against armed Islamist groups in Libya. Initially an ally of Muammar Gaddafi, Haftar led Libya's military campaign in Chad in the 1980s. Following Libya's defeat in the Chadian war, Muammar Gaddafi sacked Haftar. Haftar then became Muammar Gaddafi's opponent and went into exile in the USA for two decades before returning to Libya in 2011. Pro-Islamist militias and fighters from Misrata launched Operation Libya Dawn in 2014, resulting in their taking control of Tripoli and establishing a rival GNC government. As of early 2017, UN-led efforts to unify the rival Libyan governments under a Government of National Accord headed by Prime Minister Fayez El Sarraj have not been successful.

---

[5] Mercy Corps and The Governance Network, 'Beyond Gaddafi: Libya's Governance Context' (August 2011) available at www.mercycorps.org/sites/default/files/capacity_to_govern-libya_26_aug_2011.pdf.

Despite the arrest warrants that were issued by the ICC for Saif al-Islam Gaddafi and El Senussi on 27 June 2011, the Libyan public prosecution insisted on a domestic trial, arguing that its judiciary was capable of trying Libyan nationals for grave human rights violations. The ICC accepted an admissibility challenge for El Senussi, filed by Libyan authorities in April 2013:

> On 11 October 2013, Pre-Trial Chamber I decided that the case against Mr. Al-Senussi was inadmissible before the Court as it was subject to on-going domestic proceedings conducted by the competent Libyan authorities and that Libya was willing and able genuinely to carry out such investigation.[6]

The ICC, however, rejected Libya's admissibility challenge for Saif al-Islam Gaddafi, mainly on the grounds that the Tripoli authorities at the time were unable to secure his transfer from Zintan in order to stand trial.[7] Thirty-five other defendants were tried domestically in Libya for charges that included war crimes, the killing of protesters and corruption. Given that he was held by Zintan militias, the trial of Saif al-Islam Gaddafi was conducted in absentia, save for a few sessions in which he appeared via video link from the courtroom in Zintan.[8] Other defendants included former Prime Minister al-Baghdadi al-Mahmoudi, former Foreign Minister Abdul Ati Al Obaidi and former intelligence chief Abou Zeid Dorda. The first domestic trial of a former political figure in Libya started in June 2012. In this trial, Dorda faced human rights charges related to the killing of protesters during the Libyan uprising. His trial was suspended at the time for technical reasons.

Case 630/2012—The Trial of 37 Former Members of the Gaddafi Regime

The trial of the 37 former Gaddafi regime members began on 24 March 2014 and the verdicts were issued on 28 July 2015. Saif al-Islam Gaddafi, El Senussi, al-Mahmoudi and six other defendants were sentenced to death by firing squad for committing war crimes during the 2011 conflict. Eight others were sentenced to life imprisonment and 15 others were given prison sentences that ranged from five to 12 years. Four defendants were acquitted and one was referred to a

---

[6] International Criminal Court, 'Al-Senussi Case: Appeals Chamber Confirms Case is Inadmissible before ICC', Press Release (24 July 2014) available at www.icccpi.int/en_menus/icc/press%20and%20 media/press%20releases/Pages/pr1034.aspx.

[7] International Criminal Court, 'Public Redacted-Decision on the Admissibility of the Case Against Saif Al-Islam Gaddafi' ICC-01/11-01/11-344-Red (31 May 2013) available at www.icc-cpi.int/pages/ record.aspx?uri=1599307.

[8] Arts 241/243 of the Code of Criminal Procedure were amended to allow for this, particularly since there were no prospects for Saif al-Islam Gaddafi's transfer from Zintan to Tripoli. See M Tashani, 'Transitional Justice Chaos in Libya: The Controversial Case of Saif al-Islam Gaddafi', *The Legal Agenda*, 5 January 2017, available at http://legal-agenda.com/en/article.php?id=3344.

mental health institution. At the time of writing, the case is under review before the Court of Cassation.[9] A controversial general amnesty law was issued in 2015 by the Tobruk government, effectively allowing conditional amnesty for all Libyans for certain crimes committed since 15 February 2011.[10] Media reports in 2016 and 2017 claimed that Saif al-Islam Gaddafi was released from prison in Zintan as a direct result of the issuance of this amnesty law. Confusion surrounds the validity of the law, especially as it was issued by a government that is not recognised by all Libyans.

The trial of the 37 former Gaddafi regime members was fraught with multiple challenges and flaws. Many defendants were not informed of the charges brought against them. Several defendants did not have legal representation from the start of the trial. Those who did meet with their lawyers were subject to surveillance by prison guards, thus depriving them of confidentiality. No prosecution witnesses testified despite the fact that the court's verdict relied heavily on the testimony of witnesses. Moreover, severe delays in access to relevant material that the prosecution used to build its case prevented defence lawyers from being able to prepare their cases properly. Many documents containing evidence and testimonies were also missing.[11] The challenges that marked this trial are indicative of the problem of using weak judicial institutions to pursue cases of this magnitude and complexity.

The Prosecution of Political Leaders in Pre-transition Libya

The Gaddafi regime had a tight grip on all state institutions and prevented political opposition by adopting Law No 71 in 1972, which banned political parties. Such dictatorial laws and severe repression and intimidation of critics of the Gaddafi regime meant that there were no significant efforts to prosecute political leaders in Libya before the uprising and civil war broke out in 2011.[12] However, as veteran human rights lawyer Azza Maghur explained, there were

---

[9] The full list of those sentenced to death is as follows: Saif al-Islam Gaddafi, Muammar Gaddafi's son and right-hand man; Abdullah El Senussi, Chief of Military Intelligence; al-Baghdadi al-Mahmoudi, former Prime Minister; Mansour Daw, Security Chief; Abu Zeid Dorda, Head of Foreign Intelligence; Milad Salem Daman, Head of Internal Security Agency; Brig Gen Mondher Mukhtar al-Gheneimi; Abdul Hamid Ammar Waheda, Senussi aide; Awidaat Ghandour al-Noubi, responsible for Col Gaddafi's revolutionary committees in Tripoli. R Jawad, 'Libya Death Sentences Cast Long Shadow Over Rule of Law', *BBC News*, 12 August 2015, available at www.bbc.com/news/world-africa-33855860. See also UNSMIL and OHCHR, Case 630/2012, above n 4.

[10] Law No 6/2015. See Marwan Tashani's discussion of the complexities and implications of this law: Tashani, above n 8.

[11] UNSMIL and OHCHR, above n 4.

[12] Jerary, above n 2; interview with Lydia Vicente Márquez, Executive Director, Rights International Spain (telephone interview, 16 April 2012).

politicised and unsystematic steps taken by Muammar Gaddafi to allow prosecutions and to establish mechanisms through which victims could file human rights complaints. These efforts seriously lacked legitimacy and ultimately served as political tools to restrict opposition. For example, Muammar Gaddafi tried to bring cases against other government officials who were no longer under his control. In 2003, the Gaddafi International Charity and Development Foundation (GICDF)[13] filed charges against the Minister of Interior for human rights violations.[14] In 2004, the Ministry of Justice assigned a body to receive complaints against the Ministry. These efforts were, as Maghur explained, nothing more than overtly political manoeuvres by the Gaddafi regime to clamp down on opposition and critics of the regime.[15] Maghur also mentioned the efforts of human rights lawyer Salwa Bugaighis, who filed several 'political cases against the state during Gaddafi', particularly requesting compensation for the detained.[16]

The Search for Accountability for Abu Salim

Following the massacre of approximately 1,200 prisoners at the Abu Salim prison in 1996, the Gaddafi regime took some superficial steps to improve its international image and to show that there were efforts to hold the perpetrators accountable. This massacre, widely documented by the media and international human rights organisations, became a powerful symbol of the Gaddafi regime's repressive practices. It also contributed to the momentum that led to the popular revolt to topple Muammar Gaddafi in February 2011. As a result, pre-2011 efforts to hold to account the perpetrators of the Abu Salim massacre have trickled into post-2011 efforts to prosecute, much like the *Baraket Essahel* and *Khaled Said* cases did in Tunisia and Egypt, respectively.

Ali al Kermi was a political prisoner for 30 years, most of them spent at Abu Salim. He successfully sought financial compensation from the courts following his release in 2002. He had filed a claim in 2005 against the state for the torture and beatings he suffered in detention. Following the success of his claim, he became President of the Libyan Association for Prisoners of Conscience, where

[13] The following description is from the GICDF's website (www.gicdf.org): '[GICDF] is an international non-governmental organization, carries out developmental and humanitarian activities in the social, economic, cultural and human rights fields. GICDF was established in 2003 through the signing of its article of association in Geneva, Switzerland. Its chairman is Saif Al Islam Al Gaddafi … The Foundation adopts principles that define and guide its functions such as maintaining and protecting human rights, and fundamental liberties, developing civil society and its organizations, promoting charitable voluntary work, establishing cooperation relations among societies to consolidate the team work supporting the oppressed, the downtrodden, and the vulnerable segments in the community, such as the poor, the needy, orphans, and the handicapped. It also provides humanitarian aid for war and disaster victims wherever they are.'
[14] The newspaper article source for this is on file with Azza Maghur. Interview with Azza Maghur, veteran lawyer and human rights activist (Tripoli, Libya, 17 September 2013).
[15] ibid.
[16] ibid. Salwa Bugaighis was killed in her home in 2013.

he advocated for reparations. As Amnesty International reported, 'In 2012, a law providing for financial compensation to political prisoners detained between September 1969 and February 2011 was finally adopted'.[17] No individual political leaders were charged following al Kermi's complaint. Financial compensation was offered to the victims of Abu Salim on the condition that they would abandon their pursuit of judicial redress.[18] 'No member of the [Internal Security Agency]', Amnesty International reports, 'is known to have ever been charged or tried for committing human rights violations, including torture'.[19] Despite this, many Libyans, including al Kermi himself, have declared their wish to see the perpetrators of the Abu Salim prison massacre, especially El Senussi, tried domestically.[20]

Public pressure had been mounting for years to obtain the truth about the Abu Salim massacre. Protests in Benghazi led by families of the Abu Salim victims took place every Saturday since June 2008, in which they demanded the truth about the fate of their relatives. In response, Muammar Gaddafi appointed an investigative judge, Mohamed Bashir Al Khaddar, in 2008.[21] Nothing came of this judge's work. Maghur described him as 'a disaster'.[22] However, human rights lawyers and activists continued to push for accountability for Abu Salim. In September 2009, Libya's Defense ministry set up a panel of seven investigative judges to investigate the Abu Salim killings. At the same time, however, the government offered monetary compensation to some of the families of the Abu Salim victims 'in exchange for assurances that [they] will not pursue further legal claims in Libyan or international courts'.[23] It was clear, then, that any attempts by the Gaddafi regime to address justice for the Abu Salim victims would be contingent on a non-existent, or at best highly politicised, criminal accountability in the courts.

Politicised Courts and the Prioritisation of 'Security'

Maghur referred to *qanun mahkamit el sha'ab*, or the establishment of the People's Court in 1971, which was ostensibly set up by Gaddafi as a mechanism through which victims could file human rights complaints. Maghur explained:

> Gaddafi initiated this court because he proclaimed he wanted to stop human rights violations. Then he started to amend the law [that established the Court] until it itself

---

[17] Amnesty International, 'Rising from the Shadows of Abu Salim Prison' (26 June 2014) available at www.amnesty.org/en/latest/news/2014/06/rising-shadows-abu-salim-prison/.
[18] Amnesty International, 'Libya of Tomorrow: What Hope for Human Rights' (June 2010) 11–12.
[19] ibid 31.
[20] 'A Long Wait for Justice in Libya', *IRIN News*, 18 September 2013, available at www.irinnews.org/report/98777/long-wait-justice-libya.
[21] Maghur, above n 14; interview with Dao Al Mansouri, veteran lawyer and human rights activist (Tripoli, Libya, 18 September 2013).
[22] Maghur, above n 14.
[23] Human Rights Watch, 'Truth and Justice Can't Wait: Human Rights Developments in Libya Amid Institutional Obstacles' (12 December 2009) 4–5, available at https://www.hrw.org/report/2009/12/12/truth-and-justice-cant-wait/human-rights-developments-libya-amid-institutional.

became a human rights violation. Still, many people brought forth cases to this court for the disappeared, tortured, and killed.[24]

As became clear, the People's Court was actually established to try members of the former royal family, which Muammar Gaddafi overthrew in a coup in 1969. The Court tried prime ministers and other (over 200) officials from the deposed monarchy, including former King Idris, who received a death sentence in absentia.[25] Law 5 of 1988 institutionalised the Court, making it even more politicised:

> Many cases involved charges of illegal political activities that should have been protected under the rights to free association or speech, in particular, alleged violations of Law 71, which bans any group activity based on a political ideology opposed to the principles of the 1969 revolution that brought al-Qadhafi to power. Some cases also were against state employees accused of graft.[26]

The People's Court was finally abolished in 2005, following pressure from Libyan lawyers who refused to take part in its arbitrary and politicised procedures. The People's Court had served as a prosecution tool for the Gaddafi regime, rather than as a mechanism through which victims of the Gaddafi regime could attain justice.

Decisions made by Libya's judiciary were often ignored by the Internal Security Agency under Gaddafi. Many prisoners whose cases were successfully appealed by the public prosecution remained in detention because the Internal Security Agency, which controlled Abu Salim prison, for instance, refused to release them. Even decisions by Libya's highest court—the Supreme Court—to acquit prisoners were ignored by the Internal Security Agency. Human Rights Watch interviewed Colonel Al-Tohamy Khaled, head of the Internal Security Agency, about this refusal to release acquitted prisoners:

> Colonel Al-Tohamy Khaled, confirmed to Human Rights Watch that his agency was detaining 330 prisoners in Abu Salim prison whose sentences had ended or who had been acquitted. He said that his agency believed the men were a security risk because of their Jihadist views, and that the judges who had ordered their release 'did not understand' the situation, in some cases acquitting them on technical procedural grounds.[27]

So, even before Gaddafi's ouster, the judiciary had made some efforts that were seemingly geared towards putting an end to the practice of arbitrary detention. However, those efforts were consistently countered by the likes of the Libyan Internal Security Agency, for fear of outspoken government critics. As Khaled's statement above illustrates, the rhetoric of preserving 'security' prevailed in practice, even if it defied judicial rulings.

---

[24] Maghur, above n 14.

[25] International Crisis Group, 'Trial by Error: Justice in Post-Qadhafi Libya' (April 2013) 12.

[26] Human Rights Watch, 'Libya: Words to Deeds: The Urgent Need for Human Rights Reform' (January 2006) available at www.hrw.org/reports/2006/libya0106/5.htm.

[27] Human Rights Watch, 'Libya: 202 Prisoners Released but Hundreds Still Held Arbitrarily' (25 March 2010) available at https://www.hrw.org/news/2010/03/25/libya-202-prisoners-released-hundreds-still-held-arbitrarily.

Content and Extent of Prosecutions in Post-transition Libya

The very few, albeit high-profile, prosecutions that have taken place in Libya since Muammar Gaddafi's ouster primarily focus on crimes committed during the 2011 conflict, with the exception of the Abu Salim charges faced by El Senussi and others. Some former regime officials also faced corruption charges. Given the difficulty of access to the trial sessions, the list of charges remains ambiguous.[28] However, known charges include the embezzlement of public funds, amounting to $2.5 billion, by former Foreign Minister Al Obaidi and former head of the General People's Conference Mohamed El Zway. These were the first verdicts issued against high-level officials since Muammar Gaddafi's ouster.[29] These funds were used to compensate families of those killed in the 1988 Lockerbie plane bombing, as a way to get them to drop legal claims against Libya.[30] However, this corruption charge, which notably dates to a period from before the 2011 uprising, was dropped and Al Obaidi and El Zway were acquitted in June 2013. No explanation was given by the judge for their acquittal.[31]

Al Mahmoudi, who was Libyan Prime Minister from 2006 to 2011, was charged with funnelling $25 million of public money to Tunisia to help Gaddafi forces fighting in the 2011 conflict. Saif al Islam Gaddafi and his brother Saadi Gaddafi were also accused of 'plundering state coffers to fund extravagant playboy lifestyles abroad'.[32] The number of corruption charges, however, does not match those of the prosecutions in Egypt and Tunisia. Nevertheless, the charges against the 37 former regime members are overwhelmingly focused on crimes committed during the transition, particularly the killing of protesters and mass rape.

While some former high-profile regime officials were extradited to Libya to face trial, several escaped prosecution, thereby limiting the extent of the trials. Of note is Moussa Koussa, Libya's notorious Head of Intelligence from 1994 to 2009 and Foreign Minister from 2009 to 2011. Koussa fled to London soon after the uprising erupted, after which he spent some time in Qatar. Media reports from October 2013 indicate that he was then recruited by the Saudi intelligence

---

[28] Elham Saudi, for example, explained that her organisation, Lawyers for Justice in Libya (LFJL), faced difficulty in obtaining information on the charges. Elham Saudi in N Aboueldahab, 'Rapporteur's Report: Prosecutions, Politics and Transitions: How Criminal Justice in the Arab Spring is Shaping Transitional Justice', panel discussion, Durham Law School, 6 May 2014.

[29] 'Lockerbie Compensation: Libyan Officials Acquitted', *BBC News*, 17 June 2013, available at www.bbc.com/news/world-africa-22936678.

[30] G Shennib, 'Gaddafi Officials Acquitted but Stay Behind Bars', *Reuters*, 17 June 2013, available at www.reuters.com/article/2013/06/17/us-libya-trial-idUSBRE95G0S120130617.

[31] El Obaidi and El Zway remained in detention, however, for other human rights charges.

[32] C Stephen, 'Gaddafi Sons War Crimes Trial Begins in Libya amid Security Fears', *The Guardian*, 13 April 2014, available at www.theguardian.com/world/2014/apr/13/gaddafi-sons-war-crimes-trial-libya.

agency as an advisor.[33] This is despite Mustafa Gheriani's call in March 2011 for Koussa's extradition to Libya from London to face trial. Gheriani was the rebel leader at the time and stated that Koussa should face trial for murder and crimes against humanity.[34] This call was made six months before the capture and killing of Muammar Gaddafi in October 2011. Former judge Jamal Benour noted that many other high-level Libyan politicians left the country in 2011 and escaped prosecution. Libya had requested the transfer of Al Qadhaf Al Dam, Muammar Gaddafi's nephew and an influential figure in the Gaddafi inner circle, from Egypt to Libya to face trial. As Benour explained, Egypt refused to transfer Al Dam to Libya on the grounds that he holds Egyptian citizenship.[35]

Three main factors help explain the limited content and extent of the prosecutions. First, an enabling legal framework that is equipped to prosecute serious crimes, such as war crimes and crimes against humanity, is absent. Secondly, victims and their families do not trust the judiciary to independently carry out investigations and trials, which has limited the number of legal complaints filed. Thirdly, a dangerous security situation meant that many judges and lawyers feared for their lives when asked to represent Gaddafi regime officials and loyalists, thereby preventing fair prosecutions from taking place.

The history of efforts to pursue accountability for the Abu Salim massacre and its significant symbolic value in triggering the Libyan uprising ensured that the Abu Salim charges would emerge in the post-2011 prosecutions. El Senussi was charged for his involvement in the Abu Salim massacre, as well as in crimes committed during the 2011 conflict.[36] In fact, the pool of individuals implicated in the Abu Salim massacre significantly expanded after 2011. In June 2014, Amnesty International estimated that approximately 170 guards and officials suspected of involvement in the Abu Salim killings had been detained since 2011.[37]

Apart from the Abu Salim investigation faced by El Senussi, no major pre-transition human rights violations have figured in the post-2011 trials.[38] Similar to

---

[33] N Charara, 'Saudi Restores Libyan Spy Chief Moussa Koussa's Role as Global Shadow Broker', *Global Research*, 28 October 2013, available at www.globalresearch.ca/saudi-restores-libyan-spy-chief-moussa-koussas-role-as-global-shadow-broker/5355884.

[34] C McGreal, 'Libya Foreign Minister Moussa Koussa Must Face Atrocities Trial, Rebels Declare', *The Guardian*, 31 March 2011, available at www.theguardian.com/world/2011/mar/31/moussa-koussa-foreign-minister-trial.

[35] Interview with Jamal Benour, lawyer, former Libyan judge and prosecutor, former head of military prosecution in Benghazi, former justice coordinator for the city of Benghazi and former local council president for Benghazi, Libya (email interview, 29 March 2017).

[36] Jamal Benour stated that, to his knowledge, El Senussi was sentenced to death for his role in the Abu Salim massacre. ibid.

[37] Amnesty International, 'Libya: End Long Wait for Justice for Victims of Abu Salim Prison Killings', Public Statement, 27 June 2014, 3.

[38] However, Saadi Gaddafi, Muammar Gaddafi's son, was charged with the murder of a Libyan footballer in 2005. This trial took place in November 2015. At the time of writing, Saadi Gaddafi was still detained at Al Hadba prison. He was also one of the 37 defendants in Case 630/2012, charged with war crimes during the 2011 uprising.

Egypt and Tunisia, the human rights trials are limited to crimes committed during the uprising because, as journalist Rana Jawad argued:

> They're easier to prove. A lot of archive material was lost during the war. The memory was so fresh and alive post-war, that they're looking to address those issues first. The only old issue that we see resurfacing is Abu Salim because it was one massive thing that happened … but the other crimes, such as systematic torture and so on—they're very hard to pursue unless they track down the people who were directly involved.[39]

Maghur was emphatic about the need for appropriate legal mechanisms to prosecute human rights violations in which the state is implicated. She underlined the need for either a change in Libya's current penal code or the establishment of a transitional justice mechanism to address crimes of a massive scale:

> It is very difficult to prove human rights violations. First, it is a problem of a lack of professionalism. Second, you are prosecuting according to old laws—the old penal code. You cannot prosecute political leaders for human rights violations under the current laws. You have to really have a specialised team to work on that. We do not have this. We are using the same prosecutors who were also responsible for human rights violations. The same prosecutors who jailed people contrary to human rights standards. These special crimes are addressed as normal crimes—not as human rights violations in which the state took part. How will we establish responsibility of the state? It is very stupid of them to prosecute these people under normal laws.[40]

No Peace Without Justice (NPWJ)'s Libya Program Coordinator Stefano Moschini, however, noted that Libya decided not to establish a special court or mechanism to try former regime members. Instead, the ordinary courts are handling these cases, with organisations such as NPWJ advising the judiciary on how to prosecute war crimes and crimes against humanity.[41]

Benour, on the other hand, echoed Maghur's call for a new legal mechanism: 'In Libya today, we need a different law to implement transitional justice to properly address systematic violations.'[42] Benour added, however, that, given the severity of the crimes committed by Libya's revolutionaries in the post-2011 period, no transitional justice law could adequately address such violations. Instead, he argued, Libya must aim for national reconciliation.[43] This is because of ongoing violence in Libya, rival governments and the absence of a unified military, police force and judiciary. Benour argued that, given these significant challenges, Libya should first aim for a general amnesty to establish peace and as a way to foster national reconciliation in a deeply polarised country. 'Once a unified state with unified institutions are in place, then we can begin to establish a transitional justice mechanism to address the complex violations that have plagued the country.'[44]

---

[39] Interview with Rana Jawad, BBC journalist based in Tripoli (Tripoli, Libya, 18 September 2013).

[40] Maghur, above n 14.

[41] Interview with Stefano Moschini, Libya Programme Coordinator, No Peace Without Justice (Tripoli, Libya, 18 September 2013).

[42] Benour, above n 36.

[43] ibid.

[44] ibid.

Given the history of Libya's politicised public prosecution, victims and their families continue to refrain from filing human rights complaints for lack of trust in the judiciary. As Moschini explained:

Victims' demands for justice are quite limited because they still do not trust the institutions and the judiciary. There is no access to the trials. There was instead massive popular pressure for the political isolation law,[45] but not the same pressure for prosecutions. Also, Libyans are more focused on compensation and the return of their properties. Finally, there is a lack of awareness regarding their rights. Somebody might not even recognise torture as such.[46]

Lydia Vicente Márquez, Executive Director of Rights International Spain, made a similar observation following her work on justice in Libya: 'The concept of justice in Libya is missing. They don't even know what a crime against humanity is.'[47] Moreover, many Libyan lawyers, victims and their families were eager for a swift retributive justice regardless of the due process requirements that make the speed of such verdicts impossible. It has also prompted NPWJ and other international NGOs to implement training programmes in Libya for lawyers and judges, with a focus on fair and effective trials.[48] The International Crisis Group makes an important observation regarding the type of justice that is expected by Libyan victims and their families and the consequent distrust of the judiciary:

The main problem emerging from these prosecutions is that they are too few and— from the perspective of many armed group members—too slow. These complaints feed into the already widespread feeling that the state is unable to carry out justice. That these delays and referrals might be a healthy sign of commitment to due process often is ignored. Similarly, rather than being praised as a positive development ensuring respect for civil liberties, the December 2012 Supreme Court order that criminal courts follow proper procedures often is viewed as evidence of the judiciary's ongoing collusion in defence of Qadhafi-era officials. Many fighters as well as ordinary citizens insist on quick retribution against these officials, even if they were not directly implicated in repressing

---

[45] Political Isolation Law (2013), passed by the GNC on 5 May 2013. The law disqualifies individuals who are deemed to have been previously associated with the Gaddafi regime from holding political or public office or posts in government. LFJL expressed its concern that the exclusion of those from holding office should not be based on the mere fact that they are associated with the previous regime, but on the basis of criminal acts proven in a court of law. LFJL warned against the arbitrary application of the law, its vague language and its exemption from judicial review. LFJL stressed the need for the state to apply restraint and transparency in the application of the Political Isolation Law and reminded the state that it must only apply it to the extent consistent with its international human rights obligations. If this is not the case, this might undercut government legitimacy, undermine the rule of law and weaken efforts for national reconciliation. LFJL, 'An Eye on Human Rights in Libya', Report, December 2013.

[46] Moschini, above n 41. Justice Minister Salah Al Marghani, who is a veteran human rights activist, expressed similar views: 'there is little trust towards the judges who are still considered to be Qadhafi's judges'. Quoted in International Crisis Group, above n 25, 18.

[47] Márquez, above n 12.

[48] ibid; Moschini, above n 41. Interview with Amna Guellali, Tunisia and Algeria Researcher, Human Rights Watch (Telephone interview, 23 April 2012).

the uprising, viewing them as guilty for standing by Qadhafi. For others, swift justice for political opponents is simply the only type of justice they know.[49]

This kind of rapid retributive justice is a key characteristic of the way in which transitional justice has been pursued not just in Libya, but in other Arab Spring countries as well.[50]

A Weak Judiciary Under Threat

The dire security situation in Libya has significantly affected decisions regarding the prosecution of political leaders. There has been a string of targeted assassinations of judges and prosecutors in Libya, including the General Prosecutor in February 2014.[51] Almost all interviewees referred to the fact that judges and lawyers who agreed to be involved in a potential trial or to defend Gaddafi regime officials have received death threats. So much so that, when asked specifically about the trial of Saif al-Islam Gaddafi and El Senussi, some lawyers quietly responded that they preferred not to speak about those cases for security reasons. They added that they were approached to become involved in those cases, but that they had refused out of fear for their safety. Dao Al Mansouri, a prominent human rights lawyer who served as defence lawyer for former Head of Intelligence Abou Zeid Dorda, recalled:

> When the Dorda trial started, there were lots of threats against those involved in the case. Many of the accused were unable to find lawyers to represent them because of the security situation. The judiciary in Libya is not politicised. The judge cannot, however, work properly while the gun is aimed at his head. There are major threats from the government against the judiciary.[52]

Similarly, prosecutors are afraid to indict rebel leaders, who issued a controversial amnesty law in May 2012 to protect themselves from prosecution:

> Law 38 of 2012 on certain matters relating to transitional justice includes a complete amnesty for any 'acts made necessary by the 17 February revolution' for its 'success or protection', whether such acts are of a military, security or civil nature ... this law has terrifyingly familiar echoes of the Gaddafi era ... Impunity for violations of human rights and war crimes resulting from a sense of revolutionary legitimacy is dangerous and perpetuates the culture that existed under the Gaddafi regime, where all was justified in the name of the 1969 Revolution.[53]

---

[49] International Crisis Group, above n 25, 34–35.

[50] Reflections on justice expectations are discussed in chapter 6.

[51] Saudi, above n 28.

[52] Al Mansouri, above n 21. Al Mansouri did note, however, that there are some problems with the independence of the judiciary. The Public Prosecutor, for example, was appointed by the General National Congress, rather than by the Supreme Judicial Council.

[53] LFJL, 'LFJL Strongly Condemns New Laws Breaching Human Rights and Undermining the Rule of Law' (7 May 2012) available at www.libyanjustice.org/news/news/post/23-lfjl-strongly-condemns-new-laws-breaching-human-rights-and-undermining-the-rule-of-law/.

The acute lack of security and the multiple threats to the lives of judges, lawyers, witnesses and journalists trying to cover court hearings have contributed to the opaque nature of the trial of Gaddafi regime members. While most of the hearings were broadcast live on television, many of the sessions were interrupted by news broadcasts or other programmes.[54] Reports on the trial pointed to several problems affecting its fairness, including the absence of legal representation for some of the detainees, lack of adequate time for the defence to prepare its case and the absence of defendants—particularly Saif al-Islam Gaddafi—in the courtroom.[55] Moreover, due to fears of persecution, very few witnesses appeared in court. As a result, many submitted their testimonies in writing, which in turn impacted the credibility of the evidence examined by the judges as well as the 'overall fairness of the proceedings'.[56]

The relatively small population of Libya—approximately six million—also means that many policemen are ex-fighters from the conflict. Consequently, accountability becomes even more difficult when perpetrators join the police force as law enforcers. Elham Saudi, Director of Lawyers for Justice in Libya, noted, 'When a person claims they were tortured by a member of a militia, they go to the police and they find that their torturer is there, working as a policeman. It significantly reduces the possibilities for accountability.'[57]

Changes to the structure of judicial bodies and to judicial appointments did take place in Libya following the fall of Gaddafi. The National Transitional Council issued Law 4/2011, which modified the composition of the Supreme Judicial Council (SJC). Instead of having the justice minister as its head, the Supreme Court chief became the default head. However, the SJC remains financially dependent on the justice ministry and its leaders continue to be appointed by the legislature.[58] The changes to the judicial structure and operation in Libya were thus minor and resulted in the prosecution of political leaders taking place in pre-existing courts.[59] The legacy of arbitrary justice and public distrust in the judiciary thus continue to plague post-transition Libya, leading revolutionary militias to take matters into their own hands, as exemplified by Saif al-Islam Gaddafi's long incarceration in Zintan.

Moreover, the significant pressure on Libya to pursue criminal accountability for crimes orchestrated by a large web of Gaddafi regime officials resulted in a haphazard trial that prioritised speedy verdicts over due process. The lumping of 37 regime members in one trial, the lack of legal representation for the defendants,

---

[54] M Ellis, 'Trial of the Libyan Regime: An Investigation into International Fair Trial Standards' (November 2015) 18. See also UNSMIL and OHCHR, above n 4.

[55] His trial was in absentia, but following amendments to Libyan law, the use of video link was authorised and he was absent for 17 consecutive sessions of the trial. Ellis, above n 54, 31.

[56] ibid 44, 45.

[57] Saudi, above n 28.

[58] International Crisis Group, above n 25, 16.

[59] ibid 17.

the absence of prosecution witnesses and the lack of access to key documents all point to the prioritisation of rapid retributive justice over one where evidence is carefully examined to obtain the truth about the atrocities committed. Ultimately, the use of weak judicial institutions, particularly in the ongoing conflict in Libya, resulted in a trial that was severely compromised in both its content and extent. In her discussion on the challenges of criminal accountability in Libya, Marieke Wierda points to 'the overwhelming number of perpetrators implicated in the crimes committed under Qadhafi's government and on his orders, which were many more than could possibly be tried'.[60]

The Role of International Actors

While the role of international actors in Libya was minimal prior to the 2011 revolt against Muammar Gaddafi, the conflict that ensued quickly became an international one with the military intervention of NATO and other foreign governments. Moreover, the ICC's arrest warrants for Muammar Gaddafi, Saif-al-Islam Gaddafi and El Senussi in 2011 marked a crucial turning point in decisions regarding prosecution of political leaders in Libya. The United Nations Human Rights Council's establishment of the International Commission of Inquiry (COI) on Libya (2011–2012) was a third effort initiated by international actors and aimed at criminal accountability in Libya. The Commission investigated alleged violations of international human rights law in Libya and produced its first report under the chairmanship of Cherif Bassiouni in June 2011, with a second report following under the chairmanship of Philippe Kirsch in March 2012. Both reports are extensive and include recommendations calling for accountability for crimes committed during the 2011–12 conflict in Libya.[61] The COI, however, came under criticism for various reasons, which are explored shortly.

The interviewees differed in their opinions on whether or not the domestic prosecution of the 37 former regime members would have taken place had the ICC arrest warrants not been issued. Jerary, former Director of Communications for former Libyan Prime Minister Ali Zeidan, argued that some Libyans were relieved that Muammar Gaddafi was killed because they did not want a chaotic and sham trial 'such as the Mubarak trial in Egypt'. However, Jerary continued, Muammar Gaddafi, Saif al-Islam Gaddafi and other former regime officials would have been

---

[60] M Wierda, 'Confronting Qadhafi's Legacy: Transitional Justice in Libya' in P Cole and B McQuinn (eds), *The Libyan Revolution and its Aftermath* (Oxford, Oxford University Press, 2015).
[61] The two reports of the Commission can be found at http://mcherifbassiouni.com/investigations/libya/.

prosecuted regardless of the ICC arrest warrants.[62] Moschini echoed this view of the minimal impact of the ICC on domestic prosecutions in Libya:

> I don't think the ICC has had a positive or negative impact on the speed of prosecutions in Libya. The Saif-al-Islam case would have taken place without the ICC, but perhaps not Senussi. There has otherwise been no real impact by international actors. Collaboration between local and international NGOs is quite sensitive. There is a fear of foreign intervention.[63]

Jawad made a similar observation regarding the non-impact of international actors: 'Whether the ICC was involved or not, former regime members would have still been arrested in Libya. People need closure and accountability, regardless of the intervention of the ICC and international NGOs.'[64]

Others, such as Al Mansouri, argued that the ICC triggered domestic decisions to prosecute political leaders in Libya. He described the domestic prosecutions as a reaction to the 'foreign' ICC and the international community: 'They want the world to see they can do it.'[65] Similarly, Márquez stated that 'There is a sense of "we want to do things our way" in Libya, with limited help from abroad'.[66]

However, given the ongoing violence in Libya and the weak state of its judicial and political institutions, certain Libyans preferred to see a trial at an international tribunal such as the ICC. Salah Marghani, who was Minister of Justice between 2012 and 2014, makes this preference clear:

> I believe that the ICC or a special tribunal can play a major role in achieving justice, particularly for perpetrators of war crimes and crimes against humanity. Many such perpetrators are beyond any reach of the Libyan judiciary as they are warlords, some militia and religious leaders. In my view, the efforts of the ICC and the Public Prosecution are being hindered or blocked by international players who are either unfavourable to international justice or believe that impending justice may cause more instability. I disagree with that and I support international justice and a justice system that may involve international elements to ensure neutrality and independence of the justice delivered in politically sensitive cases.[67]

At the international level, as Marghani notes, the same actors who pushed for ICC intervention—the members of the Security Council—later abandoned such support.[68] As GJ Knoops observes, the Security Council's referral of the situation in Libya to the ICC was 'just one of the mechanisms which aimed at overthrowing the regime of Gaddafi'.[69] An arms embargo and other sanctions against the

[62] Jerary, above n 2.
[63] Moschini, above n 41.
[64] Jawad, above n 39.
[65] Al Mansouri, above n 21.
[66] Márquez, above n 12.
[67] Interview with Salah Marghani, Minister of Justice (November 2012–August 2014), Libyan jurist, human rights activist (email interview, 14 March 2017).
[68] Marghani, however, did not specify to which 'international players' he was referring.
[69] GJ Knoops, 'Prosecuting the Gaddafis: Swift or Political Justice?' [2015] *Amsterdam Law Forum* 83.

Gaddafi regime also figured prominently in the same Security Council resolution that prompted ICC intervention.[70]

Presuming regime change was the Security Council's ultimate goal in Libya, it is no surprise, then, that the capture and murder of Gaddafi in October 2011 was enough to let the furore surrounding ICC intervention in Libya wane within the UN. Peskin and Boduszynski demonstrate that such 'waxing and waning' of international support for ICC intervention in Libya is a typical result of competing policy goals. They argue that external actors' interests often converge and diverge with the needs of international tribunals, depending on 'the course of events'.[71] In the case of Libya, the conflict between Gaddafi loyalists and anti-Gaddafi revolutionaries in 2011 prompted both NATO's military intervention and Security Council Resolution 1970 as political tools to oust the Gaddafi regime. Once Gaddafi was captured and killed, the necessity of bringing Saif al-Islam Gaddafi and El Senussi to face trial in The Hague became less pressing. As Koller notes, 'the threat of punishment [in Libya] was seen as a tool for achieving a political end—the resolution of conflict'.[72] Judge Marwan Tashani notes that the toing and froing concerning the ICC's involvement played out domestically as well:

> Even dealing with the ICC has been contradictory; at times we ask that [the] ICC prosecute the perpetrators [because] our judiciary is incompetent, and at other times we demand the ICC have respect for our sovereignty, law and internal judiciary ... This confusion is not merely legal, but is primarily political. After the February revolution, the successive authorities have dealt with the issue in different ways. At the time of the NTC and the National Conference, the issue of Gaddafi's son was propagated as a criminal whose victim is an entire nation, but during the rule of the House of Representatives, he was viewed as a victim of political and military abuse that violates the law and human rights. This explains the adjustment of priorities: while the priority for the NTC and the National Conference was to bring the symbols of the former regime to justice, reconciliation with that regime has become the priority for the House of Representatives.[73]

Changes in interim governments and the emergence of rival governments in Libya, then, have played a direct role in how the Saif al-Islam Gaddafi case is being handled domestically. Given the preference of the House of Representatives or the Tobruk government for reconciliation, as Tashani notes, the general amnesty issued by this government and under which Saif al-Islam Gaddafi has allegedly been released comes as no surprise.

Further disparities in international actors' approaches to criminal accountability in Libya are revealed by the COI's findings following two intensive field missions in 2011. Kevin Heller's critique of the COI's findings highlights some

---

[70] S/RES/1970 (2011).

[71] V Peskin and MP Boduszynski, 'The Rise and Fall of the ICC in Libya and the Politics of International Surrogate Enforcership' (2016) 10 *International Journal of Transitional Justice* 272, 280.

[72] DS Koller, 'The Global as Local: The Limits and Possibilities of Integrating International and Transitional Justice' in C De Vos, S Kendall, and C Stahn (eds), *Contested Justice* (Cambridge, Cambridge University Press, 2015) 99.

[73] Tashani, above n 8.

of these disparities. For instance, following an investigation into NATO's actions during the military intervention, the COI found no evidence that a site targeted twice by NATO strikes—and resulting in 38 civilian deaths—had a military purpose. NATO refused to release gun-camera footage to the COI on security grounds. The COI made an inconclusive statement regarding this particular strike, declaring that it is 'unable to determine, for lack of sufficient information', whether the strikes were carried out as a result of 'incorrect or outdated intelligence'. Consequently, the COI refrained from drawing any conclusions as to whether NATO took 'all necessary precautions to avoid civilian casualties entirely'.[74]

Heller's critique of this particular finding—or non-finding—by the COI is incisive:

> Imagine if Qadhafi forces used artillery against a target with no evident military use; shelled the target again after non-uniformed rescuers went to help the wounded, despite having spotters who could not positively determine whether they were combatants; and then refused on national-security grounds to release video footage that could shed light on what the spotters were able to see during the second attack. It beggars belief to assume that, in such a situation, the Commission would have been 'unable to determine' whether the second attack violated the principle of distinction or the principle of proportionality. And it is even more unlikely that the Commission would have concluded that '[w]ithout further evidence to substantiate' the Qadhafi government's claims, it could not determine whether the second attack violated the government's obligation to take all feasible precautions to protect civilians.[75]

Heller concludes that, despite the COI's detailed and strong investigation into the conflict in Libya, political pressure by NATO affected some of its findings.[76] In a climate where any kind of foreign intervention—whether by states or institutions—is viewed with suspicion, it is unsurprising that attempts by international actors to push for criminal accountability in Libya have thus far failed. It is reasonable to question whether disparities such as those in the COI's findings and in the waning support of the Security Council for enforcement of the ICC arrest warrants have weakened the prospects for prosecutorial justice in Libya.

The Role of Domestic Civil Society

In the context of civil society, Saudi discussed the importance of Libyan fears of the 'foreign intervention' that Moschini and others alluded to. While there are

---

[74] Full Report of the International Commission of Inquiry to Investigate All Alleged Violations of International Law in Libya, A/HRC/19/68 (8 March 2012) para 654, as quoted in KJ Heller, 'The International Commission of Inquiry on Libya: A Critical Analysis' in J Meierhenrich (ed), *International Commissions: The Role of Commissions of Inquiry in the Investigation of International Crimes* (Oxford, Oxford University Press, forthcoming) 49.

[75] Heller, ibid, 49–50.

[76] ibid 51.

international actors with big budgets to spend on developing Libyan civil society, holding events and so on, the same international actors tread carefully in Libya because, unlike in Tunisia and Egypt, it is still unclear who the powerful domestic actors are. It is not yet clear which militias will be the new political parties. Saudi explained:

> Although [Libya] is fragile and open to international influence, Libyans have lived in paranoia for more than forty-two years and sixty-seven per cent of us were born under Gaddafi, so we know nothing other than paranoia. So there is this mechanism where on the one hand we welcome international intervention, but we are always suspecting its motives at the same time.[77]

Advocacy networks linking Libyan and international civil society organisations during Muammar Gaddafi's rule between 1969 and 2011 were thus extremely weak. Human Rights Watch and Amnesty International were—and continue to be—active in documenting human rights violations in Libya and in raising public awareness to put pressure on the Libyan government to address these violations.

The highly authoritarian and repressive policies of the Gaddafi regime, however, made it extremely difficult for such international NGOs to have any real impact on criminal accountability for high-level government officials. In 2008, for instance, a large group of Libyan lawyers, journalists and activists formed two NGOs: the Centre for Democracy and the Association for Justice and Human Rights. Despite the General People's Committee for Social Affairs' initial authorisation for the establishment of the NGOs, their registration approval was revoked within a matter of days. The Internal Security Agency has been cited as the culprit in the revocation, presumably because of the inclusion of former political prisoners and prominent human rights lawyers in the NGOs.[78]

Al Mansouri, who was President of the Centre for Democracy, was kidnapped and beaten up as a result of his efforts to establish the Centre for Democracy. He described this incident and reflected on the current state of affairs with regard to the continued—if not worsened—repercussions for human rights-related work in Libya:

> We had priorities for human rights—we wanted to peacefully address this to lessen the human rights crimes in Libya. When we set up the democratic centre it was like a message to the regime that this authoritarianism is over. There should be a constitution, freedom of expression, freedom of the media. We only worked with activists within Libya—we didn't work with Libyans in exile—staying in five star hotels.

> In June 2008, I was kidnapped from in front of my office here. I was taken away and beaten up badly. There was lots of public awareness about my kidnapping at the time. Now with the current disappearances, we don't know their fate. Armed militias are doing the kidnappings. As bad as they were, the old laws are still better than the rubbish they are drafting now, such as the transitional justice law. South Africa, Germany, Morocco,

---

[77] Saudi, above n 28.
[78] Human Rights Watch, above n 23.

Latin America—what happened there needs to happen here—we need to implement this here. There is disappearance here. There are mass graves.[79]

The attempts of Al Mansouri and numerous other lawyers and activists to establish independent NGOs to counter the Gaddafi regime's abusive policies were thus brutally crushed right up until the ouster of Gaddafi in 2011. Journalists critical of the government were also systematically targeted through arbitrary detention and beatings while detained.

With the fall of the Gaddafi regime and in the aftermath of the 2011 uprising, the stranglehold on the work of civil society has started to loosen. International NGOs, such as NPWJ, actively worked with domestic civil society actors to train Libyan legal professionals and the judiciary to improve accountability for human rights violations in Libya. The United Nations Support Mission in Libya (UNSMIL) also trained and encouraged the Libyan government to devise a prosecutorial strategy.[80] Lawyers for Justice in Libya, a group that was formed by Libyan lawyers in the diaspora and which now includes a network of lawyers in Libya, also actively monitors legal developments and makes recommendations to the Libyan government. Civil society organisations within Libya have been growing, but the level of engagement with international actors has remained low.[81] Given the legal and security challenges to the prosecution of political leaders mentioned above, most civil society organisations called for reconciliation as opposed to prosecutions.[82] Moschini noted the initial growth of civil society soon after the ouster of Muammar Gaddafi, which was quickly followed by their decline because of restrictions imposed by the government: '[Civil society] started off as 20,000 and now only 25 per cent of them operate.'[83]

Conclusion

Triggers

Had credible prosecutions been successfully carried out, the revolution would never have happened.[84]

---

[79] Al Mansouri, above n 21.

[80] United Nations Support Mission in Libya, 'Transitional Justice—Foundation for a New Libya' (17 September 2012) available at http://unsmil.unmissions.org/Default.aspx?tabid=5292&language=en-US; UNSMIL and OHCHR, above n 4. See also No Peace Without Justice, 'Libya: NPWJ Fosters Establishment of Libyan Trial Monitoring Network' (15 June 2013) available at www.npwj.org/ICC/Libya-NPWJ-fosters-establishment-Libyan-Trial-Monitoring-Network.html?utm_source=CICC+Newsletters&utm_campaign=b42a1e6c0b-August_2013_Libya_Digest_EN&utm_medium=email&utm_term=0_68df9c5182-b42a1e6c0b-356533713.

[81] LFJL Transitional Justice Programme, www.libyanjustice.org.

[82] Moschini, above n 41.

[83] ibid.

[84] Maghur, above n 14.

Maghur's statement refers to the significant role that impunity for perpetual human rights violations had in triggering the mass revolt against Muammar Gaddafi's 42-year-old regime. She echoed former Prime Minister Abdurrahim al-Keeb, who declared that 'proper justice is one of the reasons why this revolution started and one of the reasons why we ended where we are'.[85] At the centre of popular frustration was the shocking Abu Salim prison massacre in 1996, which resulted in a series of efforts by victims and lawyers to hold the perpetrators to account. It also resulted in the acquisition of financial compensation for some victims, which was, in the face of major legal and political obstacles, considered a successful attempt at ensuring some form of justice.[86] Despite the politicised nature of the move, Muammar Gaddafi's appointment of a *juge d'instruction* for Abu Salim was nevertheless in response to popular demands for justice.[87] Abu Salim was thus a highly influential trigger that led to decisions regarding prosecution, particularly for former Head of Military Intelligence El Senussi. At the time of writing, the Abu Salim massacre and Al Obaidi and El Zway's corruption trial are the only pre-transition crimes that have figured in the post-transition prosecutions.

The efforts of individual lawyers such as Salwa Bugaighis, Dao Al Mansouri and Fathi Terbil in pursuing accountability for human rights, particularly in the last decade of Muammar Gaddafi's rule, were crucial. The highly symbolic arrest of Fathi Terbil on 15 February 2011, which triggered more protests leading up to the Libyan uprising, attests to this critical role of individual lawyers in triggering decisions regarding prosecution. Moreover, despite differences of opinion on the impact of the ICC's indictments against Saif al-Islam Gaddafi and El Senussi, the tug of war between Libya and the ICC and references to Libya's eagerness to show that it can conduct the trials domestically cannot be dismissed as irrelevant factors. Libya's successful appeal regarding the admissibility of the *Senussi* case at the ICC, which resulted in the Court's approval that the Senussi trial be held in Libya, is a strong indication of how domestic decisions regarding prosecution were heavily impacted by the intervention of the ICC.[88]

Drivers

The individual lawyers mentioned above also served as key drivers of decisions regarding prosecution. In addition, despite the difficult and opaque conditions within which both international and local NGOs worked pre-transition, the advocacy efforts of organisations such as Amnesty International were vital to pressuring the government to respond. The case of Ali al Kermi is an example of this.[89] Moreover, persistent public pressure—mostly by families of the victims of

---

[85] Quoted in International Crisis Group, above n 25, 12.
[86] See Amnesty International, above n 17.
[87] Maghur, above n 14.
[88] See International Criminal Court, above n 6.
[89] See Amnesty International, above n 17.

Abu Salim and of other torture crimes in Libya—proved crucial to keeping the issue of impunity for human rights on the radar of both ordinary Libyans and the government. The tug of war for jurisdiction between Libya and the ICC is an additional factor that has had a driving role. The shadow of the ICC[90] intensified certain Libyan authorities' defiant stance on holding domestic prosecutions rather than sending former regime officials to The Hague.

Shapers

Legal challenges, a precarious security situation and a deep mistrust of the judiciary's ability to operate independently and effectively all limited the scope of the charges in the prosecutions. Moreover, a preoccupation with the crimes committed during the 2011 conflict, coupled with the adoption of a transitional justice law in December 2013, further limited the charges. Although none of the interviewees mentioned the role of the transitional justice law, its adoption has expanded the time period of the crimes addressed. It led to the cancellation of the statute of limitations for crimes committed before 1997 for political and security reasons, and allows for the investigation into the Abu Salim prison massacre, which took place in 1996.[91] Finally, the continued violence that has gripped Libya since 2011 and chaotic militia politics have formed a transition whose direction is uncertain. Significant questions of political stability plague the country, and these have effectively stalled decisions regarding the prosecution of political leaders.

However, Minister of Justice Salah Marghani reached out to the ICC in July 2014, asking it to investigate crimes committed by the Zintani and Misrati militias.[92] While, at the time of writing, there have been no major developments following this request other than the verdicts that were issued by a national court in July 2015 for Saif al-Islam Gaddafi, El Senussi and 35 others, Marghani's ICC request is indicative of two things. First, despite strong resistance to the involvement of the ICC for the case of Saif al-Islam Gaddafi and El Senussi, domestic political developments such as the deterioration of the security situation and the near collapse of the state partially reversed this resistance, at least at a certain level of the political leadership. Secondly, while Marghani did not raise the issue of Saif al-Islam Gaddafi's arrest warrant, the fact that the ICC has been called upon by the Minister of Justice to intervene means that decisions regarding prosecution are still on the political agenda. The shape of domestic prosecutions in Libya is therefore still in flux and the ICC is not completely out of the picture.

---

[90] CL Sriram and S Brown, 'Kenya in the Shadow of the ICC: Complementarity, Gravity and Impact' (2012) 12 *International Criminal Law Review* 219.

[91] Amnesty International, above n 37. The transitional justice law had not yet been adopted when the interviews were conducted in Libya in September 2013.

[92] M Kersten, 'Back Against the Wall: Libya Wants the ICC to Prosecute Wanton Militias' (21 July 2014) available at https://justiceinconflict.org/2014/07/21/back-against-the-wall-libya-wants-the-icc-to-prosecute-wanton-militias/.

5

Yemen

Unlike his counterparts in Egypt, Libya and Tunisia, Yemen's ousted President Ali Abdallah Saleh stepped down after securing his immunity from prosecution. Yemen's transition was heavily negotiated, with the involvement of several regional and international actors who were keen to prioritise political stability and to prevent violence from spilling across borders. Several years after the so-called transition, Saleh retains significant control in Yemen and the country has been reeling from a devastating war, primarily fought between the 'Arab coalition' led by Saudi Arabia and the Houthis, a Zaidi Shi'ite rebel group largely based in the north, and their allies. Prior to the outbreak of this war, Yemeni civil society activists worked hard to find ways to circumvent the immunity law, especially when it became clear that protests calling for its reversal would be completely ignored. Given the dire state of the Yemeni judiciary and the country's ambiguous and chaotic transition, other strategies for accountability were pursued through the establishment of two commissions. These commissions provided compensation for land confiscation and for forcibly retired military and security officers of the South. However, the work of these commissions and efforts to pass a transitional justice law have been halted due to the ongoing war. This chapter discusses the role that these various factors have played in the decision *not* to prosecute in Yemen.

On 27 January 2011, Yemenis took to the streets to protest President Ali Abdallah Saleh's rule. Violent clashes took place between protesters, security forces and tribesmen both loyal to and in opposition to Saleh's rule. Estimates vary regarding the death toll during several months of protests, most putting it at between 250 and 400 killed, with over 1000 injured and 100,000 displaced.[1] In November 2011, Saleh agreed to step down from his position as President of Yemen in a negotiated settlement brokered by the Gulf Cooperation Council (GCC), a political and economic sub-regional body. The settlement included a guarantee of immunity from prosecution for Saleh and his aides. The Yemeni parliament subsequently passed an immunity law for Saleh in January 2012 and power was transferred to his Vice President, Abed Rabbo Mansour Hadi, in February 2012.[2] Despite his stepping

---

[1] 'Yemen's Saleh Injured in Shelling, Seven Killed', *Reuters*, 4 June 2011, available at http://in.reuters.com/article/columns-us-yemen-idINTRE73L1PP20110603; Human Rights Watch, 'World Report 2012: Yemen. Events of 2011' (2012), available at www.hrw.org/world-report/2012/country-chapters/yemen.

[2] Law No 1/2012 Concerning the Granting of Immunity from Legal and Judicial Prosecution, Amnesty International (22 January 2012) available at https://www.amnesty.org/download/Documents/24000/mde310072012ar.pdf (in Arabic).

down from the presidency, Saleh retained his position as leader of the powerful General People's Congress Party (GPC).

Saleh had been President of Yemen for 33 years—first as President of the Yemen Arab Republic, or North Yemen, in 1978, then as President of a Yemen that unified the North and the People's Democratic Republic of Yemen in the South in 1990. However, a secessionist movement in the South turned violent and in 1994 a civil war ensued. North Yemen won the war and the South suffered social, political and economic marginalisation for decades. In 2007, a separatist movement in the South, al-Hirak, gained ground and this led to a series of violent confrontations between the southern separatists and military and security forces allied with Saleh.

Saleh's rule was marked by a number of other conflicts in Yemen. Al Qaeda has been carrying out attacks inside Yemen and originating from Yemen since 2000. The Houthis have long clashed with Yemeni state armed forces in the northern province of Saada. The Saleh regime launched a series of wars against the Houthis between 2004 and 2010, but with little success in mitigating their power.[3] General Ali Mohsen al-Ahmar led six wars against the Houthis during this time. Following the massive civil unrest of 2011 that eventually forced Saleh to transfer power to Hadi, General al-Ahmar defected and became Saleh's enemy.

Multiple internal conflicts in Yemen throughout Saleh's 33-year rule and in the six years since his ouster have thus left Yemenis wrangling with many challenges, with devastating impact on their well-being. The deep social and economic divisions between North and South Yemen throughout Saleh's rule, the multiple wars fought to suppress the southern secessionist movement and the Houthi rebellion in the north, and serious socio-economic grievances among the general Yemeni population are some of the major factors that intensified popular discontent and demands for reform. High unemployment, a water crisis, high fuel prices, internal displacement, food insecurity, rampant corruption and lack of access to health and education services as a result of violent conflict are examples of the major problems that have plagued Yemenis for many years. Yemeni journalists also suffered arbitrary detention and torture, in attempts by the Saleh regime to clamp down on the production of media reports that were critical of the government.

Thousands of army and security officers from the South, who were forced into retirement without pensions and faced severe marginalisation and exploitation by northern elites, staged street protests in 2009. Their grievances originate from their forced retirement following the 1994 war during which the Saleh regime crushed the southern secessionist movement, compounding the social, political and economic marginalisation of the South for many more years. Land and property confiscation in the South by northern elites was also a major grievance. The secessionist movement in the South, the armed Houthi rebellion in the North and attacks by Al Qaeda in the Arabian Peninsula (AQAP) were thus major markers of growing strife, instability and frustration in the years leading up to 2011.

---

[3] I Fraihat, *Unfinished Revolutions: Yemen, Libya and Tunisia After the Arab Spring* (New Haven, Yale University Press, 2016) 46–47.

The mass uprising that began on 27 January 2011 was significantly inspired by such grievances. Given Yemen's strategic importance to several regional neighbours, especially Saudi Arabia, the GCC was quick to broker a negotiated transition that would allow Saleh to step down without having to face trial, unlike his Egyptian, Tunisian and Libyan counterparts.

On 18 March 2011, peaceful anti-government protesters were shot and killed during a mass demonstration. This event became known as the 'Friday of Dignity' killings, during which Yemeni security forces allegedly killed over 45 peaceful protesters and wounded over 200 people.[4] In April 2011, Saleh, while still president, dismissed Attorney General Abdullah al-Olfy shortly after al-Olfy had requested the arrests of key suspects, including government officials, for the Friday of Dignity killings.[5] Many suspects were acquitted and the trials were criticised by international human rights organisations for being flawed.

For example, 43 out of 78 suspects indicted in June 2011 were listed as fugitives from justice. Thirty-one of them were never apprehended and the other 12 disappeared after they were provisionally released pending the outcome of the trial. Twenty-seven defendants were released on bail. In October 2011, victims' lawyers filed a motion in court demanding the indictment of at least 11 additional high-level government officials for the shootings, including Saleh, his nephew and a former interior minister. This case was sent to the Supreme Court for a decision on its validity in light of the immunity law protecting Saleh and his aides from prosecution. The trial was subsequently suspended on the basis of the immunity law.

Following the passing of the immunity law, further protests began to occur in Yemen in September 2012. These protests specifically called for the reversal of the immunity law. In response, Yemen's government ordered an investigation into the human rights violations that had occurred during the 2011 uprising and set up an investigative committee to that effect. In September 2012, the new president Hadi signed a decree authorising the creation of a commission of inquiry to investigate human rights violations during the 2011 uprising and to recommend accountability measures, including prosecutions. The Hadi government also ordered the investigation of 70 police officers suspected of being responsible for the Friday of Dignity killings. A trial commenced on the 29 September 2012 in the First Instance Court for the Western Capital District in Sanaa. However, the trial was ridden with flaws, as Human Rights Watch observed: 'The state prosecution's investigation into the Friday of Dignity massacre was marred by political interference, a failure to follow leads that might have implicated government officials, and factual errors.'[6] In October 2012, lawyers for the Friday of Dignity victims filed a motion to challenge the immunity law and called for a new investigation, seeking

---

[4] Human Rights Watch, 'Unpunished Massacre: Yemen's Failed Response to the "Friday of Dignity" Killings' (2013) available at www.hrw.org/report/2013/02/12/unpunished-massacre/yemens-failed-response-friday-dignity-killings.

[5] ibid.

[6] ibid.

to indict former president Saleh and his aides. Judge al-Sanabani, however, ruled that the motion conflicted with the immunity law and sent the case to the constitutional division of the Supreme Court for guidance, where it was stalled.

The National Dialogue Conference (NDC) was formed in 2013 with the aim of achieving consensus on a number of significant political and legal issues through consultative talks that aimed to include the various political and tribal actors in Yemen. Throughout the NDC talks, working groups debated the provisions of a draft transitional justice law that was proposed at the end of February 2012, soon after Hadi became interim president. One of the key questions was whether the law would address crimes committed since the beginning of Saleh's rule in 1978 or since the more recent 2011 uprising. Human Rights Minister Hooria Mashhour said that the transitional justice law would encourage families of victims of Saleh's rule since 1978, including those who were forcibly disappeared, to prosecute him or others either inside or outside Yemen.[7]

One of the shortcomings of the NDC process is that it failed to recognise and include the demands of major sectors of the population. Instead, it was driven by old tribal and political parties. For example, the voices of those protesting the content of the NDC negotiations, and in particular the provisions that glossed over criminal accountability for past crimes, fell on deaf ears. As Stacey Philbrick Yadav explains,

> The agreement's weaknesses were further reflected by the sit-ins and work stoppages that made up the so-called 'parallel revolution', which focused on public-sector corruption largely unaddressed by the transition. The role of the JMP—by then part of the new government—in suppressing these nonviolent forms of activism highlights the tension that has come to characterize the relationship between, on the one hand, the leaders of ossified opposition parties, and on the other hand, partisan youth and independents.[8]

Despite this, the false inclusivity of the NDC process was applauded by the USA and others. However, the transitional process in Yemen saw many problems unfold and in fact left more Yemenis dead than during the 2011 uprising itself.[9]

Meanwhile, despite their historic enmity, Saleh and the Houthis formed an alliance in the aftermath of the 2011 uprising. Saleh maintained strong political and military connections. The Houthis captured the capital city, Sanaa, and other parts of the country in September 2014, forcing Hadi to sign a Peace and Partnership Accord with them. However, with the rapid spread of Houthi control of the country in late 2014 and early 2015, Hadi was placed under house arrest in Sanaa and Yemen's parliament was dissolved.[10] As the conflict intensified, Hadi

---

[7] A Hammond, 'Yemen Minister Says Saleh Trying to Spoil Transition', *Chicago Tribune*, 22 September 2012, available at www.chicagotribune.com/news/sns-rt-us-yemen-saleh-ministerbre88 106q-20120922,0,5595875.story.

[8] SP Yadav, 'The "Yemen Model" as a Failure of Political Imagination' (2015) 47 *International Journal of Middle East Studies* 144, 145. The Joint Meeting Parties (JMP) is an alliance of opposition parties formed almost a decade before the Yemeni uprising.

[9] ibid 144, 146.

[10] Fraihat, above n 3, 49.

fled to the southern city of Aden in February 2015 and then went on to Riyadh, Saudi Arabia, in March 2015 when a coalition of GCC member states, Jordan and Morocco launched an anti-Houthi military campaign in Yemen. Saudi Arabia led this campaign through airstrikes and ground troops, with the aim of restoring the Hadi government and crushing the Houthi rebellion. Yemen has always been a security concern for neighbouring Saudi Arabia, which is keen to avoid a Houthi takeover of the country. Hadi's exile in Saudi Arabia was, however, short-lived—he returned to Aden in September 2015 to oversee the 'Arab coalition' offensive in the country.[11] In 2016, Saleh signed a deal with the Houthis, forming a supreme council that would run the country. This sparked significant international outcry, as the deal violated the terms of peace negotiations in Kuwait that year, as well as Security Council Resolution 2216, which calls on the Houthis to refrain from unilateral actions.

The Prosecution of Political Leaders in Pre-transition Yemen

Despite a provision in Yemen's constitution that allows for the prosecution of political leaders, no such prosecutions took place before the uprising that ousted President Saleh from power in 2011. Article 111 of Yemen's 1991 Constitution allows for the prosecution of the Prime Minister, his deputies and ministers following a vote of support by two-thirds of the House of Representatives.[12] In subsequent amendments to the constitution, the President was added to the list of government officials who could face prosecution. However, as all the interviewees stated, no high-level government official was prosecuted in Yemen for either corruption or human rights crimes. This was because, as activist Manal Al Qadasi and human rights lawyer Ahmed Barman put it, 'no one would dare'.[13] Political commentator Tamer Shamsan added that 'Here in Yemen, if we try to hold someone accountable, we risk our lives'.[14] Judge Ahmed Al Dhobhani recounted efforts by certain judges to refer high-level officers from the state security agencies to investigation for crimes such as torture and arbitrary detention. Such efforts never proceeded 'because those individuals were loyal to the old regime'.[15]

---

[11] 'Yemen's Exiled President Returns to Aden', *Al Jazeera*, 17 November 2015, available at www.alja-zeera.com/news/2015/11/yemen-exiled-president-returns-aden-151117102731437.html.

[12] Constitution of the Republic of Yemen, 1991, Art 111. See 'Yemen—Constitution', available at www.servat.unibe.ch/icl/ym00000_.html.

[13] Interview with Manal Al Qudsi, Programme Officer, Yemen Center for Transitional Justice (telephone interview, 21 November 2013); interview with Abdelrahman Barman, human rights lawyer, National Organisation for Defending Rights and Freedoms (Sanaa, Yemen, 22 January 2014).

[14] Interview with Tamer Shamsan, political activist, columnist (Sanaa, Yemen, 22 January 2014).

[15] Interview with Judge Ahmed Al Dhobhani, President of the Court of First Instance and member of the Yemen Judges Club (email interview, 22 March 2017).

Yemen

However, human rights lawyers have pointed out that since 2005 there have been a few efforts to prosecute senior officials in the security agencies and in the police. An example is the *Anisa Al-Shuaibi* case of 2006, who was accused of murdering her ex-husband and was taken into police custody, where she was repeatedly raped and beaten. Rizq Al-Jawfi, head of the Criminal Investigation Unit, was interrogated for his role in Al-Shuabi's illegal detention and abuse while in prison. Abdelrahman Barman described Al-Shuaibi's relentless efforts to hold a police chief to account in a court of law as a 'key case' that raised a lot of awareness in Yemen about the lack of accountability for police brutality.[16] This is despite the verdict that was issued for Al-Shuaibi: she was found innocent, but was ordered to pay one million Yemeni riyals in compensation. Ahmed Arman described this verdict as 'strange, but still regarded as a success'.[17] That the *Al-Shuaibi* case was considered a positive step towards criminal accountability for one senior police official points to the difficult environment that made even the initiation of a prosecution targeting a minister or head of state unthinkable. As with Mubarak, Ben Ali and Muammar Gaddafi, Saleh's authoritarian regime of 33 years did not tolerate opposition. The repressive consequences for those who did criticise the regime meant that there were scant efforts to prosecute political leaders in pre-transition Yemen.

The Decision *Not* to Prosecute in Yemen

Unlike Egypt, Tunisia and Libya, Yemen passed an immunity law to protect former President Saleh and his aides from prosecution.[18] This meant that, with the exception of some preliminary hearings for the 18 March 2011 killings, there were no prosecutions of former political leaders in Yemen after Saleh's ouster. There were attempts by lawyers and judges to seek the indictment of Saleh and several of his aides for the *Friday of Dignity killings* case, but the presiding judge responded that he could not proceed because of the immunity law and the case was subsequently closed.[19] This chapter thus discusses the various factors that shaped the decision *not* to prosecute former leaders in Yemen.

International actors, geopolitics, legal challenges and a heavily negotiated transition all contributed to the decision not to prosecute. The immunity law was the product of negotiations that the GCC led together with the USA, the EU, the Russian Federation and the UN Special Adviser to the Secretary General, Jamal

---

[16] Barman, above n 13.

[17] Interview with Ahmed Arman, lawyer and Executive Secretary, National Organisation for Defending Rights and Freedoms (Sanaa, Yemen, 22 January 2014).

[18] Law No 1/2012, above n 2.

[19] Interview with Letta Tayler, Senior Researcher, Human Rights Watch (telephone interview, 21 November 2013); Al Dhobhani, above n 15.

Benomar (the GCC Initiative).[20] After several months of mass protests calling for the ouster of former President Saleh in 2011, he agreed to the terms and conditions set forth in the GCC Initiative, which entered into force in November 2011. Key to this initiative was the guarantee of immunity from prosecution for Saleh and his aides, provided that they cease their involvement in Yemeni politics: 'On the 29th day after the Agreement enters into force, parliament, including the opposition, shall adopt laws granting immunity from legal and judicial prosecution to the President and those who worked with him during his time in office.'[21]

The subsequent passing of the immunity law includes the following articles:

> Article (1): Brother Ali Abdullah Saleh, President of the Republic, shall hereby be granted complete immunity from legal and judicial prosecution.

> Article (2): Immunity from criminal prosecution shall apply to the officials who have worked under the President—in state civil, military and security agencies—in connection with politically motivated acts carried out during the course of their official duties; immunity shall not apply to acts of terrorism.[22]

While the passing of this law had the full support of the international powers that negotiated the GCC Initiative, it generated deep disappointment among international and domestic human rights NGOs that prioritised criminal accountability. In addition, while the UN Special Adviser Jamal Benomar helped facilitate the GCC Initiative, some controversy surrounded the UN's support for the immunity part of the deal. George Abu Al Zulof, however, stressed the following:

> Regarding accountability, our office was very clear when this impunity law was passed— that we are against this as an office. We consider that we will not be able to turn a new page in Yemen without closing the previous period properly. Those who committed grave human rights violations should be held accountable.[23]

Judge Ahmed Al Dhobhani strongly criticised the regional and international actors involved in negotiating the immunity deal:

> The immunity law violates the Yemeni constitution ... The same international actors that called for the independence of the judiciary also pressured Yemen to issue the immunity law. Verbally, representatives of the Security Council countries, the GCC, and the UN Special Rapporteur Jamal Ben Omar typically caution against immunity as it violates the general principles of international law—as if Yemeni laws allowed immunity in the

---

[20] International Crisis Group, 'Yemen: Enduring Conflict, Threatened Transition' (3 July 2012) available at www.crisisgroup.org/en/regions/middle-east-north-africa/iraq-iran-gulf/yemen/125-yemen-enduring-conflicts-threatened-transition.aspx.

[21] The Gulf Cooperation Council Initiative, translated by the UN in International Crisis Group, ibid.

[22] Law No 1 of 2012 Concerning the Granting of Immunity from Legal and Judicial Prosecution, translated from Arabic to English by Amnesty International in 'Yemen's Immunity Law—Breach of International Obligations' (March 2012) available at www.amnesty.ca/sites/default/files/2012-03-30mde310072012enyemenimmunitylaw.pdf.

[23] Interview with George Abu Al Zulof, Country Representative, OHCHR Yemen (Sanaa, Yemen, 23 January 2014).

first place! In reality, however, those representatives are the same ones who used every political means available to pressure political actors in Yemen to pass the immunity law. Unfortunately, we are now wary of the positions of these international organisations and actors.[24]

The immunity law angered the victims of the Friday of Dignity killings, who staged mass street protests in 2011 and 2012 to demand the law's reversal, following repeated and failed attempts to prosecute. On 20 December 2011, hundreds of predominantly young Yemenis marched from the city of Ta'iz to Sanaa—the equivalent of approximately 250 kilometres—to protest the immunity deal.[25] Several protesters were killed by live ammunition from security forces allied with Saleh. This 'Life March' was followed by a second similar 'Dignity March' in January 2012, when thousands of protesters again marched in protest against the immunity deal, this time from the city of Al Hodeida to Sanaa—a distance of nearly 300 kilometres.

Despite the immunity law and the failure of these protests to reverse it, the Friday of Dignity victims continued to file legal complaints with the public prosecutor in an attempt to hold those who ordered and carried out the killings accountable. The case was originally opened in 2011 and when it became clear that the attorney general at the time, Abdullah al-Olfy, was taking the independence of the investigation seriously, he was sacked by Saleh. The court proceedings since then have been conducted in a haphazard manner, and marred with hasty acquittals and with a questionable selection of 'suspects' that did not include any high-ranking security or government officials.[26]

An Ambiguous Transition, Civil Society and Navigating the GCC Initiative

Yemen's heavily negotiated transition meant that Saleh's GPC party would retain at least half the authority over the country while the Joint Meeting Parties would serve as the other major power-sharing partner. As Yadav notes, this was a far cry from a 'substantive democratic transition'.[27] Nevertheless, the negotiated agreement was regarded as a necessary alternative to a bloody transition that would spill over into neighbouring countries and open up a power vacuum for actors such as AQAP to gain ground. The large protests of the Life March and Dignity March that constituted a powerful objection to the elite dismissal of criminal accountability

---

[24] Al Dhobhani, above n 15.

[25] Atiaf Alwazir, 'Social Media in Yemen: Expecting the Unexpected', *Al Akhbar English*, 30 December 2011, available at http://english.al-akhbar.com/node/2931.

[26] Human Rights Watch, above n 4; interview with Belkis Wille, Yemen and Kuwait Researcher, Human Rights Watch (Sanaa, Yemen, 22 January 2014); Tayler, above n 19.

[27] Yadav, above n 8, 144, 145.

for the former regime, then, were completely ignored by both regional and international actors, who prioritised domestic and regional political stability in the short term over the potentially violent repercussions of taking the decision to prosecute.

Elite politics did not always succeed in trumping Yemeni civil society demands, however. In fact, as Atiaf Alwazir argues, the Yemeni uprising was a product of over 20 years of diverse street mobilisations, sit-ins and strikes. The Law on Associations and Foundations (Law No 1/2001) facilitated the establishment of civil society organisations, an estimated 10,000 of which registered under this law.[28] While only 25 per cent of these organisations were active, a strong civil society 'culture' was present in Yemen in the decades leading up to the uprising. The southern secessionist al-Hirak movement, for example, staged many peaceful street protests, even when they were violently suppressed by armed state security officers allied with Saleh. Street protests became common in other parts of pre-uprising Yemen, particularly after 2007. Many took place in Saada, where relatives of the disappeared, journalists, political prisoners and those killed during the wars between the Houthis and Saleh loyalists protested in front of government buildings. These diverse mobilisations were held on a weekly basis—every Tuesday—to coincide with cabinet meetings.[29] In 2008, workers, teachers, professors and doctors joined in the protests and organised strikes. The Yemeni Physicians and Pharmacist Syndicate went on full strike in January 2010 to protest a fatal attack on Dr Dirham Al Qadasi, a prominent physician. As a result of the massive pressure by civil society, the government pushed for the arrest of five individuals accused of Al Qadasi's murder.[30] Also, a nationwide general strike in May 2010 forced Saleh's government to make concessions to improve the working conditions of public sector workers. Alwazir notes that one of the strengths of the Yemeni uprising is that many of the protesters (civil society leaders, activists, journalists) knew each other from the pre-2011 protests and easily formed diverse and powerful networks during the uprising: 'By the end of February 2011, over 400 coalitions were formed in Change Square in Sanaa. Liberals, leftists, Islamists, tribesmen, mothers, fathers, as well as apolitical activists formed various groups to promote change.'[31]

The perils of the heavily negotiated Yemeni transition, however, became clearer as the post-transition period progressed. Saleh continued to head his political party, the GPC. His initial sporadic political appearances, giving many Yemenis reason to believe that he still wielded power in Yemen, evolved into full-blown political engagement. Manal Al Qadasi observed that 'The problem is that our current government is a partner of the former regime—they are avoiding accountability

---

[28] International Center for Not-for-Profit Law, 'Civic Freedom Monitor: Yemen' (19 January 2017) available at http://www.icnl.org/research/monitor/yemen.html.

[29] A Alwazir, 'The Yemeni Uprising: A Product of Twenty Years of Grassroots Mobilization' in A Ghazal and J Hanssen (eds), *The Oxford Handbook of Contemporary Middle-Eastern and North African History* (Oxford, Oxford University Press, 2015) 8.

[30] ibid 8–9.

[31] ibid 10.

for prior human rights abuses'.[32] Barman summarised the Yemeni transition as follows:

> There was a political agreement between the old regime and the revolutionary parties. The old regime is still very present in today's state security. We've removed the heads and the families of the old regime, but its supporters are still there and they are influential ... In Yemen, the faces of the regime changed, but the mentality of the old regime persists ... We don't actually have a new regime in Yemen—it's the same people. If you want to create a change and open a new page, you should do it with new agents of change. Not with the same agents of the past. With them, you cannot close the past properly.[33]

These statements were made before the Saudi-led war against the Houthis in Yemen and before the consolidation of the Saleh–Houthi alliance that has since been fighting against the internationally recognised Hadi government. So, it is not only the 'mentality' of the old regime that persists: the ousted leader himself, Ali Abdallah Saleh, has made a thunderous political comeback amidst a grave humanitarian situation in the country that has left Yemen crippled by both internal and external political manoeuvrings. The immunity law, as the interviewees suggest, greatly facilitated Saleh's re-emergence as a major political actor in post-transition Yemen. Al Dhobhani added:

> The immunity law is currently the greatest challenge for the rule of law in Yemen. Its implications are not confined to impunity for a handful of individuals; rather, it extends much farther than that and strengthens the culture of corruption and impunity on a grand scale ... crimes for which there is no accountability ended up shaking people's faith in justice and encourages the perpetration of more such crimes.[34]

Al Dhobhani also noted that Saleh's political allies immediately following the uprising destroyed any attempts at a 'judicial revolution' for independence. They did so by installing individuals loyal to Saleh in positions of power in the Supreme Judicial Council. According to Al Dhobhani, 'This is because each of these parties is implicated in past crimes', and they therefore worked to ensure their protection from criminal accountability.[35]

Curiously, the UN consistently called for the implementation of the GCC Initiative in Yemen (which specifically grants immunity from prosecution for Saleh and his aides), while also calling on Yemen to pursue transitional justice measures that included criminal accountability for human rights violations.[36] A string of UN documents immediately preceding and following the signing of the GCC Initiative

---

[32] Al Qudsi, above n 13.
[33] Barman, above n 13.
[34] Al Dhobhani, above n 15.
[35] ibid.
[36] See Security Council Resolution 2014 (2011); Security Council Resolution 2051 (2012); the UN Implementing Mechanism (2011); the Human Rights Council Resolution A/HRC/18/19 (2011); the UN Security Council Presidential Statement of 29 March 2012.

reflect this bizarre contradiction. The following excerpts from a report following the UN human rights agency's visit to Yemen warrant a close look:

> 77. Launch transparent and independent investigations, in line with relevant international standards, into credible allegations of serious human rights violations committed by the Government security forces, including, but not limited to, the killing of civilians, excessive use of force against civilians, arbitrary detention, and torture and ill treatment; ensure that perpetrators are held accountable ...

> 95. Recognizing that in the present climate of violence and counter violence, much-needed investigations, particularly into excesses or abuses by the military, the security services or their affiliates will not be seen as credible or impartial, ensure that international independent and impartial investigations are conducted into incidents which resulted in heavy loss of life and injuries;[37]

These calls for accountability are reiterated in the Human Rights Council resolution of 14 October 2011, which notes Yemen's commitment to launch independent investigations into human rights violations that adhere to international standards. However, the same resolution makes the following statement:

> 7. Calls upon all parties to move forward with negotiations on an inclusive, orderly and Yemeni-led process of political transition on the basis of the initiative of the Gulf Cooperation Council;[38]

The resolution therefore calls on Yemen to pursue two conflicting goals: criminal accountability for serious human rights violations by security forces on the one hand, and the conditions set forth in the GCC Initiative on the other, which prevent the prosecution of the former president and his aides. This contradictory call reappears in subsequent UN documents:

> *Taking note* of the Human Rights Council resolution on Yemen (A/HRC/RES/18/19), and underlining the need for a comprehensive, independent and impartial investigation consistent with international standards into alleged human rights abuses and violations, with a view to avoiding impunity and ensuring full accountability, and noting in this regard the concerns expressed by the UN High Commissioner for Human Rights,

> *Welcoming* the statement by the Ministerial Council of the Gulf Cooperation Council on 23 September 2011 which called for the immediate signing by President Saleh and implementation of the Gulf Cooperation Council initiative, condemned the use of force against unarmed demonstrators, and called for restraint, a commitment to a full and immediate ceasefire and the formation of a commission to investigate the events that led to the killing of innocent Yemeni people ...

---

[37] Human Rights Council, 'Report of the High Commissioner on OHCHR's Visit to Yemen', A/HRC/18/21 (13 September 2011) available at www2.ohchr.org/english/bodies/hrcouncil/docs/18session/A-HRC-18-21.pdf.
[38] Human Rights Council, 'Resolution Adopted by the Human Rights Council', A/HRC/RES/18/19 (14 October 2011).

4. *Reaffirms* its view that the signature and implementation as soon as possible of a settlement agreement on the basis of the Gulf Cooperation Council initiative is essential for an inclusive, orderly, and Yemeni-led process of political transition ...[39]

UN Security Council Resolution 2051 (2012) repeats conflicting demands for accountability and for compliance with the GCC Initiative that calls for immunity:

1. *Reaffirms* the need for the full and timely implementation of the GCC Initiative and Implementation Mechanism in accordance with resolution 2014 (2011);

7. *Stresses* that all those responsible for human rights violations and abuses must be held accountable, and underlining the need for a comprehensive, independent and impartial investigation consistent with international standards into alleged human rights abuses and violations, to prevent impunity and ensure full accountability;[40]

Despite these clauses in the UN documents that call for conflicting paths to individual criminal accountability in Yemen, the Transitional Justice Working Group at the NDC made use of these documents to advocate for criminal accountability. The Working Group essentially referred to the clauses that call on Yemen to fulfil its international legal obligations by ensuring that those responsible for human rights violations are held accountable. This strategy, according to Hamza Al Kamali, a member of the Transitional Justice Working Group, is a means to circumvent the immunity law by citing these clauses in the Working Group's recommendations to the NDC. Al Kamali explained that 'The UN is a tool for us—the youth and civil society—an important tool to put pressure on the president to set up an investigative commission and to ensure accountability'.[41] Such attempts to circumvent the immunity law in Yemen are akin to the circumvention strategies pursued in Chile, Argentina and Uruguay to overcome those countries' amnesty provisions. As Engstrom and Pereira observe, 'in many countries, amnesty provisions are circumvented rather than overturned'.[42]

Moreover, the immunity law in Yemen, according to some interpretations, is not all encompassing, as it might initially appear. Abu Al Zulof, for instance, explained that the Transitional Justice Working Group's recommendations aimed to link the immunity law with political activity by ensuring that politically active individuals would be stripped of their immunity. Here, 'politically active' means 'to take high

---

[39] Security Council Resolution 2014 (2011). Similar contradictory calls regarding accountability and Yemen's international human rights obligations continued to emerge in subsequent UN documents, such as the Agreement on the Implementation Mechanism for the Transition Process in Yemen in Accordance with the Initiative of the GCC, the UN Security Council Presidential Statement of 29 March 2012 and Security Council Resolution 2051 (2012).

[40] Security Council Resolution 2051 (2012).

[41] Interview with Hamza Al Kamali, member of the Transitional Justice Working Group, National Dialogue Conference (Sanaa, Yemen, 22 January 2014).

[42] P Engstrom and G Pereira, 'From Amnesty to Accountability: The Ebb and Flow in the Search for Justice in Argentina' in F Lessa and LA Payne (eds), *Amnesty in the Age of Human Rights Accountability: Comparative and International Perspectives* (Cambridge, Cambridge University Press, 2012) 122.

positions in the government, or *manasib 'olyah*.[43] In other words, the immunity law currently in place only pertains to high-level government officials:

> This means that we can—despite the immunity law—address human rights violations committed by other personnel from the previous regime, such as the security forces. There are other political groups, such as Islah, that were part of the 1994 civil war and they worked with the previous regime and they committed violations as well. So this means that if there are investigations conducted, their leaders, or those who were involved and decided to continue to be involved in the political scene in the country could be held accountable and prosecuted. Or, from the very beginning, they could choose either to step down from political life or face prosecution.[44]

Whether such other mid- to low-ranking officers will be prosecuted in Yemen remains an open question, particularly given the fragile security situation and the judiciary's weak and politicised disposition. Moreover, it leaves unresolved the question of lack of accountability for high-level officials at both the domestic and international level.

'A Different Kind of International Intervention': Geopolitics and the Role of International Actors

Human rights lawyers argue that the political interests of certain international and regional actors directly led to immunity for high-level government officials in Yemen. Arman, for instance, stated: 'The immunity law is a product of politics at the international level.'[45] Belkis Wille of Human Rights Watch agreed: 'The reason that the immunity law exists is because of international actors.'[46] Abu Al Zulof provided three explanations regarding the question of the role of international and geopolitical actors in Yemen in severely limiting the prospects for prosecuting former leaders:

> First, Yemen's location in the Arabian Peninsula—being close to the Gulf States and Saudi Arabia—means that any instability in Yemen will affect the neighbouring countries. So I think the GCC countries are very much concerned that what will happen in Yemen will negatively affect them. They are doing their utmost to reach an agreement peacefully. They are against the prosecutions because they were allies with the previous regime.

> Secondly, the GCC countries didn't pay a lot of attention to the complete dismantlement of the previous regime because the previous regime shares half of the authority over the country. The reason is that the alternative was not acceptable to the GCC countries. The alternative was the key opposition group—al-Islah, which is the Yemeni branch of

---

[43] Abu Al Zulof, above n 23. '*Manasib 'olyah*' is the Arabic term for 'high-level positions'.
[44] ibid.
[45] Arman, above n 17.
[46] Wille, above n 26.

the Muslim Brotherhood. From a political point of view, they were not so much moti-vated to have a regime that is Muslim Brotherhood. There is the right wing of al-Islah, such as the Zindani. Their ideology is very much in line with Al Qaeda. So there is an extremist wing in al-Islah so they were concerned that this would have bad consequences for instability in Yemen.

The third reason is related to the international community. For Europe, the EU, and the United States the key concern was Al Qaeda in the Arabian Peninsula's unification with the Saudi branch and their ability to build their own bases. For the Western countries, any instability in Yemen is an opportunity for AQAP to expand and control more areas. So the political agenda supersedes the human rights agenda for these powers.

The impunity law was the price to be paid for stability in Yemen. This is what makes Yemen different from other countries. In Libya, NATO intervened. This wasn't possible in Yemen. In Yemen you have weak government and institutions, more than 50 million pieces of small arms in Yemen. On top of that you have Al Qaeda and the tribal powers. All these elements pushed towards a scenario not to have the international community come and end the conflict. It's a different kind of international intervention.[47]

Others commented on the role of specific actors, such as Saudi Arabia, in directing a substantial part of domestic politics in Yemen to suit their interests. For exam-ple, Shamsan criticised regional and international actors for contributing to the decades-long political chaos in Yemen:

Saudi Arabia doesn't want to see a stable and successful state in Yemen because they don't want the Saudi people to see a successful, democratic model elsewhere ... The UN is controlled by big powers which are run by institutions, not individuals. They build their decisions based on studies. Europe views us—the Third World—as barbaric, reactionary. They're fine with an almost collapsed state—it's in their interests. So long as it is 'stable' enough not to cause too many problems for them.[48]

Omar Own lamented this state of affairs by referring to the weakness of Yemeni President Hadi: 'Ten states control Yemen. Our president merely acts as the coordinator.'[49] Shamsan also charged Yemenis—and Arabs in general—with fail-ing to build a democratic state that could hold its leaders accountable. 'We in the Arab world,' Shamsan observed, 'make a dictator out of a democratic leader. And that is because we don't have democratic institutions to ensure a leader remains democratic.'[50] In sum, Yemen's grappling with internal tribal politics while also fielding external power wrangling meant that 'the impunity law was the price to be paid for stability in Yemen'.[51]

However, avoidance of criminal accountability for crimes committed in Yemen was not confined to Yemeni and regional actors. In September 2016, the UK

---

[47] Abu Al Zulof, above n 23.
[48] Shamsan, above n 14.
[49] Interview with Omar Own, consultant, UNDP Yemen; NGO expert (Sanaa, Yemen, 22 January 2014.
[50] Shamsan, above n 14.
[51] Abu Al Zulof, above n 23.

rejected an EU proposal to launch an international inquiry into civilian deaths in Yemen as a result of the Saudi-led military campaign against the Houthis.[52] Given the £3 billion worth of weapons the UK has sold to Saudi Arabia for use in the war in Yemen since 2015, it is no surprise that the British government is averse to such an international inquiry that may result in its ministers being held legally accountable for serious human rights violations.[53] Moreover, documents obtained by Reuters in October 2016 reveal that American government officials have serious concerns about the potential for the USA to also be held accountable for its military aid to Saudi Arabia for the war in Yemen. Officials cited the expansion of the term 'aiding and abetting' war crimes in the 2013 ruling against former Liberian president Charles Taylor. The expansion of the term's definition included 'practical assistance, encouragement or moral support' as sufficient to determine liability for war crimes.[54] This expanded definition of aiding and abetting war crimes could lead to a criminal investigation into the responsibility of American and British government officials in contributing to the perpetration of crimes in Yemen.

Legal Challenges and a Weak Judiciary

While Yemen's Constitution guarantees judicial independence (Article 147 of the 1994 Constitution and Article 206 of the 2015 Constitution), there is extensive executive power meddling in the judiciary's affairs. The Ministry of Justice and the President appoint and remove judges at their discretion, and judges are forcibly transferred if they issue rulings unfavourable to the government. Saleh's dismissal of Attorney General Abdullah Al Olfy is one example of such a practice. The Supreme Judicial Council regulates the appointment, transfer, promotion and protection of judges. However, its leadership is heavily controlled by the executive. Saleh himself served as the President of the Supreme Judicial Council until 2006, when the judiciary and external donors pressured him into handing over the position to the Chief Justice of the Supreme Court.

Weak institutions are a significant factor in the shaping of decisions not to prosecute in Yemen. Split along tribal lines, the judiciary rarely takes action with regard to controversial cases that implicate high-level officials. Barman noted that 'The judiciary in Yemen has many challenges. You will find a good judge, but he's also corrupt. You will find a good judge, but he is not powerful. You will find a powerful judge, but he is not knowledgeable.'[55] This politicisation of the judiciary, coupled

---

[52] J Doward, 'UK Accused of Blocking UN Inquiry into Claim of War Crimes in Yemen', *The Guardian*, 25 September 2016, available at www.theguardian.com/world/2016/sep/24/yemen-britain-human-rights-inquiry.

[53] ibid.

[54] Special Court for Sierra Leone, Judgment, Case No SCSL-03-01-A (10766-11114) (26 September 2013) available at www.rscsl.org/Documents/Decisions/Taylor/Appeal/1389/SCSL-03-01-A-1389.pdf.

[55] Barman, above n 13.

with corruption and nepotism, left Yemenis with a weak judicial institution to which very few turned in their quest for justice. The aborted Friday of Dignity killings case is a tragic illustration of this. Al Dhobhani emphasised that certain judges and prosecutors attempted to take advantage of the new atmosphere created by the 2011 uprising—an environment which he explained was conducive to a 'judicial revolution' in 2011–12. Judges called for the pursuit of investigations into crimes committed by politicians and leaders of the former regime, but such efforts were quickly crushed by Saleh's allies.[56] Al Dhobhani places great importance on the role of the Yemeni judiciary in any effort to achieve transitional justice:

> We do not want to hurt anyone or sentence anyone to death. We want judicial justice for all those responsible for wrongdoing. We want a transitional justice to forgive and to respect the law. We need to heal the wounds of victims that have been superficially stitched and have allowed gangrene to spread. An independent judiciary is the foundation for justice.[57]

Barman also noted that security forces destroyed many of his organisation's archives during the revolution, making it particularly difficult to provide the evidence required to prosecute.[58] A lack of direct evidence linking Saleh and other high-level government officials to crimes such as the Friday of Dignity killings thus significantly weakened prospects for prosecution in the immediate aftermath of Saleh's ouster.

Moreover, problems of security in Yemen have specifically targeted the judiciary. Judges and prosecutors have been, and continue to be, assassinated.[59] Judges, prosecutors, lawyers and other legal professionals actively protested alongside anti-government demonstrators during the uprising, mainly demanding judicial independence and protection.[60] Even in cases where officials who hold high-level governmental positions are supportive of the push for criminal accountability of political leaders, their goals are quashed by other, more powerful, actors. Wille explained that the Ministry of Legal Affairs and Ministry of Human Rights are strongly against the immunity law and support a comprehensive transitional justice law and the ratification of the Rome Statute. However, they are the two weakest ministries in terms of power, and thus have had little, if any, influence on decisions regarding prosecution.[61] A high-level government position is not tantamount to a position of power.

Finally, there is a serious problem of capacity in the judiciary. Apart from the absence of war crimes, crimes against humanity and genocide in the criminal code, the prosecution of ordinary crimes is highly unlikely. As Arman explained,

---

[56] Al Dhobhani, above n 15.

[57] ibid.

[58] Barman, above n 13.

[59] Abu Al Zulof, above n 23.

[60] E Gaston and N Al Dawsari, 'Justice in Transition in Yemen: A Mapping of Local Justice Functioning in Ten Governorates' (Washington DC, United States Institute for Peace, 2014).

[61] Wille, above n 26.

there are only 700 judges in Yemen and 2700 members of the judiciary, who have four months' annual leave. He added:

> This is a very, very low number of judges for a population of twenty-two million. One judge has 200 or more cases per month. There is no time to deal with all these cases. There is also a problem of law enforcement—the police do not enforce judicial decisions. Judges are powerless.[62]

As a result, many cases have lingered with the judiciary for 20 or more years.[63]

The Yemen Judges Club was established in 1991, when it was known as the Judges' Forum. It is a voluntary association, with representation across all Yemeni governorates, and aims to push for judicial independence and better work allowances. However, soon after its formation, Saleh ordered that the head of the Supreme Court—his ally—should also head the Yemen Judges Club. Consequently, the Club was inactive for many years.[64] After the 2011 uprising, however, the Club became active again, documenting violations against its members and reaching out to the International Association of Judges for advocacy efforts related to judicial independence and the protection of Yemeni judges. In May 2013, the Club won a case filed with the Supreme Court, in which it objected to the Minister of Justice's control over appointments at the Supreme Judicial Council.[65] As the Club became more active and independent in its operations, it also began to face severe repercussions for its work. Its most prominent member, the veteran Judge Abdul Jalil Noman, led the Club's fight for judicial independence in 2013 and was subsequently killed in an attack at the Military Hospital in Sanaa. Gunmen affiliated with Al Qaeda allegedly shot and killed him, his wife and 50 other patients and hospital staff.[66]

Post-uprising prospects, then, are also grim: courts do not function 20–60 per cent of the time because of judges' strikes and judge absenteeism, driven by a lack of motivation, major discontent with their working conditions and serious threats against them.[67] While the Supreme Judicial Council in Yemen has control over the judicial budget—something which other countries in the region continue to struggle for—its weak capacity and executive interference in its leadership overshadows its ability to perform its functions effectively. As Hesham Nasr, Jill Crystal and Nathan Brown note:

> There are 223 offices with human working power of 800 prosecutors. In this regard, Yemen has particular need of infrastructural development ... In Yemen, there is particular need for work related to buildings, equipment and human resources (administrative and judicial) in order to provide for the basic needs of effective public prosecution function.[68]

---

[62] Arman, above n 17.

[63] Shamsan, above n 14.

[64] AA Al Dhobhani, 'A Report on the Violations of Judicial Independence in Yemen between September 2014 and March 2016' (March 2016) 3.

[65] ibid.

[66] ibid 8.

[67] Gaston and Dawsari, above n 60, 7.

[68] H Nasr, J Crystal and NJ Brown, 'Criminal Justice and Prosecution in the Arab World', Programme on Governance in the Arab Region (UNDP, October 2004) 8, available at ftp://pogar.org/LocalUser/pogarp/judiciary/criminaljustice-brown-e.pdf.

It is not surprising, then, that even lower-profile prosecutions in Yemen since the 2011 uprising have not progressed. Many Yemenis instead turn to non-state community dispute resolution mechanisms to address their legal claims. Reparations through the Commission to Consider and Address Land Issues (the Land Commission) have also served as a potential alternative to criminal justice in the courts. The purpose of this commission and its impact is discussed in the next section.

Content and Extent of Decisions Regarding Prosecution

Despite the immunity law and the challenges discussed above, efforts are being made in Yemen to seek accountability for political leaders—whether in the form of prosecutions, truth commissions or reparations, or through other transitional justice mechanisms. Al Kamali's explanation of the Transitional Justice Working Group's efforts is one example of this, as is the draft transitional justice law, the discussion of which was short lived because of the subsequent outbreak of war. However, when asked about the time period of the crimes to be covered within a transitional justice framework, the picture begins to look similar to those of Egypt, Tunisia and Libya. A focus on crimes committed during the transition, namely, the killing of peaceful protesters in 2011, has left the subject of pre-transition crimes to be dealt with by the non-existent transitional justice law. A number of explanations for this limited scope of crimes have emerged.

First, prosecuting crimes committed during the 2011 uprising is, as Al Kamali explained, easier and more practical than prosecuting earlier crimes. It is easier because 'all the various political factions who continue to wield power in Yemen were involved in pre-2011 crimes. 2011 crimes are more straightforward—the killing of protesters, full stop'.[69] Letta Tayler observed that the question of how far back the transitional justice law should go was a 'key sticking point' for the same reasons that Al Kamali identified. Consequently, Tayler explained that '[Human Rights Watch's] position ... ideally start[s] with the most recent violations because they are fresh and easiest to prosecute ... We'd rather see that than no [transitional justice] law at all'.[70] Helen Lackner similarly points to the controversy over the extent of the transitional justice law in the negotiations that took place between 2012 and 2013 and at the NDC:

The main disagreement concerned article 4, which stated that the provisions of the law would apply to events from 26 September 1962 onwards in the former [Yemen Arab

[69] Al Kamali, above n 41.
[70] Tayler, above n 19.

Republic] and from 30 November 1967 in the former [People's Democratic Republic of Yemen], up until the date the law was enacted. Had this been passed by parliament, it would have annulled the validity of Saleh's immunity law.[71]

Efforts have emerged, however, to include as many pre-2011 crimes as possible. Abu Al Zulof explained some of the manoeuvres taken to try and ensure that a more inclusive set of crimes are addressed by the transitional justice law than were addressed under negotiation in 2013 and 2014. He described these efforts by referring to the example of enforced disappearances and land confiscations, of which there are many in Yemen. He stated that:

> As an office, we are supporting expansion of the [transitional justice law's] mandate to include crimes committed before 2011. But there are so many limitations, including the text of the GCC agreement. We are trying to overcome these limitations through the national dialogue. The decision they reached now is that the grievances of the past—their impact is still ongoing today and will be addressed in the new draft of the transitional justice law. For example, for cases of enforced disappearances, the families are still suffering from this ongoing crime. The president will consider the national dialogue recommendations and those who were affected will at least be compensated.

Abu Al Zulof emphasised that enforced disappearances and land confiscations are both 'ongoing' crimes and that 'families are still suffering as a result of these crimes, so there is a need [for the transitional justice law] to address these grievances, which have been around since 1994'.[72] Barman also discussed the inclusion of 'ongoing' crimes:

> The transitional justice working group will go back to previous years but only for 'ongoing crimes'—land confiscation, enforced disappearances, and so on. Not torture and extra judicial killings. This is because the current political forces in Yemen are implicated in these crimes.[73]

Since the Houthi takeover of the country in 2014 and the ensuing full-blown war involving the Saudi-led military coalition, however, movement on the transitional justice law has halted.

Nevertheless, two commissions to address pre-uprising grievances stand out as among the few relatively successful efforts to provide a form of transitional justice in Yemen. These are the Commission on the Forcibly Retired in the Southern Governorates and the Land Commission, both established by Presidential Decree No 2/2013. Following the violent conflicts between the Saleh government and its allies against the southern secessionist movement throughout the 1990s and 2000s, many military and security officers in the South lost their jobs through

---

[71] H Lackner, 'Yemen's "Peaceful" Transition from Autocracy: Could it Have Succeeded?' (Stockholm, International IDEA, 2016) 54.
[72] Abu Al Zulof, above n 23.
[73] Barman, above n 13.

unfair termination of contracts and were thus forced into retirement without pensions. They faced 'cultural, economic and political marginalisation and exploitation by northern elites', causing them to lead a series of street protests together with other forcibly retired state employees, as well as unemployed youth, journalists and other southerners who had suffered at the hands of the Saleh government.[74] Between 2013 and 2014, more than 150,000 applications for compensation were filed and between 95,000 and 100,000 claims were declared valid by the Commission on the Forcibly Retired in the Southern Governorates.[75] Jens Kambeck summarises the success of this commission in responding to the claims filed:

> By November 2014, the Commission [had approved] 17,261 valid claims. All claim-holders are entitled to participate in the financial settlement process. This includes, for example, the continuation of the payment of regular pensions, a new calculation of pensions or salaries in cases where the years in service or ranks had not been calculated correctly, compensation payments, etc. Out of the above valid claims, 13,304 applicants are entitled to reinstatement in their former positions or to promotion into higher ranks.[76]

In addition to the grievances of these forcibly retired army officers in the South, land and property theft was another major grievance that also stemmed from decades of economic marginalisation of the South. Addressing land and property theft was, as Jon Unruh argues, an important symbol of social justice in Yemen, even if it did not result in concrete legal action to return property.[77] Soon after the establishment of the Land Commission, more than 90,000 claims were filed. President Hadi then issued Decree No 253/2013, which established a compensation fund for confiscated land issues and dismissed civil, security and military servants in the southern governorates since July 1994.[78] However, the Houthi-led war in 2015 halted the work of the commissions.

While these two commissions are headed by judges, their mandate does not include a criminal accountability mechanism. The fund established by Hadi in 2013 thus signifies an important reparations effort that acknowledges the wrongful dismissal of army officers as well as the unlawful land confiscations that have taken place since the 1994 war against southern secession. It also represents one, if not the only, transitional justice mechanism to date that has addressed pre-uprising grievances in a systematic manner.

---

[74] J Kambeck, 'Returning to Transitional Justice in Yemen: A Backgrounder on the Commission on the Forcibly Retired in the Southern Governorates' (Center for Applied Research in Partnership with the Orient, 26 July 2016) 7.

[75] ibid 9.

[76] ibid 11.

[77] JD Unruh, 'Mass Claims in Land and Property Following the Arab Spring: Lessons from Yemen' (2016) 5(1) *Stability: International Journal of Security and Development* 2.

[78] Kambeck, above n 77, 22.

Conclusion

In contrast to the corresponding section in the chapters on Egypt, Libya and Tunisia, this section distinguishes between the trigger, driving and shaping factors that led to the decision *not* to prosecute former leaders in Yemen. Using the various factors laid out in this chapter, it is useful to review the pre- and post-uprising factors and actors that led to prosecutorial decisions and drove them in the direction of immunity rather than criminal accountability. Finally, this section reviews the factors that shaped decisions regarding prosecution, in particular the content and extent of transitional justice decisions. The implications of these triggers, drivers and shapers for the transitional justice field of scholarship and practice, including their impact on the peace versus justice debate, will be examined in the next chapter.

Triggers

For regional and international actors, political stability in Yemen and the containment of non-state actors such as AQAP were vital to prevent a bloody transition that could spill over borders. The GCC Initiative, which was borne out of these concerns, triggered the decision not to prosecute political leaders in Yemen. It produced an immunity law that contradicted the provisions of the Yemeni constitution and went against the wishes of victims, their families and supporters.[79] Unlike in Egypt, Libya and Tunisia, popular demands to hold Saleh accountable for crimes committed before and during the uprising rang hollow. These demands, however, could also be regarded as triggers that prompted regional and domestic politicians to issue the immunity law and to uphold it so as to lay the question of prosecuting Saleh to rest.

Drivers

A corrupt and non-independent judiciary, a weak and fragmented justice system, and internal and external politics are just some of the principal drivers behind decisions not to prosecute. Wille mentioned that international actors in support of the immunity law would not fund local organisations that sought criminal accountability.[80] There are, then, active efforts to steer away from decisions to prosecute political leaders in Yemen. However, civil society and human rights

---

[79] See 'Yemenis Protest against Immunity for Saleh', *Al Jazeera*, 22 January 2012, available at www.aljazeera.com/news/middleeast/2012/01/201212210178891840.html.

[80] Wille, above n 26.

activists, particularly those who participated in the Transitional Justice Working Group of the National Dialogue Conference, worked hard to find ways to circumvent the immunity law and to ensure some form of accountability—even if this has meant through the use of a transitional justice mechanism other than prosecutions. Al Kamali's account of these efforts regarding the navigation of the GCC Initiative and the various UN mechanisms attests to this.[81]

Shapers

The overtly negotiated transition in Yemen and the country's complex history of tribal politics resulted in a number of major obstacles to both accountability for pre-2011 crimes and the prosecution of political leaders in general. The most obvious is the immunity law. However, despite the fact that the immunity law was negotiated as a compromise that would see Saleh's removal from power— and from politics altogether—a different transition unfolded in Yemen. As Tayler explained: 'This deal may have avoided bloodshed in the immediate term, but it certainly did not remove Saleh and his allies from power in the dramatic way that I think many who backed this immunity deal had hoped.'[82]

The shaping factors that impacted the decision not to prosecute in Yemen, including the limited scope of crimes addressed in the negotiations, are similar to the factors that triggered and drove the decisions. As human rights lawyers have explained, senior security and police officials are essentially the only individuals who could be held accountable for crimes. International actors—mainly the GCC—and internal politics, particularly the Saleh–Houthi alliance, played major roles in limiting both the content and the extent of potential prosecutions in this way. They helped ensure that high-level government officials, especially Saleh and his aides, would not be tried. But the ambiguous nature of the transition itself significantly shaped decisions regarding prosecution in Yemen. From the removal of the Public Prosecutor presiding over the Friday of Dignity killings case to the negotiators of the immunity law and to the continued assassination of judges and prosecutors, it is clear that while Saleh was removed from his position as head of state, he and individuals loyal to him continued to exert influence on the transition itself. As a result, they also influenced the direction of decisions regarding prosecution by directly interfering in the judiciary's work. Moreover, the precarious security situation in Yemen, long described as being on the brink of another civil war and now fully engaged in such a war, further compounded efforts to ensure that the immunity law remains in place.

That said, many Yemenis, particularly from the South, had better success in achieving a form of social justice. The Land Commission and the Commission

---

[81] Al Kamali, above n 41.
[82] Tayler, above n 19.

on the Forcibly Retired in the Southern Governorates are two examples of serious efforts to address pre-uprising socio-economic grievances. However, it remains to be seen whether the 'ongoing' crimes of enforced disappearances and land theft in other parts of the country will be taken into account by a transitional justice mechanism once the current war comes to an end. For now, movement on the transitional justice law and on the compensation fund for the two commissions has been halted as the country reels from continued airstrikes and attacks by both the Houthis and their allies and the Saudi-led military campaign, backed by weapons and training from the UK and the USA.

6

Reckoning with Transitional Justice

Criminal accountability in the form of trials occupies an important space in the transitional justice of Egypt, Libya, Tunisia and Yemen. Even in countries where leaders have not been toppled, such as Morocco, Bahrain and Syria, questions surrounding the possibility of prosecutions remain prevalent. Thousands of journalists, activists, political dissidents and civil society actors continue to be detained and tried in military and civilian courts throughout the region. In the year following the military coup in Egypt, which overthrew President Mohammed Morsi in 2013, more than 600 of his Muslim Brotherhood supporters along with Morsi himself were put on trial. They were sentenced to death in what was the largest mass death sentencing in Egypt's history.[1] The financial reconciliation deals in Egypt and Tunisia were driven in part by a desire to avoid the prosecution of business tycoons with deep connections to the former and current governing elites. In response to the proposed financial reconciliation bill in Tunisia, mass street protests and a passionate national debate about the merits of criminal accountability ensued. The trial of 37 high-level members of the Gaddafi regime is under review at Libya's Court of Cassation. Confusion abounds surrounding the release of Saif al-Islam Gaddafi following a general amnesty law. Yemenis sought to circumvent the immunity law despite all the obstacles they faced. There is no question, then, that decisions regarding prosecution were central to the Arab Spring.

The importance of negative emotions in transitional justice helps explain the symbolic significance of prosecutions in the Arab Spring. Michaela Mihai's assertion that resentment and indignation are 'politically relevant' emotions for transitional societies explains, in part, the value that Arab civil society, victims, and incoming and outgoing elites have placed on retributive justice. The philosophical and practical meaning of justice will never be defined in the same way by different actors in different contexts. This book has thus focused on *prosecutorial justice*—which is in and of itself a very complex and contested form of justice—in order to illuminate questions of retributive transitional justice. The book in no way attempts to use analysis of prosecutorial justice to make generalisations about justice as it is understood under other transitional justice mechanisms. However, by focusing on justice in the form of criminal trials, questions about it and about

---

[1] 'Egyptians Reel from Mass Death Sentence', *Al Jazeera*, 29 April 2014, available at www.aljazeera.com/news/middleeast/2014/04/egyptians-react-mass-death-sentence-201442951751626248.html.

the foundational assumptions of transitional justice emerge. To what extent can we speak of a 'transition' in the Arab Spring countries, particularly one that does not have attributes typical of the paradigmatic transitions that have largely shaped the transitional justice field? How can effective prosecutions run their course without pre-existing institutional structures that are equipped to implement and oversee them and other transitional justice processes? To what extent can we refer to a 'global accountability norm' when international actors pursue it in one context (Libya) but completely ignore it in another (Yemen)?[2]

This chapter explores these and other questions through a critique of mainstream transitional justice theory with a focus on prosecutions. The findings generated from interviews in each of the four case studies presented in the previous chapters challenge the predominant understanding that transitional justice uniformly occurs in liberalising contexts. The conclusions drawn therefore build on the growing literature that claims that transitional justice is an under-theorised field and needs to be further developed to take into account non-liberal and complex transitions. This chapter advances four principal arguments for how the Arab region cases present the strongest challenge yet to the transitional justice paradigm.

First, the nature of the transitions that took place in the Arab region was non-paradigmatic in that they did not constitute a shift from violent dictatorships to liberal democracies. This warrants a rethinking of transitional justice and its pursuit in varied contexts. Transitions that are at once ruptured as well as negotiated, where the heads of state were ousted but 'deep state' institutions remained intact, produced a complex set of decisions regarding the prosecution of political leaders. Moreover, the shift to a renewed form of repressive, non-liberal rule in several Arab region transitions undermines mainstream transitional justice theory's presumption of a 'return to a liberal state'.[3]

Secondly, the Arab region cases demonstrate that both domestic and international actors pursue competing accountability agendas. Domestic and international wrangling over if, when and how to pursue prosecutions points to the diverse goals of transitional justice actors. This weakens claims that a uniform global accountability norm has gained ground. The contradictory role of international actors in Libya and Yemen—pushing for criminal accountability in the former and immunity in the latter—exemplifies the need to deconstruct the varied objectives of transitional justice actors. Some actors pursue prosecutions within a transitional justice framework that is advocated by international human rights organisations. Many other actors, however, use transitional justice as either a façade to appease public anger without achieving meaningful accountability

---

[2] This question is, of course, more complex than a simple dichotomy and is discussed later in this chapter.
[3] RG Teitel, *Globalizing Transitional Justice: Essays for the New Millennium* (Oxford, Oxford University Press, 2014).

or as a weapon to silence political dissent post-transition. Both scenarios are a product of transitions that, unlike their Latin American counterparts, are marked by a return to—or a renewed form of—repressive rule and continued human rights violations.[4] They also resuscitate the long-debated dilemma surrounding the merits of pursuing peace or justice, or both.

Thirdly, the limited content and extent of the investigations and prosecutions that have taken place in all four case studies further underline the need to develop transitional justice theory. The emphasis on accountability for corruption and economic crimes in Egypt and Tunisia, for instance, points to a practice of selective accountability in order to avoid the prosecution of a more comprehensive set of crimes, particularly those of a civil and political nature. This practice of scapegoating is used by political leaderships with the aim of producing an authoritative image of a break with the former regime. In reality, however, the influence of the *feloul* in Egypt, the *anciens nouveaux* in Tunisia and former President Saleh's political manoeuvrings in Yemen reveal otherwise. The very limited human rights prosecutions that have taken place thus point to the elite-controlled nature of the transitions. Moreover, the focus on crimes committed during the transition in the investigations and trials that have taken place leaves decades of human rights violations unaccounted for.[5] This contributes to the propagation of conflicting narratives regarding legacies of past atrocities, furthering the use of transitional justice to entrench authoritarian rule.

Fourthly, the Arab region cases demonstrate the perils of pursuing prosecutions in the midst of a highly contentious transition. Weak and politicised judiciaries crippled by executive power meddling and inadequate legal frameworks are a principal challenge to the pursuit of fair prosecutions. A rethinking of transitional justice therefore needs to take into account the absence of pre-transition

---

[4] Tunisia is often cited as the exception to this. Nevertheless, the flawed prosecutions, continued politicisation of the judiciary and the re-emergence of *ancien régime* officials in Tunisia's leadership warrant a cautious assessment of the Tunisian transition. See, eg, Human Rights Watch, 'Flawed Accountability: Shortcomings of Tunisia's Trials for Killings during the Uprising' (January 2015) 1, available at www. hrw.org/report/2015/01/12/flawed-accountability/shortcomings-tunisias-trials-killings-during-uprising. More optimistic accounts of the Tunisian transition as a role model for other Arab Spring countries include Editorial, 'Tunisia Becomes a Beacon of Hope', *Boston Globe*, 17 February 2015, available at www.bostonglobe.com/opinion/editorials/2015/02/16/tunisia-becomes-beacon-hope/q4ZJ0VuX-6LljqmYXjcj4pK/story.html; 'Tunisia Polls Offer Arab Spring Ray of Hope', Middle East Eye, 28 October 2014, available at www.middleeasteye.net/news/tunisia-polls-offer-arab-spring-ray-hope-1988403914.

[5] These human rights violations have been documented by many Egyptian civil society organisations, including the Egyptian Organization for Human Rights (www.eohr.org); the Cairo Institute for Human Rights Studies (www.cihrs.org); the Egyptian Initiative for Personal Rights (www.eipr.org); the Arabic Network for Human Rights Information (http://anhri.net); and the Nadeem Center for the Treatment and Rehabilitation of Victims of Violence (http://alnadeem.org). They have also been documented extensively by Amnesty International and Human Rights Watch. For accounts of systematic torture in Egypt, see, eg, Human Rights Watch, 'Behind Closed Doors: Torture and Detention in Egypt' (July 1991) available at www.hrw.org/sites/default/files/reports/Egypt927.pdf; Human Rights Watch, 'Work on Him Until he Confesses: Impunity for Torture in Egypt' (30 January 2011) available at www. hrw.org/report/2011/01/30/work-him-until-he-confesses/impunity-torture-egypt.

democratic institutions and what this means for criminal accountability prospects in such non-paradigmatic transitional contexts.

The key factors that triggered, drove and shaped decisions regarding the prosecution of political leaders in Egypt, Libya, Tunisia and Yemen have been identified in previous chapters. As explained in chapter 1, the trigger–driver–shaper mechanism is used as a general prism of analysis. Far from comprehensive, it is a prism through which the research collected is analysed and by which an explanation is developed of how decisions regarding the prosecution of political leaders emerged and evolved before, during and after the highly contentious period of transition.[6] First, it is worth briefly reviewing the triggers, drivers and shapers identified in each case study. An analysis of the implications of the case study findings for transitional justice follows.

Egypt

The criminal cases of Emad El Kebir and Khaled Said were triggers that opened up the possibility of holding the police, a much-feared arm of the Ministry of Interior, criminally accountable. In addition, the Kifaya movement in 2005 and the 6 April Youth Movement in 2008 served as triggers in the form of social movements that grew over time and were marked by periodic protests, or 'mini-uprisings'.[7] Emad El Kebir, Khaled Said, the Kifaya and the 6 April movements thus served as some of the most influential trigger factors that led to the 2011 uprising and stronger demands for criminal accountability and social justice.

During and immediately after the 2011 uprising, public pressure and individual plaintiffs, particularly those working in established NGOs, were the major drivers of decisions regarding prosecution in Egypt. Sustained protests forced interim authorities to allow some highly symbolic prosecutions in order to appease public anger and to create an image of a break with the past. Individual lawyers also played a significant role in initiating prosecutions, thus simultaneously serving as triggers. Together, these triggers and drivers pushed the judiciary and interim military authorities to respond by allowing certain prosecutions of high-level government officials.

A number of shapers impacted on the content and extent of decisions regarding prosecution in Egypt. Explicit demands for socio-economic accountability by the protesters, a politicised judiciary and public prosecutor, a weak legal framework and a military-controlled transition all shaped the limited content and extent of prosecutions in Egypt.

---

[6] See the Methodology section in chapter 1.

[7] The Mahalla strike and protests in 2008 is often described as an uprising or revolt. See O El Sharnoubi, 'Revolutionary History Relived: The Mahalla Strike of 6 April 2008', *Ahram Online*, 6 April 2013.

Tunisia

At least three events in Tunisia's past triggered the momentum behind decisions to prosecute the country's leaders. The 1978 general strike, the Baraket Essahel torture practices in 1991 and the Gafsa revolt of 2008 each fuelled resistance to repression and civil society advocacy for accountability for human rights violations. Moreover, public pressure during the uprising and also immediately following Ben Ali's ouster was the strongest trigger that led to decisions to prosecute.[8]

The Groupe de 25's early efforts, immediately following Ben Ali's ouster, were successful in driving decisions regarding prosecution. Continued protests and pressure from victims' families made it difficult for interim authorities to ignore the question of prosecutions. The appeasement of public anger was therefore also a key driver of decisions regarding prosecution.[9]

The shapers in Tunisia included the dire socio-economic situation, which led to an emphasis on corruption and economic crimes in the charges, and the prospect of a Truth and Dignity Commission, which many relied on as the mechanism that would cover the human rights violations that the prosecutions thus far failed to address. Much like Egypt, financial reconciliation with corrupt business tycoons, and a politicised judiciary and public prosecutor also limited the content and extent of prosecutions. Furthermore, a lack of command responsibility provisions led to many acquittals and light sentences. Finally, a transition that increasingly saw the return of the *anciens nouveaux*—ex-Ben Ali regime officials—meant that human rights prosecutions in particular, but also corruption prosecutions, would be limited to protecting those with former regime ties.

Libya

The 1996 Abu Salim prison massacre and the impunity its perpetrators enjoyed for years served as a powerful trigger for subsequent decisions regarding prosecution. Moreover, the highly symbolic arrest of Fathi Terbil on 15 February 2011 attests to the critical role of individual lawyers in triggering decisions regarding prosecution. The International Criminal Court's (ICC) issue of arrest warrants for

---

[8] Interview with Amna Guellali, Tunisia and Algeria Researcher, Human Rights Watch (telephone interview, 23 April 2012); interview with Solène Rougeaux, Director, Avocats Sans Frontières, Tunis Office (Tunis, Tunisia, 25 April 2012); interview with Abderrahman El Yessa, Democratic Governance Advisor, UNDP Tunisia (Tunis, Tunisia, 26 April 2012); interview with Anis Mahfoudh, Human Rights Officer, OHCHR, Tunisia (Tunis, Tunisia, 27 April 2012); interview with Habib Nassar, Middle East and North Africa Director, International Center for Transitional Justice (New York City, New York, 18 May 2012); interview with anonymous senior employee of the Tunisian Ministry of Foreign Affairs (2012).

[9] Nassar, above n 8.

three Libyan high-level officials was also cited as a factor that triggered domestic decisions to prosecute.

Individual lawyers also drove decisions regarding prosecution by filing legal complaints and participating in protests calling for accountability. In addition, the advocacy efforts of organisations such as Amnesty International were vital to pressuring the government to respond by allowing the public prosecution to initiate investigations and trials. Persistent public pressure—mostly by families of the victims of Abu Salim and of other torture crimes in Libya—were also influential in driving decisions to prosecute.

Legal challenges, a precarious security situation, and a deep mistrust of the judiciary's ability to operate independently and effectively all contributed to the limited content and extent of the prosecutions. The continued violence that has gripped Libya since 2011, chaotic militia politics and rival governments constitute a transition whose direction is uncertain and in which decisions regarding prosecution are in flux.

Yemen

International actors, preoccupied with the preservation of political stability in Yemen and the region, triggered the decision not to prosecute political leaders in the form of an immunity law.[10] Unlike in Egypt, Libya and Tunisia, popular demands to hold Saleh accountable for crimes committed before and during the uprising rang hollow. These demands, however, were also triggers that prompted regional and domestic politicians to issue the immunity law so as to lay the question of prosecuting Saleh to rest. A corrupt, fragmented and tribal judiciary and domestic and regional politics were some of the principal drivers behind decisions not to prosecute. International actors and internal politics played a major role in limiting both the content and the extent of potential prosecutions. They helped ensure that high-level government officials, particularly Saleh and his regime, would not be tried. But the ambiguous nature of the transition itself significantly shaped decisions regarding prosecution in Yemen. From the removal of the Public Prosecutor presiding over the Friday of Dignity killings case to the negotiators of the immunity law and the continued assassination of judges and prosecutors, it is clear that while Saleh was removed from his position as head of state, he and individuals loyal to him continued to exert influence on the transition itself.[11] As a result, they also influenced the direction of decisions regarding prosecution.

---

[10] Law No 1 of 2012 Concerning the Granting of Immunity from Legal and Judicial Prosecution, Amnesty International (22 January 2012) available at https://www.amnesty.org/download/Documents/24000/mde310072012ar.pdf (in Arabic).

[11] PRI, for example, reports: 'Saleh, a strongman who ran Yemen for 33 years, stepped down in 2011 after a wave of popular protests. But if demonstrations drove him from office, they failed to

Moreover, the precarious security situation in Yemen, compounded by the ongoing war, worsened the prospects for any reversal of the immunity law.

* * *

The factors identified in each case study above reveal that while the triggers and drivers—particularly in Egypt, Libya and Tunisia—are marked by traditional motives for a more just, liberal democratic order, the shapers paint a more complex picture that presents a significant challenge to mainstream transitional justice theory. The various shaping factors that pushed and pulled decisions regarding the prosecution of political leaders in different, and even opposing, directions are a strong indication that different actors have been fiercely battling each other for competing visions of transitional justice—and of criminal justice in particular.

Rather than serving as a 'liberalising ritual', transitional justice can be—and, indeed, has been—employed by both pre- and post-transition leadership figures as a political tool to consolidate or renew repressive rule.[12] On the other hand, actors such as domestic human rights organisations and individual lawyers push for prosecutions within a transitional justice framework that they regard as an opportunity for genuine accountability for past atrocities. For the leadership figures exerting control over the transition so as to preserve the status quo or to consolidate their power, the absence of independent judicial institutions to carry out investigations and trials was an essential factor that aided their cause. For human rights actors vying for individual criminal accountability for former leaders and other high-level government, police and military officials, weak and politicised judiciaries have obviously posed a major obstacle to their cause.

Non-paradigmatic Transitions

The complex nature of the transitions that took place in the Arab region warrants a rethinking of transitional justice and of its pursuit in varied contexts. The Arab transitions do not fall within the paradigmatic framework for transitions that is marked by a shift from authoritarian to liberal democratic rule. Ahmed Nader Nadery warns that 'we must take care to distinguish the nature of each transition,

---

drive him from power. Thanks to the flawed immunity deal he signed in exchange for resigning, Saleh still lives in Yemen, heads its biggest political party and retains a network of well-placed friends, family and cronies'. PRI, 'The Man Accused of Stealing $60 Billion from Yemen is Still There and Wielding Power', *The World*, 2 April 2015, available at www.pri.org/stories/2015-04-02/man-accused-stealing-60-billion-yemen-still-there-and-wielding-power.

[12] T Obel Hansen, 'Transitional Justice: Toward a Differentiated Theory' (2011) 13 *Oregon Review of International Law* 1.

lest we mistakenly import the lessons of one context into another'.[13] Transitions that are both ruptured and negotiated, where the heads of state are ousted but the oppressive state institutions remain intact, produce a complex set of decisions regarding the prosecution of political leaders. They are, as Nassar and others have described them, 'ambiguous transitions'.[14] The ambiguity in Libya and Yemen primarily lies in the uncertain direction of the politics of the transitions, the ongoing violent conflicts there and the actors that hold sway in decisions regarding prosecution. In Egypt and Tunisia, the continued presence of certain influential political actors and institutions, despite dramatic changes at the head-of-state level, has shaped decisions regarding prosecution. The police, military, state security agencies and judiciary are among such institutions that largely escaped reform and have morphed into renewed versions of authoritarianism.[15]

The shaping role of such deep state institutions points to the divergent objectives of various transitional justice actors. Their lingering influence on decisions regarding prosecution puts into question the merits of the transitional justice industry's advocacy for accountability mechanisms rooted in liberal values. Lingering or remnant political actors include, but are not limited to, the judiciary, military and Mubarak loyalists in Egypt; the judiciary and the *anciens nouveaux* politicians in Tunisia; and Saleh and his political and tribal loyalists in Yemen. Gaddafi loyalists make up part of General Haftar's army in Libya. Cherif Bassiouni usefully summarises the ambiguity of the Arab Spring transitions:

> The difficulty in the Arab world is that there have not been fundamental changes in the different countries' political systems because previous regimes, whenever removed, have either simply survived, morphed into the new regimes or continued to hold influence over what appear to be new regimes. Consequently, there is a vested interest in both the old and new regimes to avoid publicizing past misdeeds and to cover up human rights violations and, for that matter, crimes under national and international law … the interests of actors in prior regimes remain powerful in those Arab states where change has occurred.[16]

It is important to note here that the ambiguity of the Arab Spring transitions is not new. In the early transitional justice literature, scholars tended to explain the likelihood of prosecutions based on whether or not the country in question

---

[13] AN Nadery, 'Editorial Note: In the Aftermath of International Intervention: A New Era for International Justice?' (2011) 5 *International Journal of Transitional Justice* 171.

[14] H Nassar, 'Transitional Justice in the Wake of the Arab Uprisings: Between Complexity and Standardisation' in KJ Fisher and R Stewart (eds), *Transitional Justice and the Arab Spring* (London, Routledge, 2014).

[15] There have been constitutional amendments that, to some degree, strengthen the independence of the judiciary. Despite these amendments, however, political alliances and the absence of the separation of powers remain. See, eg, International Bar Association Human Rights Institute, 'Separating Law and Politics: Challenges to the Independence of Judges and Prosecutors in Egypt' (February 2014); International Commission of Jurists, 'The Independence and Accountability of the Tunisian Judicial System: Learning from the Past to Build a Better Future' (May 2014).

[16] M Cherif Bassiouni, 'Editorial' (2014) 8 *International Journal of Transitional Justice* 325, 335–36.

experienced a ruptured or a negotiated transition. This approach has waned. As scholars took a closer look at what happened in the Latin American transitions, it became clearer that even in the orthodox ruptured case of Argentina, where an explicit military defeat took place, the transition was both ruptured and pacted. The Argentinian military and the post-transition governments negotiated decisions regarding prosecution, resulting in the initial wave of amnesties, which were then followed by many prosecutions—some of which were still taking place at the time of writing. Skaar's account of the role of judicial reform over time is useful here, as it highlights the relationship between the ebbs and flows of prosecutions in Argentina and developments in the establishment of the independence of the judiciary over time.[17] The 'paradigmatic transition' from 'violent conflict to peace and democracy', then, was never an adequate framework for the analysis of varied transitions and their transitional justice decisions.[18]

Given the non-paradigmatic nature of these transitions, is it helpful to speak of a *transition* to begin with? While Thomas Carothers' critique of the transition paradigm is made within the context of the democratisation discourse and practice, it nevertheless provides an important analytical framework for transitional justice and the Arab Spring. Carothers observes that most states labelled as 'transitional' are in fact not transitioning to liberal democracy; they may be considered formerly authoritarian, but that does not mean they are on an inevitable and definitive path to democracy.[19] He critiques the tendency of policy makers to assess a state's 'progress' in its transition through a prescribed measurement of democratisation that many states do not necessarily follow.[20] Instead, most states tend to fall within a 'gray zone' marked by a 'precarious middle ground between full-fledged democracy and outright dictatorship'.[21] They do not neatly follow the paradigmatic transitional path from authoritarianism to liberal democracy. Carothers warns: 'The continued use of the transition paradigm constitutes a dangerous habit of trying to impose a simplistic and often incorrect conceptual order on an empirical tableau of considerable complexity.'[22]

Moreover, Carothers continues, some of the principal components of a democratising society, such as judicial reform and civil society strengthening, do not conform to rational sequences resulting in democratisation. Rather, they are 'chaotic processes of change that go backwards and sideways as much as forward, and do not do so in any regular manner'.[23] This is unsettling for policy makers. It is

---

[17] E Skaar, *Judicial Independence and Human Rights in Latin America* (New York, Palgrave MacMillan 2011).

[18] C Bell, C Campbell and F Ni Aolain, 'Justice Discourses in Transition' (2004) 13 *Social and Legal Studies* 305, 310.

[19] T Carothers 'The End of the Transition Paradigm' (2002) 13 *Journal of Democracy* 5, 7.

[20] ibid 8.

[21] ibid 18.

[22] ibid 15.

[23] ibid.

particularly unsettling for transitional justice practitioners, who seek to implement a transitional justice framework in 'transitional' societies with a view to setting them on a non-existent path to democracy. As Catherine Turner notes, transitional justice's weakness lies in its binary oppositions: the assumption that we are moving from a state of war (violence) to a state of peace (law), and the false assumption that violence and law are mutually exclusive.[24]

The temporal significance of transitions therefore needs to be examined in the context of the Arab Spring countries if we are to better understand how transitional justice processes unfold. Transitional countries apply an exceptional justice to deal with exceptional circumstances.[25] Teitel describes this policy as 'extraordinary justice'.[26] In the Arab Spring cases, however, the circumstances calling for justice were not exceptional as such. In fact, they were the norm for the decades since independence from colonial rule. The protesters in Egypt, Libya, Tunisia and Yemen were struggling against post-colonial authoritarianism. The popular nature of the uprisings thus prompted Hamid Dabashi to declare the end of post-colonialism, whilst acknowledging the open-ended nature of the Arab Spring 'transitions'.[27] Nassar points to this important difference between the Arab Spring transitions and others that preceded them: the Arab region is dealing with the legacy of atrocities committed under multiple regimes, whereas most transitions in the rest of the world have dealt with the legacy of a single regime or conflict.[28] Nassar's observation is important as it indicates the impossibility of a 'return to a liberal state'[29] because in all four case studies there was no liberal state to begin with. The decades of atrocities committed under multiple regimes, Nassar argues, will require creativity that today's transitional justice models do not offer.[30]

National dialogue attempts aimed at forming truth and reconciliation mechanisms in Egypt, Libya and Yemen have faltered because of the controversial question of how far back the past they should go. Have Egypt, Libya, Tunisia and Yemen been in 'transition' since independence? Is this why Tunisia's Truth and Dignity Commission (TDC) mandate extends to crimes committed since 1955? Such questions make it more difficult to apply the transitional justice paradigm to the Arab region cases, especially as transitional and post-transitional political actors are often implicated in the multiple legacies of atrocities, making effective accountability measures that much more challenging. The heavy focus in the

---

[24] C Turner, *Violence, Law and the Impossibility of Transitional Justice* (Oxford, Routledge, 2016) 69, 166.

[25] H van der Merwe and MB Lykes, 'Transitional Justice Processes as Teachable Moments' (2016) 10 *International Journal of Transitional Justice*, 361, 362.

[26] RG Teitel, *Transitional Justice* (Oxford, Oxford University Press, 2000) 6.

[27] H Dabashi, *The Arab Spring: The End of Postcolonialism* (London, Zed Books, 2012); N Aboueldahab, 'The Legacy of Bandung: The Arab Spring in Perspective' in L Eslava, M Fakhri and V Nesiah (eds), *Bandung, Global History and International Law: Critical Pasts and Pending Futures* (Cambridge, Cambridge University Press, forthcoming).

[28] Nassar, above n 14, 59.

[29] Teitel, above n 26, 67.

[30] Nassar, above n 14, 59.

investigations and prosecutions thus far on crimes committed during the transition is a strategy led by elites to further bury the past (their past) and instead foreground the exceptional circumstance—that is, the temporary period of the uprisings in 2010 and 2011 that led up to the ouster of all four leaders.

This question of transitioning *from what* and transitioning *to what* is worth briefly visiting here.[31] Catherine Turner draws attention to the temporality of transitional justice in the critical scholarship. She refers to 'the extent to which we can ever speak of a before and after of transition, and the ways in which past, present and future intersect in the transitional context'.[32] Rosemary Nagy's account of the South African Truth and Reconciliation Commission and of the Saddam Hussein trial in Iraq is also insightful in that she points out the selective focus on crimes committed within a certain period as well as the problem of continued political violence, human rights violations,and socio-economic inequalities. Nagy explains:

> Transitional justice ... implies a fixed interregnum period with a distinct end; it bridges a violent or repressive past and a peaceful, democratic future. Notions of 'breaking with the past' and 'never again', which align with the dominant transitional mechanisms, mould a definitive sense of 'now' and 'then'. This can problematically obscure continuities of violence and exclusion. ... In Iraq and Afghanistan the transition is constructed as being 'from' a repressive police state under Saddam Hussein or 'from' cycles of war and repression culminating in the Taliban regime. This neatly avoids the current matter of foreign military intervention and implies that the transitional problem has to do with 'then' and not the 'now' of occupation, insurgency, and the war on terror ... Although prosecution, vetting, reparation and truth-telling are taking or will take place in the midst of violence and insecurity, the concern of these transitional mechanisms is the history before 2001 in Afghanistan and before 2003 in Iraq. The 'to' of transitional justice is thus insulated from the current reasons for instability.[33]

The question of time, then, emerges as a contentious feature of transitional justice decisions, which, as Nagy illustrates above, already has a history of limiting decisions regarding prosecution. The patchy extent of the prosecutions in Egypt, Libya, Tunisia and Yemen demonstrate that decisions regarding prosecution have for the most part been guided by a reckoning with the transition itself, rather than with what brought about the transition to begin with.

Many of the challenges to the prosecution of political leaders in pre-transition Egypt, Libya, Tunisia and Yemen are, with a few important exceptions, similar to the post-transition challenges to prosecution. These challenges include lack of judicial independence, crimes that continue to be orchestrated and/or perpetrated by the regime, violent crackdowns on civil society, victims' fear of the repercussions

[31] See R Nagy, 'Transitional Justice as Global Project: Critical Reflections' (2008) 29 *Third World Quarterly* 275; C Turner, 'Transitional Justice and Critique' in D Jacobs, C Lawther and L Mofrett (eds), *Research Handbook on Transitional Justice* (Surrey, Edward Elgar, forthcoming 2017).
[32] Turner, ibid.
[33] Nagy, above n 31, 280.

for filing complaints against high-level government officials and legal obstacles, such as the absence of command responsibility provisions. The continued existence of these challenges is indicative of the ambiguous nature of the transitions and the role this plays in shaping decisions regarding prosecutions and making them more limited. In other words, without a definitive resolution of these challenges, the so-called transition offers no real change in its institutions and human rights practices. Consequently, decisions regarding prosecution remain severely limited and politicised.

Despite these challenges, however, pre-transition efforts to hold perpetrators to account have, with the exception of Yemen, trickled into post-2011 efforts to prosecute. Egypt's *Khaled Said* case, Tunisia's *Baraket Essahel* case, and Libya's *Abu Salim prison massacre* case are all examples of prosecutions targeting mid-to-high-level government and police officials that, despite an exceedingly difficult and repressive environment for civil society to work within, were revived post-transition.[34] Of note here is that the incidents that led to these iconic cases were also cited as major triggers that eventually led to decisions to prosecute high-level officials in Egypt, Libya and Tunisia. These triggers, which were marked by the public outrage they created and the tireless efforts of civil society and individual lawyers to ensure accountability for them, were milestones in the long and difficult road to accountability for political leaders in these countries. This is why it is crucial to identify pre-transition triggers and to analyse their impact, if any, in subsequent decisions to prosecute former political leaders. They point to the significant role that public pressure and civil society efforts play in sustaining the momentum behind certain iconic cases over time, which also in one way or another served as triggers of post-transition decisions to prosecute political leaders.

Decisions to prosecute former leaders were taken in three of the four case studies. If transitional justice was only pursued in a liberalising direction, what could explain the opaque and politicised prosecutions of Mubarak, Ben Ali, Saif al-Islam Gaddafi and their aides? While there is no single answer to this question, calls for greater attention to the various claims of transitional justice are important for a better understanding of the motives behind prosecution decisions in the Arab region. Rather than serve as a mechanism to help transitional societies overcome past atrocities, decisions regarding the prosecution of political leaders in the Arab region exhibit a divergence in objectives from the classical cases of Latin America.[35] They largely represent transitions to non-liberal and repressive rule, contrary to the liberalising ritual of transitional states elsewhere.[36]

In the case of Egypt, for instance, transitional justice has been used to entrench repressive rule and to propagate conflicting historical narratives regarding legacies

---

[34] See chapters 2–4 for details on each of these cases.

[35] It is important to re-emphasise here that the Latin American cases should not be considered as a homogeneous set of transitions. The Latin American transitions varied considerably both in how they unfolded and in the transitional justice decisions they undertook. However, mainstream transitional justice theory has elevated certain cases to 'core' status, thereby shaping the field considerably.

[36] Again, perhaps, with the exception of Tunisia.

of injustice. Since the toppling of former President Mubarak in 2011, both military-backed transitional governments (2011–12 and again in 2013–14) and the one-year rule of President Morsi (2012–13) oversaw widespread human rights abuses. In November 2012, Morsi issued a highly controversial presidential decree that effectively removed the separation of executive, legislative and judicial powers.[37] A repressive protest law, which grants security forces sweeping powers to ban protests through the use of lethal force, effectively putting an end to any kind of dissent and freedom of assembly, was issued in 2013 under the interim President Adly Mansour.[38] Moreover, the biggest mass killing in Egyptian modern history, the Raba'a massacre of August 2013 where over 800 Muslim Brotherhood supporters were killed, continues to be marked by impunity.[39] On the other hand, since the ouster of President Morsi by the military in July 2013, thousands of people have been arrested and detained without trial, while crackdowns on student protesters, journalists the media and NGOs are endemic and have become institutionalised.[40] At a mass trial in 2014, the judge sentenced 683 alleged Muslim Brotherhood supporters to death—the largest mass death sentencing in recent times.[41] There is no doubt that the trial was highly politicised: it lasted eight minutes, the majority of defendants were absent, the judge did not review evidence and defence lawyers were not allowed to cross-examine witnesses.[42] The trial was presided over by Judge Saeed Yousef, fittingly also known as *al gazzar* ('the butcher').[43]

In Tunisia, most of the 20 senior government officials who faced prosecution have been set free.[44] Ousted Tunisian President Ben Ali continues to live in Saudi Arabia, which has ignored all extradition requests from Tunisia. In Libya, 37 former regime officials, including Saif al-Islam Gaddafi and El Senussi, were tried and verdicts were issued in 2015. In Yemen, repeated calls for Saleh to be put on trial have been ignored. Saleh's continuous violation of the terms of the immunity

---

[37] For an English translation of the constitutional declaration, see 'English Text of Morsi's Constitutional Declaration', *Ahram Online*, 22 November 2012, available at http://english.ahram.org.eg/NewsContent/1/64/58947/Egypt/Politics-/English-text-of-Morsis-Constitutional-Declaration-.aspx. After intense protests, this decree was annulled in December 2012.

[38] Law 107/2013. For more on the human rights implications of this law, see Amnesty International, 'Egypt: New Protest law Gives Security Forces Free Rein' (25 November 2013), available at www.amnesty.org/en/news/egypt-new-protest-law-gives-security-forces-free-rein-2013-11-25.

[39] For a detailed report on this massacre, see Human Rights Watch, 'All According to Plan: The Rab'a Massacre and Mass Killings in Egypt' (12 August 2014) available at www.hrw.org/node/127942.

[40] S Abdel Kouddous, 'Egypt's 1984' (Sada, Carnegie Endowment for International Peace, 28 October 2014), available at http://carnegieendowment.org/sada/index.cfm?fa=show&article=57051&solr_hilite=.

[41] See n 1 above.

[42] M Michael and M Thabet, 'Egypt Mass Trial: Judge Sentences 683 to Death in Single Mass Trial', *Huffington Post*, 28 April 2014, available at www.huffingtonpost.com/2014/04/28/egypt-mass-trial_n_5224509.html.

[43] N Aboueldahab, 'Egypt: Justice on Death Row', *Al Jazeera*, 17 July 2014, available at www.aljazeera.com/indepth/opinion/2014/07/egypt-transitional-justice-201471693143435510.html.

[44] C Gall, 'Questions of Justice in Tunisia as Ousted Leaders are Freed', *New York Times*, 16 July 2014, available at www.nytimes.com/2014/07/17/world/africa/questions-of-justice-in-tunisia-as-ousted-leaders-are-freed.html.

agreement—namely, that he disengage from practising politics—has been met with silence.

It is clear, then, that the Arab region transitions do not constitute a return to a liberal state, nor do they constitute a transition in a new liberalising direction. Instead, they are marked by regimes that have reincarnated into themselves. Despite this ambiguous state of affairs, a break with the past has taken place *to some extent* in each case study, and formal decisions to prosecute political leaders or not have been taken. The toppling of leaders as a result of a massive uprising and the subsequent initiation of a political transition constitute this partial break, although the drastic measures taken to remove any and all remnants of the Gaddafi regime have meant that a more comprehensive break has taken place in Libya. However, the absence of pre-existing institutional structures that are equipped to implement genuine transitional justice measures means that it is time to assess whether we should discard the transition paradigm altogether[45] or call for an internal transformation of the paradigm so that it accommodates such varied contexts.

Whose Transitional Justice?

Globally, the number of prosecutions of political leaders has increased significantly.[46] Since 1990, more than 85 heads of state have been prosecuted.[47] The subsequent prosecutions of Mubarak and Ben Ali add to these numbers. But the statistic on its own overlooks the complex motives behind such trials and, perhaps more importantly, it overlooks how and why various actors struggle for competing visions of transitional justice. The unfolding of transitional justice in the Arab region, and particularly decisions regarding prosecution, has been politically charged.

As the case studies demonstrate, various factors pushed and pulled decisions regarding the prosecution of political leaders in different and even opposing directions. These drivers and shapers are thus examples of the different actors that fiercely battled each other for competing visions of transitional justice—and of criminal justice in particular. Obel Hansen rightly urges a closer examination of the 'horizontal expansion' or 'proliferation' of transitional justice actors to better understand these competing transitional justice discourses and practices.[48]

---

[45] Carothers, above n 19, 17.

[46] EL Lutz and C Reiger (eds), *Prosecuting Heads of State* (New York, Cambridge University Press, 2009).

[47] ibid 2. Lutz and Reiger state that 67 heads of state were prosecuted between 1990 and 2008. At least three additional heads of state have been prosecuted since 2008, along with a slew of other high-level political leaders.

[48] T Obel Hansen, 'The Vertical and Horizontal Expansion of Transitional Justice: Explanations and Implications for a Contested Field' in S Buckley-Zistel, TK Beck, C Braun and F Mieth (eds), *Transitional Justice Theories* (Abingdon, Routledge, 2014) 108.

The Arab region cases present an important opportunity to better examine the nuances of transitional justice.

The key domestic actors involved in decisions regarding prosecution were individual lawyers, civil society organisations and victims on the one hand, and the judiciary, transitional and post-transitional leadership officials on the other.[49] The former group of actors shares the motive of seeking criminal accountability for former leaders; the latter group of actors has largely attempted to block prosecutions, or at least to severely limit their content and extent. As a result, a highly contentious process of prosecution took shape in the Arab region cases, with these two groups of actors often clashing with each other. Subotic identifies three domestic groups of actors in the overall process of decisions regarding prosecution, which are also useful in describing the competing domestic actors in the Arab region:

> how elites go about engaging in transitional justice is the result of specific domestic power structures and coalitions. The contested process of transitional justice adoption defines domestic elites along three major groups: justice resisters, justice instrumentalists and true believers. Which domestic group comes out on top in the domestic political battle will determine what approach to transitional justice elites undertake and to what policy effect.[50]

The various civil society actors, lawyers, interim elites, military actors and judges largely fall within the three categories outlined by Subotic above. The unfolding of decisions regarding prosecution before, during and immediately after the Arab Spring uprisings is thus marked by such tensions between justice resisters, justice instrumentalists and true believers.

The interview responses across the four case studies indicate that civil society actors advocated for fair and effective prosecutions of former leaders. Given the repressive environment within which civil society actors had to work, however, their primary role, particularly in the pre-transition period, was to document human rights violations by the regime and its associated state agencies. The objective was to raise awareness and put pressure on governments to change their human rights practices. Eid and El Shewy explained that, despite working with a politicised judiciary, the aim of civil society documentation was to have enough evidence so that 'one day', when an independent judiciary is in place, 'we will be able to prosecute'.[51] As a result, documentation was the 'most powerful tool' for a civil society struggling under authoritarian rule.[52] Scholars differ on the extent to

---

[49] The military is a crucial additional factor in the case of Egypt.

[50] J Subotic, 'Bargaining Justice: A Theory of Transitional Justice Compliance' in Buckley-Zistel et al, above n 49, 128.

[51] Interview with Gamal Eid, human rights lawyer, activist and Director of the Arabic Network for Human Rights Information (Cairo, Egypt, 8 December 2013); interview with Mohamed El Shewy, Transitional Justice Programme Officer, Egyptian Initiative for Personal Rights (telephone interview, 24 November 2013).

[52] El Shewy, ibid; see chapter 3 for a more detailed discussion of the responses regarding the role of civil society and documentation.

which civil society actors impact decisions regarding prosecution. The findings from the Arab region cases largely confirm Pion-Berlin and others' contention that political leadership preferences trump those of 'interest groups', or civil society and other domestic actors.[53] This does not, however, diminish the impact of civil society pressure in driving prosecutions.

Discussions in the emerging scholarship on transitional justice decisions in the Arab region largely overlook this proliferation of actors that drive and shape transitional justice decisions. One example is Line Khatib's critique of the rise of political Islamists in the Arab Spring countries and the allegedly harmful challenge they pose to the transitional justice process. However, casting Islamists as opponents of a liberal transitional justice process diminishes the crucial role they played in shaping and challenging the scope of these processes. For instance, what does the rise of Islamism in the Arab Spring reveal about the shortcomings of transitional justice, or even of international human rights? How should we understand the tensions between 'communal forms of justice', as promoted by the Islamists Khatib examines, and individual freedoms in the context of transitional justice and political Islamism?[54] Khatib seems to solely explore whether Islamism is an appropriate political ideology for the pursuit of transitional justice, while being largely uncritical of the so-called universal concepts of justice and of transitional justice itself.[55] Moreover, many accounts point to the central role Islamists in Tunisia played in expanding the mandate of the TDC to cover both the Bourguiba and Ben Ali eras, during which Islamists were heavily repressed.[56] Many of the Abu Salim prisoners in Libya were also Islamists and their families have pushed for criminal accountability for years. The deconstruction of the various domestic actors involved in decisions regarding prosecution is thus vital to understanding that the origins of competing agendas of transitional justice are much more complex than simply battling visions between liberal proponents of transitional justice and 'illiberal' actors.

Domestic and International Advocates of Competing Visions of Transitional Justice

The pursuit of individual criminal accountability for past atrocities in transitional justice contexts often draws the involvement of international actors. Much has

---

[53] D Pion-Berlin, 'To Prosecute or to Pardon? Human Rights Decisions in the Latin American Southern Cone' in NJ Kritz (ed), *Transitional Justice: How Emerging Democracies Reckon with Former Regimes*, vol 1 (Washington DC, United States Institute of Peace 1995) 83–84.

[54] L Khatib (2014) 'Challenges of Representation and Inclusion: A Case Study of Islamist Groups in Transitional Justice' in Fisher and Stewart, above n 14, 135.

[55] ibid.

[56] G Barbone in N Aboueldahab, 'Rapporteur's Report: Prosecutions, Politics and Transitions: How Criminal Justice in the Arab Spring is Shaping Transitional Justice', panel discussion, Durham Law School, 6 May 2014, available at www.academia.edu/8738334/Rapporteurs_Report_Prosecutions_Politics_and_Transitions_-_How_criminal_justice_in_the_Arab_Spring_is_shaping_transitional_justice; CK Lamont, 'The Scope and Boundaries of Transitional Justice' in C Sriram (ed), *Transitional Justice in the Middle East and North Africa* (Oxford, Oxford University Press, 2016) 95.

been discussed about the role of international NGOs such as Amnesty International and Human Rights Watch, regional bodies such as the Inter-American Commission on Human Rights, international tribunals such as the ICC and intergovernmental bodies such as the UN and its various agencies as some of the key international actors that work to promote accountability for past human rights violations. This promotion is often conducted through transnational networks made up of these actors and that work to ensure accountability at the domestic level, where possible, or at the international level, where necessary. The prevailing assumption is that international (or 'transnational') actors actively seek the fulfilment of a well-established and shared norm—that of individual criminal accountability, or the global accountability norm.[57]

International actors, particularly in the case of Libya and Yemen, thus constitute another set of influential actors that drove and shaped decisions regarding prosecution. Their objectives, however, were not consistent throughout all four Arab region cases. Libya and Yemen demonstrate that the influence of international actors on domestic decisions regarding prosecution can have—and, indeed, has had—very different outcomes. The involvement of the ICC in Libya, although fiercely resisted by certain domestic actors, drove domestic decisions to prosecute 37 high-level members of the former Gaddafi regime.[58] The involvement of the GCC, the US, the EU and the UN had the opposite effect in Yemen, where they championed the negotiation of a deal granting immunity for the former president and his aides. Thanks in large part to the Yemeni immunity law, domestic efforts to launch prosecutions of former political leaders for human rights violations committed before and during the 2011 uprising have been continuously blocked.[59] Just as there are competing objectives regarding criminal justice among domestic actors, so too are there competing accountability preferences among international actors. The starkly opposing justice strategies in Libya and Yemen, often by the very same international actors, weaken the international community's claim to a global accountability norm.

Why did some of the same international actors who advocated for criminal accountability in Libya almost simultaneously back an immunity deal in Yemen? The UN Security Council requested the ICC to investigate crimes committed

---

[57] See C Collins, 'Grounding Global Justice: International Networks and Domestic Human Rights Accountability in Chile and El Salvador' (2006) 38 *Journal of Latin American Studies* 711; ME Keck and K Sikkink, 'Transnational Advocacy Networks in International and Regional Politics' (1999) 51 *International Social Science Journal* 89; P Arthur, 'How "Transitions" Reshaped Human Rights: A Conceptual History of Transitional Justice' (2009) 31 *Human Rights Quarterly* 321, 359; K Sikkink, 'Patterns of Dynamic Multilevel Governance and the Insider–Outsider Coalition' in D Della Porta and S Tarrow (eds), *Transnational Protest and Global Activism: People, Passions and Power* (Oxford, Rowman & Littlefield 2005); M Finnemore and K Sikkink, 'International Norm Dynamics and Political Change' (1998) 42 *International Organization* 887; F Lessa and LA Payne (eds), *Amnesty in the Age of Human Rights Accountability: Comparative and International Perspectives* (New York, Cambridge University Press, 2012).

[58] Of those domestic actors, the Zintani militias, who continue to hold Saif al-Islam Gaddafi in custody, have been the most strongly opposed to ICC intervention.

[59] Law No 1 of 2012, above n 10.

in Libya while stopping short of such a request with regard to Yemen. While the Security Council was swift in its issuance of Resolution 1970 (2011), which referred the situation in Libya to the ICC, no such action was taken with regard to Yemen, despite the regime's implication in the perpetration of grave crimes.[60] The GCC countries, the US and the EU had decided that 'the impunity law was the price to be paid for stability in Yemen',[61] especially because of the threat posed by Al Qaeda in the Arabian Peninsula and the general instability and violence in Yemen. The geopolitics of Libya, on the other hand, are such that the international community endorsed both the ICC's involvement and domestic efforts to prosecute because they were deemed less of a threat to the stability of Libya and the region.[62] Moreover, the ICC was a tool to help nudge regime change in Libya.

The Libyan and Yemeni cases reveal that, even in circumstances of severe domestic repression and limited interaction between domestic and international civil society, international actors can still significantly influence accountability decisions at the domestic level. At the same time, those same international actors exercise varying degrees of power that yield different outcomes related to prosecutorial decision making. In the case of Yemen, for instance, the GCC was an external actor whose accountability preference (immunity for Saleh and his aides) overwrote domestic civil society's accountability preference (prosecution of Saleh and his aides). In the Libyan case, the 'shadow of the ICC', or the threat of the ICC's involvement, stirred some domestic judicial activity, albeit within a complicated political and security environment.[63]

It is worthwhile revisiting Koskenniemi's analysis of the politics of international law and the consequent selectivity of international actors. For instance, he refers to the Security Council's 'notorious selectiveness'[64] when pushing for collective

---

[60] This is particularly true for the 'Friday of Dignity' attack that took place in Yemen on 18 March 2011. See Human Rights Watch, 'Unpunished Massacre: Yemen's Failed Response to the "Friday of Dignity" Killings' (2013), available at https://www.hrw.org/report/2013/02/12/unpunished-massacre/yemens-failed-response-friday-dignity-killings.

[61] Interview with George Abu Al Zulof, Country Representative, OHCHR Yemen (Sanaa, Yemen, 23 January 2014).

[62] Ironically, the Security Council has not moved to pressure Libya to cooperate with the ICC, despite requests from the Court's Chief Prosecutor, Fatou Bensouda. Violent conflict has since gripped the country. Similar Security Council inaction in Sudan prompted the Chief Prosecutor to formally put the case on hold: 'Given this Council's lack of foresight on what should happen in Darfur, I am left with no choice but to hibernate investigative activities in Darfur as I shift resources to other urgent cases, especially those in which trial is approaching. It should thus be clear to this Council that unless there is a change of attitude and approach to Darfur in the near future, there shall continue to be little or nothing to report to you for the foreseeable future': F Bensouda in her statement on the situation in Darfur to the Security Council in December 2014. See UN News Centre, 'Security Council Inaction on Darfur "can only embolden perpetrators"—ICC prosecutor' (12 December 2014) available at www.un.org/apps/news/story.asp?NewsID=49591#.VbwfYyTaH7U.

[63] Interview with Azza Maghur, lawyer and human rights activist (Tripoli, Libya, 17 September 2013); interview with Dao Al Mansouri, lawyer and human rights activist (Tripoli, Libya, 18 September 2013).

[64] M Koskenniemi, *The Politics of International Law* (Oxford, Hart Publishing, 2011) 84.

security actions in certain countries and not in others. 'Selectivity,' he argues, 'is unavoidable.'[65] While Martti Koskenniemi makes this statement in the context of his discussion on collective security, it is equally applicable to international criminal law. It points to his overarching argument that law is a product of politics:

> It is an uninteresting truism that delegations couch decisions in legal garb to make them look respectable. That is the point of law ... The question is never about security versus something else, but about 'whose security' and 'at what cost'?[66]

It is crucial, then, to examine the divergent objectives of not only transitional justice actors, but especially transitional justice actors in varying transitional contexts. The stark contrast between the accountability preferences of the so-called international community in Libya and Yemen is an example of competing accountability agendas that are contingent on state interests. The immunity deal in Yemen was inspired by a strong desire on the part of the GCC to ensure a relatively peaceful transition on the basis that Saleh would remove himself from politics. On the other hand, the Security Council referred the Libyan situation to the ICC, signifying a clear preference for the marginalisation of the Gaddafi regime, even whilst the conflict was raging.[67] Once Muammar Gaddafi had been captured and killed, the Security Council's support for an ICC trial of Gaddafi regime members waned significantly, a clear indication of the political motivations behind the Security Council's initial referral.[68]

While domestic elites often use transitional justice to score political points, as Subotic observes, international actors also pursue conflicting justice agendas motivated by their political interests.[69] This is hardly surprising. Geopolitics was one of the key factors responsible for the existence of the immunity law in Yemen. Arman's statement was clear: 'The immunity law is a product of politics at the international level.'[70] Wille of Human Rights Watch agreed: 'The reason that the immunity law exists is because of international actors.'[71] In Yemen, domestic support for justice—particularly in the form of prosecutions—was strong, but international pressure was not.[72] Many contend that the long-standing peace versus

---

[65] ibid 88.

[66] ibid 100, 111.

[67] The ICC arrest warrants for Muammar Gaddafi, Saif-al-Islam Gaddafi and Abdullah El Senussi were issued in June 2011. At the time, the conflict was still ongoing and neither Gaddafi nor any of the other senior Gaddafi regime members had been captured.

[68] V Peskin and MP Boduszynski, 'The Rise and Fall of the ICC in Libya and the Politics of International Surrogate Enforcership' (2016) 10 *International Journal of Transitional Justice* 272.

[69] Subotic, n 50, 134–35.

[70] Interview with Ahmed Arman, lawyer and Executive Secretary, National Organisation for Defending Rights and Freedoms (Sanaa, Yemen, 22 January 2014).

[71] Interview with Belkis Wille, Yemen and Kuwait Researcher, Human Rights Watch (Sanaa, Yemen, 22 January 2014).

[72] This, of course, refers to international pressure at the international relations level. International human rights organisations, such as Amnesty International and Human Rights Watch, have consistently called for prosecutions.

justice debate in transitional justice and international criminal law scholarship explains the decision not to prosecute in Yemen.[73]

However, explaining the divergent decisions regarding prosecution as a product of the peace versus justice debate is misleadingly simplistic. The reductionist notions of peace and justice that plague such analyses overlook the importance of diversified understandings of peace and justice. For example, Sharp explains how the 'transitional justice as peacebuilding' narrative only works where the concepts of justice and peace are synonymous with a liberal justice and a liberal peace. He argues:

> insofar as the goals of liberal international peacebuilding and the historical goals of transitional justice are essentially one and the same, transitional justice as peacebuilding may be little more than a dressed up tautology. More darkly, an amorphous 'transitional justice as peacebuilding' narrative may prove useful to autocratic regimes that would seek to use the tools and rhetoric of transitional justice to consolidate abusive regimes in the name of peace, just as victors have often done in the name of justice.[74]

There is a need to reconceptualise transitions. One way is to conceive of transitions as moving towards a 'positive peace' or 'popular peace', in which questions of social justice are foregrounded in transitional justice decisions.[75] Given the now long-standing tendency to exclude or overlook problems of economic violence in transitional justice practice, a popular peace where 'everyday problems faced by ordinary individuals and communities' are taken into account in a peacebuilding or transitional justice process would help strengthen prospects for security

---

[73] See, eg, I Fraihat and B Hess, 'For the Sake of Peace or Justice?' in CL Sriram (ed), *Transitional Justice in the Middle East and North Africa* (Oxford, Oxford University Press, 2016), in which they argue for a 'holistic' application of transitional justice mechanisms in Libya and Yemen, rather than allowing the peace versus justice divide to guide the choice of transitional justice mechanisms to implement. For more on the peace versus justice debate, see, eg, N Roht-Arriaza and J Mariezcurrena (eds), *Transitional Justice in the Twenty-first Century: Beyond Truth versus Justice* (Cambridge, Cambridge University Press, 2006); CL Sriram, *Confronting Past Human Rights Violations: Justice versus Peace in Times of Transition* (London, Frank Cass, 2004); Lessa and Payne, above n 57. See also Pion-Berlin, above n 53; G Bass, *Stay the Hand of Vengeance: The Politics of War Crimes Tribunals* (Princeton, Princeton University Press, 2000); Human Rights Watch, 'Uganda: No Amnesty for Atrocities. Turning a Blind Eye to Justice Undermines Durable Peace' (27 July 2006) available at www.hrw.org/news/2006/07/27/uganda-no-amnesty-atrocities; DF Orentlicher, 'That Someone Guilty Be Punished: The Impact of the ICTY in Bosnia', Open Society Justice Initiative (International Center for Transitional Justice, July 2010); L Vinjamuri, 'Justice, Peace and Deterrence in the Former Yugoslavia', Background Paper (European Council on Foreign Relations, November 2013) available at www.ecfr.eu/page/-/IJP_BosniaHerzegovina.pdf. On why there have been few prosecutions for human rights violations, Cherif Bassiouni, writing in 2002, notes: 'The answer is that justice is all too frequently bartered away for political settlements … the practice of impunity has become the political price paid to secure an end to the ongoing violence and repression. In these bartered settlements, accountability to the victims and the world community becomes the object of political trade-offs, and justice itself becomes the victim of realpolitik': C Bassiouni (ed), *Post-conflict Justice* (Leiden, Brill-Nijhoff, 2002) 7–8.

[74] DN Sharp, 'Emancipating Transitional Justice from the Paradigmatic Transition' [2015] *International Journal of Transitional Justice* 150, 151.

[75] D Roberts, 'Post-conflict Peacebuilding, Liberal Irrelevance and the Locus of Legitimacy' (2011) 18 *International Peacekeeping* 410.

and peace.[76] These everyday problems include access to social services and economic and social rights. This point is discussed further in the next section.

Limited Accountability and Foregrounding Social Justice

The limited content and extent of the investigations and prosecutions that took place in all four case studies further underline the need to develop transitional justice theory. The emphasis on accountability for corruption and economic crimes in Egypt and Tunisia, for instance, points to a practice of selective accountability in order to avoid the prosecution of a more comprehensive set of crimes, particularly those of a civil and political nature. Moreover, certain highly symbolic individuals, such as Mubarak and Ben Ali, were prosecuted while several others were not. This practice of scapegoating is used by political leaderships with the aim of producing an authoritative image of a break with the former regime. In reality, however, the influence of the *feloul* in Egypt, the *anciens nouveaux* in Tunisia and former President Saleh's political manoeuvrings in Yemen reveal otherwise. The same political leaderships sought to limit prosecutions in order to shield themselves from being held accountable for a past they are implicated in. The very limited human rights prosecutions that have taken place thus point to the elite-controlled nature of the transitions.

Nagy offers an important reminder that transitional justice is, by its nature, a selective process due to resource, time and political constraints.[77] While these constraints are pertinent to the Arab region case studies and have been discussed thus far as shaping factors, the political constraints of the Arab region prosecutions require a close examination because of their significant role in limiting the extent of the investigations and trials. By prosecuting only a handful of individuals for a significantly limited set of crimes, those actors shaping the prosecutions aim to create the impression of a symbolic break with the former regime in order to neutralise an outraged public that demanded the prosecutions in the first place. Moreover, the limited selection of individuals that faced investigation and prosecution points to a prosecutorial strategy that is motivated by elite preferences and leadership interests rather than by the merits of the so-called global accountability norm. Finally, the focus on crimes committed during the transition in the investigations and trials that have taken places leaves decades of human rights violations unaccounted for.[78]

---

[76] David Roberts as cited in Sharp, above n 74, 164.

[77] Nagy, above n 31, 276.

[78] Tunisia's TDC may become an exception to this. Isabel Robinson explains the importance of 'quasi-judicial' powers of the TDC and the expanded scope of the crimes to be covered: 'Created in December 2013, the TDC was launched in June 2014 and will run for four years, with the possibility of

Before discussing the implications of the emphasis on corruption and socio-economic crimes in the Arab Spring prosecutions, it is worth clarifying what is meant by 'corruption'. Isabel Robinson usefully sums up the difference between grand and low-level corruption:

> corruption can ... be understood as a systematic and structurally entrenched phenomenon that affects all social interactions. In this regard, it is important to distinguish between high-level or 'grand' corruption, involving appropriation of large sums of money by heads of state and senior officials, and low-level corruption—also referred to as 'administrative' or 'petty' corruption—which takes place 'at the implication end of politics, where citizens meet public officials'.[79]

In the Arab Spring case studies, both grand and low-level types of corruption took place and contributed to the 'visibility' that several interviewees referred to when explaining the impetus behind demands for accountability. The investigations and prosecution charges, however, pertain to the 'grand corruption' that Robinson mentions.

The content and extent of decisions regarding the prosecution of political leaders demonstrate that the Arab region is beyond recent debates calling for the merging of the two sets of rights in transitional justice mechanisms. Vasuki Nesiah laments the absence of sufficient consideration of Pinochet's harmful macroeconomic policies in his trial. She argues that the Chilean and South African cases show that transitional justice often backgrounds systemic factors such as economic and racial structures: 'rather than shining a light on them as enabling conditions of human rights abuse ... [they] deter and distract from structural violence'.[80] Sharp notes that economic violence has been the 'blind spot of transitional justice' as it is rarely scrutinised in comparison to human rights violations,

---

a one-year extension ... The law aims to address past human rights violations committed by previous regimes, in particular the regime of former President Zine al-Abidine Ben Ali, who ruled from 1987 until the revolution in January 2011. During this time, Ben Ali's extended family reportedly embezzled millions and, by 2010, controlled approximately 20 per cent of private sector profits in Tunisia. In addressing corruption, the TDC will combine investigation, arbitration and reform functions. The Commission is mandated to investigate violations committed by the state and organized groups from July 1955 to December 2013 ... The significant powers of the TDC regarding arbitration and vetting effectively mean that the TDC's work vis-a-vis corruption is characterized by a quasi-judicial nature. This is not necessarily a new phenomenon; indeed, there have been truth commissions that have had subpoena powers (including for individuals or documents and other objects) and search and seizure powers. However, it is certainly the first time that a truth commission has been given such far-reaching powers vis-a-vis corruption': I Robinson, 'Truth Commissions and Anti-Corruption: Towards a Complementary Framework?' (2015) 9 *International Journal of Transitional Justice* 1, 13, 16.

[79] I Robinson, 'Truth Commissions and Anti-corruption: Towards a Complementary Framework?' (2015) 9 *International Journal of Transitional Justice* 1.

[80] V Nesiah, 'The Trials of History: Losing Justice in the Monstrous and the Banal' in R Buchanan and P Zumbansen (eds), *Law in Transition: Human Rights, Development and Transitional Justice* (Oxford, Hart Publishing, 2014) 305. Nesiah notes that, despite a sharp rise in poverty under Pinochet's rule, 'it is striking that the impact of Pinochet's macroeconomic policies is not part of Chile's transitional justice story' (295–96).

which are under intense scrutiny.[81] Abou-El-Fadl draws attention to Egypt as an example of how conventional transitional justice falls short of addressing the former regime's violation of social and economic rights.[82] The 'invisibility' of the economic dimension of transitional justice is further highlighted by Miller, who argues that its inclusion would help ensure a more comprehensive accountability that would prevent renewed violence and inequality.

Various scholars have proposed several explanations for why social and economic rights have not been included in most transitional justice processes in other parts of the world. For example, transitional justice is largely based on traditional international human rights law, which has long viewed economic and social matters as 'entitlements' rather than 'rights'.[83] Other explanations include the difficulty in ascribing responsibility to individuals for economic crimes and that social justice is a longer-term political process that short-term transitional justice mechanisms cannot fully take into account.[84] Moreover, discussions on the inclusion of economic and social rights in transitional justice mechanisms focus on their place in truth commissions and reconciliation deals, with limited reflections on their place in criminal prosecutions. As Makau Mutua notes, despite significant efforts to incorporate socio-economic justice into transitional justice mechanisms,

> the human rights idiom speaks largely in the language of the entitlements that are germane to a liberal, market democracy. It focuses on the so-called core rights that are essential to securing the people against political tyranny, but does little to ward off the privations that come from economic despotism.[85]

The Arab Spring prosecutions, on the other hand, show that, contrary to most transitional justice experiences in other parts of the world,[86] corruption and socio-economic crimes figured quite heavily in the charges. Moreover, despite strong demands for accountability for civil and political rights, they have taken a much more limited form, largely focusing on crimes committed during the transition (as in Egypt, Libya and Tunisia), or they have been dismissed almost entirely (as in the case of Yemen). The reasons for this particular content and extent—or shape—of decisions regarding prosecutions are complex, as presented by the

[81] DN Sharp, 'Addressing Economic Violence in Times of Transition: Toward a Positive-Peace Paradigm for Transitional Justice' (2012) 35 *Fordham International Law Journal* 780, 782.

[82] R Abou-El-Fadl, 'Beyond Conventional Transitional Justice: Egypt's 2011 Revolution and the Absence of Political Will' (2012) 6 *International Journal of Transitional Justice* 318.

[83] L Arbour, 'Economic and Social Justice for Societies in Transition', Second Annual Transitional Justice Lecture hosted by the Center for Human Rights and Global Justice at New York University School of Law and by the International Center for Transitional Justice, New York University School of Law, 25 October 2006.

[84] L Waldorf, 'Anticipating the Past? Transitional Justice and Socio-Economic Wrongs' (2012) 21 *Social and Legal Studies* 171.

[85] M Mutua, 'What is the Future of Transitional Justice' (2015) 9 *International Journal of Transitional Justice* 1, 4.

[86] The few exceptions here include the trial of General Augusto Pinochet (Chile), Alberto Fujimori (Peru), Suharto (Indonesia) and Joseph Estrada (Philippines).

findings in each case study. A number of conclusions can be drawn from them. First, a brief review of the explanations for the content and extent of the prosecutions is worthwhile here, followed by a discussion of their implications for transitional justice research and practice.

The Content and Extent of Decisions Regarding Prosecution: A Recap

Egypt experienced an elite-controlled transition, whereby the military and other state agencies worked to ensure that investigations and trials did not extend 'too far' so as not to harm their political interests and subject themselves to prosecution. Linked to this explanation is the role of a politicised judiciary in blocking certain controversial cases. A third factor is that the victims, activists and lawyers who were active in pursuing prosecutions were preoccupied with the more recent crimes of 2011 because they were 'fresher' and therefore easier to prosecute.[87] Fourthly, the absence of an enabling legal framework and other legal challenges, such as the requirement of direct evidence, have made human rights prosecutions particularly difficult, thereby limiting the extent of individuals on trial. Fifthly, the emphasis on corruption and economic crimes was used as a means to scapegoat certain high-level individuals to deflect attention from the lack of accountability for a more comprehensive set of human rights violations and their perpetrators.

In Tunisia, a number of explanations for the content and extent of prosecutions have emerged. A combination of the relative success of workers' movements, a history of a very visible and rampant corruption, specific public demands for social justice, and a weak judiciary and legal framework all limited the scope of charges and the selection of individuals held accountable. Moreover, the anticipation of a truth and reconciliation commission, along with the highly controversial proposed financial reconciliation bill, resulted in a waning of the emphasis on trials pertaining to corruption and economic crimes in the latter phase of the post-transitional period.

The very few prosecutions that have taken place in Libya since Muammar Gaddafi's death have focused primarily on crimes committed during the 2011 conflict.[88] The number of corruption charges does not match that of the prosecutions in Egypt and Tunisia. Instead, the charges are overwhelmingly focused on human rights crimes committed during the transition, particularly the killing of protesters and mass rape. Three main factors help explain the limited content and extent of the prosecutions. First, an enabling legal framework that is equipped

---

[87] Eid, above n 51.
[88] See, eg, United Nations Support Mission in Libya (UNSMIL) and Office of the United Nations High Commissioner for Human Rights (OHCHR), 'Report on the Trial of 37 Former Members of the Qadhafi Regime (Case 630/2012)' (21 February 2017) 19–20.

to prosecute serious crimes such as war crimes and crimes against humanity is absent. Secondly, victims and their families do not trust the judiciary to carry out investigations and trials independently, which has limited the number of legal complaints filed. Thirdly, a dangerous security situation means that many judges and lawyers fear for their lives when asked to represent Gaddafi regime officials and loyalists.

International actors, geopolitics, legal challenges and a fairly ambiguous transition all contributed to the decision not to prosecute in Yemen. Weak judicial institutions were a significant factor that shaped the decisions not to prosecute. Moreover, problems of security in Yemen have also infiltrated the judiciary. Judges and prosecutors have been—and continue to be—assassinated.[89] The strong involvement of the military in politics is yet another factor that has severely restricted progress towards prosecutions. As a result, even in cases where officials who hold high-level governmental positions are supportive of the push for criminal accountability of political leaders, their goals were quashed by other, more powerful, actors. Despite the immunity law and the challenges discussed above, there are efforts in Yemen to seek accountability for political leaders—whether in the form of prosecutions or through truth commissions and other transitional justice mechanisms. A focus on crimes committed during the transition, namely, the killing of peaceful protesters in 2011, has left the subject of pre-transition crimes to be dealt with by the non-existent transitional justice law. A number of explanations for this limited scope of crimes emerged.

First, prosecuting crimes committed during the 2011 uprising is, as Al Kamali explained, easier and more practical. It is easier because 'all the various political factions who continue to wield power in Yemen were involved in pre-2011 crimes. 2011 crimes are more straightforward—the killing of protesters, full stop'.[90] Tayler observed that the question of how far back the transitional justice law should go was a 'key sticking point' for the same reasons that Al Kamali identified.[91]

Secondly, a lack of direct evidence linking Saleh and other high-level government officials to crimes such as the Friday of Dignity killings case significantly weakened the prospects for prosecution. The destruction of evidence that Barman mentioned is also a contributing factor.[92]

Thirdly, and perhaps most importantly, the complex and uncertain nature of Yemen's transition significantly impacted on decisions regarding prosecution, effectively resulting in the immunity law.

---

[89] Abu Al Zulof, above n 61.

[90] Interview with Hamza Al Kamali, member of the Transitional Justice Working Group, National Dialogue Conference (Sanaa, Yemen, 22 January 2014).

[91] Interview with Letta Tayler, Senior Researcher, Human Rights Watch (telephone interview, 21 November 2013).

[92] ibid.

Rethinking Transitional Justice Theory and Practice

Despite the many challenges that have marked the trials and the overall transitional justice process in the Arab region, they present a crucial opportunity to develop transitional justice theory and practice. The Arab Spring cases demonstrate that addressing socio-economic crimes is a possibility, even within a difficult and opaque judicial and authoritarian environment.[93] While scholars and practitioners have been consumed with cautioning transitional countries against neglecting the incorporation of socio-economic rights crimes in their transitional justice mechanisms, the case studies examined here demonstrate that corruption and economic crimes were foregrounded in many of the investigations and trials.[94] Robins makes a similar observation:

> While the politics that accompany transitional justice deny the social and the economic as justice issues, the Arab Spring has confronted the discourse with transitions driven by slogans such as 'bread, freedom and dignity'. The revolutions in Egypt and Tunisia were catalysed by graduate unemployment and rapid rises in the prices of basic foods. This presents both a challenge and an opportunity for approaches to justice in transition, in terms of looking beyond electoral democracy and civil and political rights.[95]

Given the vast extent of corruption, which involved the embezzlement of tens of millions of dollars in Egypt, Libya, Tunisia and Yemen, some authorities, especially those in Egypt, decided to settle for reconciliation deals.

Through such deals, business tycoons such as Hussein Salem and former presidents such as Mubarak would pay the state the money they gained illicitly and this money would be used to help rebuild Egypt's battered economy. Legal steps were taken to facilitate these reconciliation deals, particularly SCAF Decree No 4 of 2012, which 'gives immunity from criminal prosecution to businessmen accused of corruption under Mubarak and offers them the chance to settle their cases with government commissions'.[96] Wageeh explained that the military justified these

---

[93] S Robins, 'Mapping a Future for Transitional Justice by Learning from its Past' (2015) 9 *International Journal of Transitional Justice* 181, 186: 'While the politics that accompany transitional justice deny the social and the economic as justice issues, the Arab Spring has confronted the discourse with transitions driven by slogans such as "bread, freedom and dignity". The revolutions in Egypt and Tunisia were catalysed by graduate unemployment and rapid rises in the prices of basic foods. This presents both a challenge and an opportunity for approaches to justice in transition, in terms of looking beyond electoral democracy and civil and political rights. In Tunisia, for example, the Organic Law on Transitional Justice has created a novel class of transitional justice actor by defining groups of individuals who have been socially marginalized or excluded as "collective victims".'

[94] See P Gready and S Robins, 'From Transitional to Transformative Justice: A New Agenda for Practice' (2014) 8 *International Journal of Transitional Justice* 339. They argue, however, that socio-economic crimes are best addressed through reparations, which can offer both 'corrective and distributive justice' (347, 356).

[95] Robins, above n 93, 186.

[96] M Abdelrahman, *Egypt's Long Revolution: Protest Movements and Uprisings* (New York, Routledge, 2014) 130.

reconciliation deals as a means to protect capitalism and restore economic security. Rather than imprison individuals for such grand corruption and economic crimes, the reconciliation deals proved somewhat popular among a public eager to improve an economy 'in tatters'.[97] Tunisia took similar steps toward reconciliation deals with corrupt business tycoons and former Ben Ali regime officials in order to revive its economy. Its proposed Reconciliation Bill effectively offers immunity from prosecution in exchange for a portion of illicit gains to be returned to the state. At the time of writing, the Tunisian government, headed by Essebsi, is still trying to pass this bill, despite significant resistance to it among ordinary Tunisians.

Several implications, then, can be gleaned for transitional justice theory and practice. First, the daily visibility of corruption and unequal access to economic resources was—and continues to be—a major factor in the way the Arab region conceptualises injustice. As Emile Gabory noted in the context of the French Revolution, 'Generations forget more quickly spilled blood than stolen goods'.[98] From a transitional justice policy standpoint, it is worth considering Sharp's call for reconceptualising transitions as transitions to 'positive peace', in which questions of resources and inequality are foregrounded and help 'to ensure that a greater balance is struck between a wider range of justice concerns'.[99] A stronger analysis of the few significant cases in which corruption and socio-economic crimes were the focus of prosecutions, as in the Asian examples cited by Lutz and Reiger and now in the Arab region as well, is therefore needed.[100]

Secondly, the inclusion of socio-economic accountability does not necessarily imply a more comprehensive transitional justice process is in place. The Arab Spring cases, specifically Egypt and Tunisia, where the trials are at a more advanced stage compared to Libya and Yemen, demonstrate that the inclusion of socio-economic crimes is not sufficient by itself to ensure a more comprehensive accountability mechanism. On the contrary, due to scapegoating strategies to appease public anger and to foment a symbolic 'break' with the past, the focus on corruption and socio-economic crimes has served as a means to protect interim and post-transitional authorities from prosecution for human rights crimes. In this sense, the prosecution of political leaders for corruption crimes reflects the use of transitional justice for strategic purposes.[101]

Thirdly, the focus on crimes committed during the transition, particularly in Egypt and Yemen, risks marginalising certain narratives regarding legacies of past injustices. Moreover, this limited content of the trials furthers the use of

---

[97] Interview with Tamer Wageeh, Director, Economic and Social Justice Unit, Egyptian Initiative for Personal Rights (Cairo, Egypt, 8 December 2013).

[98] A Gabory, *Les Guerres de Vendée* (Paris, Robert Laffont, 1989) 1063. Quoted in J Elster, 'Emotions and Transitional Justice' (2003) 86 *Soundings: An Interdisciplinary Journal* 17, 27.

[99] Sharp, above n 74, 160.

[100] Lutz and Reiger, above n 46, 280–82.

[101] See T Risse, SC Ropp and K Sikkink (eds), *The Power of Human Rights. International Norms and Domestic Change* (Cambridge, Cambridge University Press, 2007) 15.

transitional justice to entrench authoritarian rule. Michael Wahid Hanna warns against the detrimental consequences of the fabrication of historical narratives in Egypt. There, conflicting narratives on past atrocities have already had negative consequences and have derailed an already flawed transitional justice process.[102] For example, a few months after Egypt's worst mass killing at Raba'a Al Adawiyah Square in Cairo, the military-backed government erected a monument representing the military and the police instead of the victims of the mass killing. It was an attempt to 'revise history rather than confront it'.[103] Despite the ongoing televised hearings that were launched in November 2016, it will be a long time before Tunisia's TDC yields results, including trials, as it was only established in June 2014. It may, however, become an example of how to expand the content and scope of the crimes through a specialised mechanism that is separate from the ordinary courts where the trials have thus far been conducted.[104]

Fourthly, the uses of the limited criminal sanction, as proposed by Teitel and Orentlicher, fall short of explaining the limited extent of the investigations and trials in the Arab region case studies. Teitel defines the limited criminal sanction as a practice of criminal investigations and prosecutions followed by little or no penalty. She identifies this practice as a partial process 'that distinguishes criminal justice in transition', because it does not result in full punishment.[105] The merits of the limited criminal sanction, Teitel continues, is that it offers a 'pragmatic resolution of the core dilemma of transitions; namely, that of attributing individual responsibility for systemic wrongs perpetrated under repressive rule'.[106] Orentlicher warns against the cynical use of prosecutions as a scapegoating practice. 'This might happen,' she explains, 'if prosecutions were directed against only low-level participants in a system of past atrocities or if patently political considerations infected the determination of defendants.'[107] The strategic limitation of prosecutions for the sake of preserving the 'return to a liberal state'[108] and the broader stability of the transition itself offer only a partial explanation for the decisions regarding the extent of individuals who faced investigation and prosecution in the Arab region.

The problem with the limited criminal sanction argument is that it does not take into account non-paradigmatic transitions that do not constitute a shift to

---

[102] M Wahid Hanna, 'Egypt and the Struggle for Accountability and Justice' in Fisher and Stewart, above n 14.

[103] K Faheem and M El Sheikh, 'Memory of a Mass Killing Becomes Another Casualty of Egyptian Protests', *New York Times*, 13 November 2013, available at www.nytimes.com/2013/11/14/world/middleeast/memory-egypt-mass-killing.html.

[104] It should be noted here that in Tunisia, most trials of former political leaders were conducted in military courts. See Human Rights Watch, 'Flawed Accountability: Shortcomings of Tunisia's Trials for Killings during the Uprising' (January 2015) available at www.hrw.org/report/2015/01/12/flawed-accountability/shortcomings-tunisias-trials-killings-during-uprising.

[105] Teitel, above n 26, 99.

[106] ibid 100.

[107] D Orentlicher, 'Settling Accounts: The Duty to Prosecute Human Rights Violations of a Prior Regime' in Kritz, above n 53, 410.

[108] Teitel, above n 26, 67.

liberal rule. As an anonymous interviewee explained, the practice of selective prosecutions in Egypt and Tunisia was a strategy aimed at 'sacrific[ing] a part of the
regime to save the regime'.[109] The starkly opposing motivations behind Teitel's
description of the limited criminal sanction and the ways in which it has unfolded
in the Arab region suggest the need for a serious reconsideration of the various
and competing claims of transitional justice agents. Teitel further suggests that
where prosecutions fail to provide full accountability, other mechanisms that
recognise and condemn past atrocities can have transformative impact, 'the public establishment of which liberates the collective'.[110] But where there is a strong
and very public demand for a retributive justice in the courts, the 'mere exposure
of wrongs'[111] would fall far short of meeting victims' expectations and desires.
Moataz El Fegeiry and others have noted that for the Arab Spring protesters, justice means retribution, while reparations and truth commissions do not hold as
much significance. People are not so much concerned with the justice process
itself as with the outcome, such as imprisonment.[112]

On the other hand, Koskenniemi suggests that selective trials that are also show
trials—in the sense that they do not establish a full picture of the truth about past
atrocities—are sufficient for the mere recognition that suffering was inflicted and
wrong.[113] Koskenniemi outlines the limits of criminality, especially as an inevitable focus on individual leaders may 'serve as an alibi for the population at large to
relieve itself from responsibility'.[114] Instead, or as a complement to criminal trials,
he argues that truth commissions are able to address context in a way that criminality, especially in the form of prosecutions, cannot.[115] It is too early to assess
whether transitional justice mechanisms other than prosecutions will become
acceptable for victims in all the Arab region case studies. The merits of the limited

---

[109] Interview with anonymous senior expert on transitional justice in Egypt, International Center
for Transitional Justice (14 June 2013).

[110] Teitel, above n 26, 101.

[111] ibid.

[112] Aboueldahab, above n 56. Even in Libya, where the progress of prosecutions has been much
slower than in Egypt and Tunisia, the selective extent of criminal accountability was institutionalised early on. The International Crisis Group's report on Libya explains: 'Overshadowing the security situation has been the lack of accountability for crimes committed by rebel fighters during and
after the 2011 conflict. Rather than being investigated, those suspected of such acts often are hailed as
national heroes. The state's unwillingness or inability to look into the unlawful killing of prisoners of
war throughout 2012 has contributed to the fighters' feeling of operating above the law. Although this
might be a prudent course of action to avoid an open confrontation between government forces and
independent armed groups, it inevitably carries the risks of entrenching lawlessness and becoming a
trigger of violence. The [National Transitional Council] in effect gave legal sanction to impunity in
May 2012 when it amnestied those who had committed crimes—including murder and forced displacement—during the uprising.' Law 38/2012 on 'Special Procedures during the Transitional Period'
grants immunity from prosecution to 'revolutionaries' for 'military, security and civilian acts required
by the 17 February Revolution' committed with the 'purpose of leading the revolution to victory'. International Crisis Group, 'Trial by Error: Justice in Post Qadhafi Libya' (April 2013) 28.

[113] Koskenniemi, above n 64, 178.

[114] ibid 181.

[115] ibid 179.

criminal sanction, however, need to be re-examined when selective trials—both in content and extent—instead have a negative impact on the course of transitions and on the stability of the state. The polarisation of Egyptian society, for example, is in many ways tied to those with loyalties to the Mubarak regime and those who have a strong desire to see more radical change and a clearer break with the authoritarian past. The result is a highly contentious justice process that has largely contributed to the suffering, rather than the healing, of victims and their families.

The Legacy of Deep State Institutions

The Arab region cases demonstrate that a rethinking of transitional justice needs to take into account the absence of pre-existing democratic structures and what this means for criminal accountability prospects in such transitional contexts. As we have seen, the challenges of pursuing prosecutions during highly contentious transitions are many. Weak and politicised judiciaries that are crippled by executive power meddling and by an inadequate legal framework further worsen prospects for fair and effective prosecutions. Prosecutions of political leaders in times of transition typically provide a major opportunity for the use and abuse of transitional justice for political ends. These ends are intimately tied to the nature of the transition, which, as explained throughout this book, does not fall neatly within the paradigmatic shift from authoritarian rule to liberal, democratic rule.

The Arab region cases therefore present transitional justice—and criminal prosecutions in particular—as a process that prioritises politics over due process, strengthens repression and buttresses the overall disregard for the rule of law and for the establishment of truth about past atrocities. This process has seen the use of military trials in Egypt to silence opposition, arbitrary and non-transparent judicial decisions in Libya, questionable acquittals in Tunisia and an immunity law against the will of many Yemenis, with detrimental political and security consequences. The lack of appropriate legal frameworks has led to questionable acquittals and a very limited set of trials, in both content and extent. The abuse of transitional justice—currently and largely understood as a liberalising process— has instead strengthened repressive rule post-transition, effectively turning transitional justice and its prosecution mechanism on its head. Nesiah aptly describes the motivations behind transitional justice decisions: 'transitional justice initiatives anchor a political horizon that bends towards historical closure and away from historical accountability'.[116]

The argument that previously existing democratic institutions, particularly functioning judiciaries, are necessary in order for adequate trials to take place post-transition falls significantly short in explaining the context of the Arab region. Teitel warns against political justice and unfair trials, and calls attention to

---

[116] Nesiah, above n 80, 293.

the necessity of democratically functioning institutions in order to avoid such a scenario.[117] Similarly, Lutz and Reiger argue that 'accountability by itself is neither sufficient nor possible absent other functioning democratic institutions, including an independent judiciary'.[118] It is useful to recount Huyse's assessment of the Belgian, Dutch and French experiences in addressing their past atrocities following World War II. Huyse argues that the democratic institutions and structures that existed prior to the four years of repressive rule in those countries were able to survive and were not completely eliminated: 'four years of occupation and collaboration were insufficient time for the authoritarian regime's legal culture and codes to take root'.[119] This may explain the speed with which prosecutions were initiated.[120] On the other hand, Huyse points to Central and Eastern Europe—particularly Czechoslovakia, Poland and Hungary—where communist regimes lasted for 40 years. This meant that decision making on crime and punishment was much slower because 'The legal culture created by communism was firmly established and [proved] hard to eradicate'.[121]

The UN's solution to the lack of the democratically functioning institutions needed to carry out fair prosecutions is to establish international and hybrid tribunals. It proposes the following in its guidance note on transitional justice:

> States emerging from years of conflict or repressive rule may be unable or unwilling to conduct effective investigations and prosecutions. In such situations, international and hybrid criminal tribunals may exercise concurrent jurisdiction ... The ICC operates on the basis of the principle of complementarity articulated in article 17 of the Rome Statute. As such, it should also contribute to the development of national capacities to bring alleged perpetrators of international crimes to justice.[122]

A special tribunal or hybrid tribunal could, as the UN suggests, overcome the problem of a state's inability to carry out prosecutions due to a legacy of weak and corrupt institutions. Such a tribunal would not work, however, if the concerned state were unwilling to carry out prosecutions or to provide the evidence required to conduct prosecutions internationally. This leaves the question of the absence of democratically functioning institutions and a state's consequent inability to carry out fair prosecutions unresolved. Indeed, it is a very real issue in Egypt, Libya, Tunisia and Yemen, as the intelligence agencies, the police and other state security agencies have either refused to submit or destroyed evidence requested by the courts to carry out prosecutions of former leaders. In Tunisia, President Essebsi's office made clear that it would not allow access to the presidential archives should

---

[117] Teitel, above n 26.

[118] Lutz and Reiger, above n 46, 4.

[119] L Huyse, 'Justice after Transitions: On the Choices Successor Elites Make in Dealing with the Past' in Kritz, above n 53, 111.

[120] ibid.

[121] ibid.

[122] Guidance Note of the Secretary General, 'United Nations Approach to Transitional Justice' (March 2010) available at www.unrol.org/files/TJ_Guidance_Note_March_2010FINAL.pdf.

the TDC decide to pursue legal cases against its members. The problem, then, is not just weak and corrupt judiciaries. Where judiciaries are functioning, a non-cooperative police or intelligence force could seriously hamper the proceedings of a trial.

Sharp argues that scholarly deliberations on the shortcomings of mainstream transitional justice's assumptions 'go to the heart of the field's potential to serve as an instrument for the consolidation of more democratic societies grounded in positive peace'.[123] As such, transitional justice is often regarded as an important component of a democratisation process. But in Egypt, Tunisia, Libya and Yemen, it was the very lack of democratically functioning institutions—and in particular the judiciary—that in large part led to the uprisings and prevented fair prosecutions from taking place. It is unclear, then, how Teitel and others, including those from the critical literature, such as Sharp and Obel Hansen, would explain the possibility of having democratically functioning institutions in place during a phase of the 'fledgling liberal state',[124] particularly when the lack of such institutions was the reason the transitions occurred in the first place. The transitions in the Arab Spring were exceptional only insofar as they were the first ever massive, popular uprisings against dictatorial governments. The decades of authoritarian rule until then were the 'norm'. There was no liberal state to begin with—certainly not in the political sense.

The socio-economic well-being of a country also adversely impacts the ability of judiciaries and other institutions to carry out a transitional justice process that is acceptable to victims. The prospects for redress for human rights violations are grimmer, scholars suggest, when pursued in poor countries with a lack of adequate access to justice. The poorer the country, the lower the chances that transitional justice, and in particular costly prosecutions, will be pursued.[125] Nagy argues that in such cases, and especially where judiciaries are weak and corrupt, international law should play a role in ensuring some form of accountability.[126] However, Mutua argues that the implementation of such transitional justice 'blueprints' by international actors is 'a paternalistic and imperialistic approach that should be rejected out of hand'.[127] Instead, Mutua continues, societies should distance themselves from a desire for revenge against the perpetrator and instead seek ways to address 'the injured soul of the victim, and the corruption of the nation's moral fiber'.[128]

---

[123] DN Sharp, 'Interrogating the Peripheries: The Preoccupations of Fourth Generation Transitional Justice' (2013) 26 *Harvard Human Rights Journal* 149, 178.

[124] Teitel, above n 26.

[125] See TD Olsen, LA Payne and AG Reiter, 'The Justice Balance: When Transitional Justice Improves Human Rights and Democracy' (2010) 32 *Human Rights Quarterly* 980; G Dancy and E Wiebelhaus-Brahm, 'Bridge to Human Development or Vehicle of Inequality? Transitional Justice and Economic Structures' (2014) 9 *International Journal of Transitional Justice* 51.

[126] Nagy, above n 31, 226.

[127] Mutua, above n 85, 5.

[128] ibid.

Still others, such as Chandra Sriram, point to the merits of institutional reform before the implementation of transitional justice processes. Citing the example of Chile, she argues:

> the introduction of judicial reforms such as changes relating to judicial appointments, the size and composition of the Supreme Court, and the power of military courts played an important role in stimulating increased activism by domestic courts to try Pinochet era-crimes.[129]

Sriram further argues that transitional justice is more likely to be successful in promoting a 'normative environment conducive to democratic institution-building', rather than promoting deep structural changes.[130] Sriram concludes that, given the negative impact of transitional justice on democratic institution building in certain contexts, transitional justice may not be 'the most appropriate instrument in all transition contexts'.[131] As discussed in chapter 4, former Libyan judge Benour emphasised the significant challenge posed by the absence of a unified judiciary, police force, military and other state institutions. He suggested that a general amnesty in Libya is needed first in order to allow for much needed national reconciliation. This, he argues, is a precondition for the establishment of a transitional justice mechanism that could effectively address the country's complex violations committed before, during and after the tumultuous transition of 2011.[132]

These are serious points to ponder for Egypt, Libya, Tunisia and Yemen. As Abu Al Zulof noted, many judges and prosecutors in Yemen belong to the previous regime, making any prosecution attempts almost impossible without the necessary changes in the judiciary. These changes include reform, full independence and capacity building for judges regarding due process procedures, particularly for human rights prosecutions.[133] Aziz describes the Egyptian judiciary as 'politically vulnerable' and 'facially independent', used and abused by a shrewd military to create a false appearance of transition.[134] The result, Aziz observes, is 'a nation firmly in the grasp, both politically and legally, of its military—with the judiciary's blessing'.[135] Consequently, Aziz argues, there was no political transition in Egypt and therefore one cannot speak of a transitional justice process.[136]

Aziz's contention, however, presupposes that a certain type of transition must take place in order for transitional justice to unfold. However, the case study

---

[129] V Arnould and C Sriram, 'Pathways of Impact: How Transitional Justice Affects Democratic Institution-Building', Policy Paper (Project on the Impact of Transitional Justice on Democratic Institution-building, October 2014) available at www.tjdi.org.

[130] ibid.

[131] ibid.

[132] Interview with Jamal Benour, lawyer, former Libyan judge and prosecutor, former head of military prosecution in Benghazi, former justice coordinator for the city of Benghazi, and former local council president for Benghazi, Libya. (Email interview, 29 March 2017).

[133] Abu Al Zulof, above n 61.

[134] S Aziz, 'Theater or Transitional Justice: Reforming the Judiciary in Egypt' in CL Sriram (ed), *Transitional Justice in the Middle East* (New York, Oxford University Press, 2016) 210.

[135] ibid 211.

[136] ibid.

findings demonstrate that a transitional justice process does take place in ambiguous, non-paradigmatic transitions. The fact that decisions regarding prosecution were taken—even in the case of Yemen, where an immunity law was passed—provides ample material that challenges the predominant understanding of transitional justice as a liberalising process. The absence of pre-existing democratic institutions, particularly a functioning and independent judiciary, is a significant factor that distinguishes the Arab region transitional justice processes from transitions elsewhere, particularly in Latin America. That said, the evolution of the Argentinian judiciary over time is an example of how, even in a radically different political transition, such as that of Argentina, judicial reform had a significant impact on decisions regarding prosecution. The initial absence of trials in post-transition Argentina is attributed to, among other factors, politically biased courts. It took decades for judicial reform to materialise, which in turn opened up prosecutions after the initial lull.[137] In sum, to speak of the total absence of a transition in the Arab region case studies is to miss a crucial point: the use of transitional justice processes, and of prosecutions in particular, to consolidate authoritarian, non-liberal rule and to emphasise one historical narrative on past atrocities over another. The absence of pre-existing democratic structures has contributed to this state of affairs in the Arab region, but it has not single-handedly shaped decisions regarding prosecution, as the case studies have thus far demonstrated.

The impact of this legacy of authoritarian and repressive institutions has far-reaching consequences on both transitions and transitional justice. As Carothers observed with regard to Eastern Europe and sub-Saharan Africa, 'the specific institutional legacies from predecessor regimes strongly affect the outcomes of attempted transitions'.[138] Democracy-building efforts have traditionally focused on the redistribution of state power as opposed to state building, leaving deep state legacies in place.[139] The same problem applies to transitional justice efforts—the institutions that implement the transitional justice process are the same institutions that are implicated in past atrocities. Carothers' critique of the false assumption that transitional countries build on already coherent, functioning states is thus crucial for the Arab region cases. So-called reforms of deep state institutions, such as the state security sector, are often only aesthetic in nature. Building state institutions—even from scratch[140]—is thus a difficult but highly necessary task for transitional countries that plan to pursue any kind of meaningful justice that adequately reflects their local realities. Before concluding, it is worth briefly visiting the Moroccan case of transitional justice, as it raises additional questions about the nature of transitions and their impact on decisions regarding prosecution.

---

[137] Skaar, above n 17, 11.
[138] Carothers, above n 19, 16.
[139] ibid.
[140] ibid 8–9.

Morocco: Transitional Justice for a Quasi-transition?

Morocco was the first Arab country to undergo a transitional justice process. Launched under unique circumstances that did not involve a massive anti-government uprising, as in the Arab Spring, Morocco's truth commission was established soon after King Mohamed VI's accession to the throne in 1999. Following consultations with civil society, the Equity and Reconciliation Commission, or l'Instance Equité et Réconciliation (IER), was established by the monarchy in November 2003. Its mandate generally aimed to address human rights violations since Moroccan independence in 1956 until the death of King Hassan II in 1999. King Hassan II ruled Morocco from 1961 to 1999. Ominously known as the Years of Lead, this period saw ruthless and systematic human rights violations, including enforced disappearances, torture, arbitrary detention and killings of political opponents. The Years of Lead were thus marked by fear and the victimisation of thousands of Moroccans. With the ascension of King Mohamed VI to the throne following this dark period, the IER was seen as an effort to delineate a break with King Hassan II's regime.

The IER constituted almost two years of investigations into enforced disappearances, arbitrary arrests, torture and sexual violence. As a result, 742 cases of enforced disappearances were confirmed; 325 of them were declared killed by security forces during riots and an additional 173 died while in illegal detention.[141] The IER also concluded that 9,779 cases of rights abuses had taken place, including unlawful killings, forced disappearances and sexual abuse.[142] A reparations budget of $50–70 million was distributed among victims and their families; however, this compensation was restricted to victims of arbitrary detention and to the relatives of those forcibly disappeared.[143]

One of the most lauded initiatives of the IER was the decision to hold seven public hearings, which were broadcast on both television and radio. Victims and their families from across Morocco aired their grievances publicly; however, they were required to sign a form beforehand stating that they would not name any perpetrators. While the public hearings promoted an important national debate about human rights in Morocco, their scope was limited, particularly as the IER was not authorised to investigate crimes committed in the Western Sahara. Moreover, no criminal prosecutions were allowed.

Morocco's experience with transitional justice is thus described either as a laudable democratic initiative or as a public relations 'scam' for the new king.[144]

---

[141] Instance Equité et Réconciliation, 'Summary of the Final Report' (Casablanca, Imprimerie Najah al-Jadida, 2006) 11.

[142] L Wilcox, 'Reshaping Civil Society through a Truth Commission: Human Rights in Morocco's Process of Political Reform' (2009) 3 *International Journal of Transitional Justice* 49, 58.

[143] E Wiebelhaus-Brahm, '"Early" Transitional Justice in the Arab World: Lessons Learned' (2016) 23 *Middle East Policy* 56.

[144] ibid.

In the absence of a democratic transition—whether in the form of an overhaul of the government and its leader or in the context of a dramatic uprising that ousted the leader, Morocco's experience with transitional justice ironically begins to look somewhat similar to the Arab Spring: tightly controlled by governing elites for the purpose of consolidating power, as opposed to the pursuit of a genuine transitional justice process. The specific prohibition of naming perpetrators and hence the complete absence of prosecutions prompted criticism of the politicised motives of the IER. The absence of a dialogue with perpetrators makes even the IER's reconciliation efforts incomplete. If the aim is to reconcile, the partial testimonies of victims of torture and arbitrary detention fall far short of a genuine reconciliation effort. While the public hearings are often described as the most powerful and successful component of the IER, particularly in stimulating debate and dialogue about human rights in Morocco, the issue of unveiling the 'truth' remains unresolved as only a part of the stories were told. The prohibition of naming perpetrators thus points to the monarchy's control over how far the IER was able to extend accountability.

Morocco's experience thus points to the use of transitional justice to bring about 'reconciliation' without threatening the core of the regime. It constitutes yet another example of a transition that does not conform to the paradigmatic transition in mainstream transitional justice discourse. The decision to establish the IER was ultimately driven and shaped by a monarchy proclaiming its wish to improve its human rights practices. This top-down liberalisation contrasts with the Arab Spring's grassroots pressure and mobilisation aimed at criminal accountability, at least in its very early stages following the ouster of state leaders. The IER, then, served as a strategy to protect government officials from punishment and from internal resistance that would shake the stability and security of the country.[145] The Egyptian and Tunisian political authorities, on the other hand, endorsed prosecutions as a scapegoating strategy that was also aimed at protecting certain government officials from punishment. Whether in Morocco or the Arab Spring countries, transitional justice was used as a political tool to control a transition, consolidate authority and keep dissent at bay.

Conclusion

The non-paradigmatic transitions of the Arab Spring warrant a rethinking of transitional justice and its pursuit in varied contexts. The shift to a renewed form of repressive, authoritarian rule in several Arab region countries undermines mainstream transitional justice theory's presumption of a 'return to a liberal state'.[146] A rethinking of transitional justice must therefore take several issues into account.

---

[145] This stability and security rhetoric was typical in the Moroccan case.
[146] Teitel, above n 3.

First, the field of transitional justice must confront the difficult question of how to transform the 'transition' paradigm so that it accounts for radically varied contexts, or whether to discard the transition paradigm altogether.

Secondly, the pursuit of competing accountability agendas by both domestic and international actors weakens global accountability norm claims. The number of prosecutions of former political leaders may be increasing, but this does not take into account whether other senior level officials who oversaw massive human rights violations have also been prosecuted. Nor does it take into account the motives behind the trials, their content and extent, and the push for accountability in some instances but not in others.

Thirdly, the emphasis on corruption and economic crimes and the very limited focus on civil and political rights crimes are driven by the elite-controlled nature of the transitions and point to a practice of scapegoating certain high-level officials for a certain set of crimes to show that there has been a break with the former regime. This, in effect, reinforces the use of transitional justice as a tool of entrenching authoritarian rule rather than as a mechanism to attain accountability or to establish the truth and acknowledge the suffering of victims.

Finally, a rethinking of transitional justice must seriously account for the absence of pre-existing democratic structures.

The similarity of the challenges to prosecution in pre-transition Egypt, Libya, Tunisia and Yemen to those in the post-transition period is indicative of the ambiguous nature of the transitions. Without a definitive resolution of these challenges, the so-called transition offers no real change in its institutions and human rights practices. As a result, decisions regarding prosecution remain severely limited and politicised. However, certain iconic human rights cases in pre-transition Egypt, Libya and Tunisia served as major triggers, or turning points, that led to decisions to prosecute high-level officials in those three countries. These cases targeting pre-transition high-level officials have, with the exception of Yemen, trickled into post-2011 efforts to prosecute. Marked by the public outrage in response to the original crimes and the persistent efforts of civil society and individual lawyers to see the cases through, these triggers were milestones in the long and difficult road to accountability for political leaders in these countries. This is why it is crucial to identify pre-transition triggers and to analyse their impact, if any, in subsequent decisions to prosecute former political leaders. Such analysis debunks false generalisations that are quick to identify 'failed transitional justice' or 'failed transitions' without assessing some of the roots of the challenges transitional countries face. These roots are found in the array of trigger, driving and shaping factors identified in each case study.

The various factors that pushed and pulled decisions regarding the prosecution of political leaders in different directions strongly represent the battle for competing visions of transitional justice, and criminal justice in particular. Discussions in the emerging scholarship on transitional justice decisions in the Arab region largely overlook the proliferation of actors that drive and shape transitional justice decisions. Instead, many of them attribute competing accountability agendas to differences between Islamists and secularists. The deconstruction of the various domestic actors involved in decisions regarding prosecution, however, has demonstrated that the origins of competing accountability agendas are far more complex. Various actors, including but not limited to the Islamists, act as justice resisters, instrumentalists and true believers.[147] Moreover, the starkly opposing justice strategies in Libya and Yemen weaken the international community's claim to a global accountability norm. The international community's divergent goals, however, may appear less contradictory when explained within the peace versus justice debate. Nevertheless, the outcome thus far has seen anything but peace or justice in either Libya or Yemen. Consequently, the peace versus justice dichotomy is unhelpful in examining the complexity of factors impacting decisions regarding prosecution in Libya and Yemen. As Sharp contends, neither peace nor justice is a monolithic concept.[148]

The content and extent of decisions regarding the prosecution of political leaders demonstrate that the Arab region is beyond recent debates calling for the merging of the two sets of rights in transitional justice mechanisms. The case studies do, however, demonstrate that addressing socio-economic crimes is a possibility even within a difficult and opaque judicial and authoritarian environment. At the same time, the focus on corruption and socio-economic crimes has served as a means to protect interim and post-transitional authorities from prosecution for human rights crimes. This goes back to the argument that ambiguous transitions that lack a definitive break with the past manifest themselves in prosecutions, as remnants of the former regime attempt to shield themselves from the courts for their responsibility in past atrocities. The merits of the limited criminal sanction, then, need to be re-examined when selective trials (both in content and extent) instead have a negative impact on the course of transitions and on the healing of victims.

Scholars of both the mainstream and critical transitional justice strands argue that some degree of democratically functioning institutions, particularly the judiciary, is necessary in order for fair trials to take place. However, when the lack of such institutions was a major reason for the transitions occurring in the first place, this argument falls short in explaining the course of transitional events in the Arab region. The absence of pre-existing democratic institutions, particularly a functioning and independent judiciary, is a significant factor that distinguishes the Arab region transitional justice processes from transitions elsewhere. The ambiguity of the transitions has led some to conclude that transitions simply did not take place in the Arab region.[149] However, to speak of the total absence of a transition in the Arab region case studies is to miss a crucial point: the use of transitional justice processes and of prosecutions in particular to consolidate authoritarian,

---

[147] Subotic, above n 50.
[148] Sharp, above n 74.
[149] RG Teitel, 'Transitional Justice and the Power of Persuasion: Philosophical, Historical and Political Perspectives', paper presented to the Panel, American Political Science Association annual conference, Chicago, September 2013.

non-liberal rule and to emphasise one historical narrative on past atrocities over the other. In sum, the transitional justice paradigm needs to redefine what is meant by 'transition' by expanding its currently very limited parameters to better reflect the mosaic of transitional countries.

These arguments have profound implications for the study of transitional justice because they weaken long-standing assumptions of the liberalising directions of transitions and of transitional justice. From the outset, it was clear that the Arab Spring transitions—many of which are still ongoing—already pointed to the shortcomings of the prevailing assumptions of the liberal roots of transitional justice. Indeed, there is a fundamental tension between the liberal roots of transitional justice and the illiberal leanings of key socio-political actors.[150] In recent scholarship, these illiberal socio-political actors, who pose a challenge to the practice of liberal transitional justice, are overwhelmingly identified as Islamists.[151] Scholars of transitional justice in the Arab region have largely stopped short of adequately discussing the use and abuse of transitional justice by other, secular political actors, most notably the military. The binary analyses that have emerged, pitting the secularists against the Islamists, are therefore unhelpful in taking stock of how the Arab Spring is shaping transitional justice more broadly. As Mutua argues, 'Dogmatic universality is a drawback to an imaginative understanding of transitional justice'.[152]

---

[150] This tension is referred to by several authors in Fisher and Stewart, above n 14.
[151] See Line Khatib and Elham Manea in Fisher and Stewart, above n 14.
[152] Mutua, above n 85, 5.

7

Conclusion

All too often, transitional justice looks back and looks forward without looking at the present. This tendency compromises the ability of transitional justice actors to make a realistic assessment of whether a transitional society is equipped to deal with the past and the future. Regardless of the support of international organisations, problems of deep state institutions and of domestic actors battling for rival versions of justice persist. In the Arab region cases examined in this book, the past was not dealt with properly because the future is being shaped by the political interests of the current transitional and post-transitional authorities. Wary of their own involvement in past atrocities, attempts to ensure due process and criminal accountability have faced many obstacles. The transitional justice processes that have unfolded, and in particular the prosecution of political leaders, have thus been hijacked by the demons of the past that have morphed into the present.

Victims of the past have largely been marginalised, while new victims have been created by crimes of the transition and post-transition period. Ongoing atrocities, such as enforced disappearances, arbitrary detention, killings and torture, target human rights activists and political opponents. Lawyers, judges and activists who work to ensure accountability for former leaders have been attacked, sometimes fatally, as in Libya and Yemen. In Tunisia, the presidency made clear that the presidential and interior ministry archives are off limits for the Truth and Dignity Commission's investigations into crimes committed by its members. In Egypt, thousands of activists, journalists, civil society leaders and political opponents have been detained, tried in military courts and tortured. Hundreds have been forcibly disappeared. Former political leaders and police chiefs in Egypt, Tunisia and Yemen have been released through questionable acquittals. For example, in Egypt, following a highly politicised six-year trial, Mubarak was released and allowed to return to his mansion in Cairo. These are blatant reminders that the premise of transitional justice itself is constantly being challenged, often violently.

The shift to a renewed form of repressive, non-liberal rule in several Arab region transitions undermines mainstream transitional justice theory's presumption of a 'return to a liberal state'.[1] The Arab region cases demonstrate that both domestic

---

[1] RG Teitel, *Globalizing Transitional Justice: Essays for the New Millennium* (Oxford, Oxford University Press, 2014).

and international actors pursue competing accountability agendas, thereby weakening global accountability norm claims. The limited content and extent of the investigations and prosecutions that have taken place in all four case studies underline the need to further develop transitional justice theory. The emphasis on accountability for corruption and economic crimes and a much more limited form of accountability for civil and political crimes in Egypt and Tunisia, for instance, points to a practice of finding scapegoats for certain crimes in order to avoid prosecution for a more comprehensive set of crimes. The very limited human rights prosecutions that have taken place thus point to the elite-controlled nature of the transitions. Moreover, the focus on crimes committed during the transition in the investigations and trials that have taken place leaves decades of human rights violations unaccounted for.[2] The Arab region cases demonstrate the perils of pursuing prosecutions during highly contentious transitions. Weak and politicised judiciaries crippled by executive power meddling and inadequate legal frameworks are a principal challenge to the pursuit of fair prosecutions. A rethinking of transitional justice therefore needs to take into account the absence of pre-existing democratic institutions and what this means for criminal accountability prospects in such non-paradigmatic transitional contexts.

Pre-transition efforts to hold perpetrators to account have, with the exception of Yemen, trickled into post-2011 efforts to prosecute. Egypt's *Khaled Said* case, Tunisia's *Baraket Essahel* case and Libya's *Abu Salim prison massacre* case are all examples of prosecutions targeting mid-to-high-level government and police officials that, despite an exceedingly difficult and repressive environment for civil society to work within, were revived post-transition. Of note here is that the incidents that led to these iconic cases were also cited as major triggers that eventually led to decisions to prosecute high-level officials in Egypt, Libya and Tunisia. These triggers, which were marked by the public outrage they created and the tireless efforts of civil society and individual lawyers to ensure accountability for them, were milestones in the long and difficult road to accountability for political leaders in these countries. These iconic cases impacted subsequent criminal accountability efforts, as we have seen with the re-emergence of the *Khaled Said, Baraket Essahel* and *Abu Salim* cases in the post-uprising period. They also point to the significant role that public pressure and civil society efforts played in sustaining

---

[2] These human rights violations have been documented by many Egyptian civil society organisations, including the Egyptian Organization for Human Rights (www.eohr.org), the Cairo Institute for Human Rights Studies (www.cihrs.org), the Egyptian Initiative for Personal Rights (www.eipr.org), the Arabic Network for Human Rights Information (http://anhri.net) and the Nadim Center for the Treatment and Rehabilitation of Victims of Violence (http://alnadeem.org). They have also been documented extensively by Amnesty International and Human Rights Watch. For an account of systematic torture in Egypt, see, eg, Human Rights Watch, 'Behind Closed Doors: Torture and Detention in Egypt' (July 1991), available at www.hrw.org/sites/default/files/reports/Egypt927.pdf; Human Rights Watch, 'Work on Him Until he Confesses: Impunity for Torture in Egypt' (30 January 2011) available at www.hrw.org/report/2011/01/30/work-him-until-he-confesses/impunity-torture-egypt.

the momentum behind certain iconic cases over time. Looking to the future, these actors will continue to be crucial to any process involving the prosecution of political leaders, and to transitional justice in general.

Ambiguous transitions are not a novelty. However, the Arab region cases provide renewed importance for the need to rethink transitional justice and its purpose in varied contexts. This book's inquiry into pre-transition efforts to prosecute political leaders illustrates the similarity of the challenges to prosecutions in pre- and post-transition Egypt, Libya, Tunisia and Yemen. The absence of a return to a liberal state and the multiple legacies of atrocities raise a critical question: what are these countries transitioning from and to? The 2010/11 uprisings that constituted the Arab region transitions were not so much 'exceptional' as they were a culmination of decades-long grievances. They were a powerful expression of protest against the 'norm' of systematic abuses, against the 'norm' of authoritarian rule. Elections and constitutional referenda in Egypt and Tunisia did not necessarily signify an end to authoritarianism or the crystallisation of democracy. The interviewees were clear on the nature of the transitions, often lamenting that 'it is the same regime', 'we have the same courts and the same human rights abuses', 'we have removed the heads of the regime, but the mentality of the regime persists', transitional justice has been used to 'sacrifice a part of the regime to save the regime'.

The view that there has been no meaningful transition must be taken seriously. Social change has not translated into political change[3] and, as a result, civil society has reverted to pre-transition strategies of advocacy.[4] Whether in Morocco or the Arab Spring countries, transitional justice was used as a highly political tool to control a transition, consolidate authority and keep dissent at bay. It will, arguably, fail on all three counts. A transitional society is already treading on fragile ground. The abuse of transitional justice to entrench authoritarianism makes these societies all the more vulnerable to popular discontent and general insecurity. Economic protests and strikes continue in both Egypt and Tunisia. Violent attacks by extremist groups plague all four countries. Libya is deeply and violently polarized, and Yemen is reeling from a multi-state military campaign and from its own internal conflicts. This is not to say, of course, that such abuse of transitional justice is entirely to blame for this state of affairs; but the analysis of decisions regarding prosecution in particular and transitional justice in general points to the importance of examining non-paradigmatic transitions more rigorously. Is there a paradigmatic transition? Or has it diminished completely with the rise of non-liberal transitions?

---

[3] Interview with Wael Eskandar, prominent blogger, independent journalist and media commentator, and member of the Kaziboon campaign, which called for accountability for crimes committed by the Egyptian military (Cairo, Egypt, 8 December 2013).

[4] Interview with Mohamed El Shewy, Transitional Justice Programme Officer, Egyptian Initiative for Personal Rights (telephone interview, 24 November 2013).

Using empirical analysis gathered from actors on the ground, this book has demonstrated that the foundational assumptions of the transitional justice paradigm are significantly weakened and that a rethinking of the paradigmatic transition needs to take shape. The paradigmatic shift from violent, authoritarian rule to liberal, democratic rule is extremely restrictive in how transitional justice is imagined and how transitions actually unfold. Nevertheless, paradigmatic transitions have largely shaped the transitional justice field of research and practice. Are transitions so complex that it would be best to explain them as 'unspecified change'?[5] Should we not qualify transitions, then, as failed, stalled, progressing or successful? What does this mean for the study and practice of transitional justice? Is justice something that is always 'to come', something to which societies must continually strive?[6] The pursuit of justice in various countries and through various mechanisms—whether through truth commissions, prosecutions, reparations programmes or lustration—points to the importance of the *process* of justice itself. In South Africa, Argentina, Romania, Rwanda and 'established democracies', such as Canada and New Zealand, the pursuit of transitional justice has not known an end point. While its lack of finality may be frustrating for advocates of transitional justice, it points to the importance of managing justice expectations of policy makers, practitioners and victims alike. Such examples from around the world also point to the perils of formulating transitional justice policies that are based on a restrictive transition paradigm. A reckoning with the past is thus always relevant, regardless of whether an uprising or tumultuous transition has occurred.

The ubiquity of non-liberal and ambiguous transitions, the multiple legacies of human rights violations and the particular content and extent of decisions regarding prosecution underline the need to re-examine transitional justice and to further develop its theory and practice. The conflicting roles of regional and international actors, particularly in the cases of Libya and Yemen, also reveal that transitional justice itself is not a consistently applied phenomenon that is rooted in so-called universal, liberal values such as the 'global accountability norm'. The case studies thus serve as a strong reminder that transitional justice is indeed a political project and cannot be described or understood to be post-political.[7] While critical transitional justice scholarship challenges transitional justice, it does not appear in institutional form or in transitional justice practice.[8] The Arab region cases presented in this book demonstrate the strong need for this to change.

---

[5] DN Sharp, 'Emancipating Transitional Justice from the Paradigmatic Transition' (2015) *International Journal of Transitional Justice* 150, 155.

[6] C Turner, *Violence, Law and the Impossibility of Transitional Justice* (Oxford, Routledge, 2016).

[7] H Franzki and MC Olarte, 'The Political Economy of Transitional Justice. A Critical Theory Perspective' in S Buckley-Zistel, TK Beck, C Braun and F Mieth (eds), *Transitional Justice Theories* (Abingdon, Routledge, 2014) 202.

[8] V Nesiah, 'Cashing in the Blue Chips' in A Orford and F Hoffman (eds), *The Oxford Handbook of the Theory of International Law* (Oxford, Oxford University Press, 2016).

INDEX

www.ingramcontent.com/pod-product-compliance
Lightning Source LLC
Chambersburg PA
CBHW050445280326
41932CB00013BA/2243